VOICES FOUND

Voices Found: Free Jazz and Singing contributes to a wave of voice studies scholarship with the first book-length study of free jazz voice. It pieces together a history of free jazz voice that spans from sound poetry and scat in the 1950s to the more recent wave of free jazz choirs. The author traces the developments and offers a theory, derived from interviews with many of the most important singers in the history of free jazz voice, of how listeners have experienced and evaluated the often unconventional vocal sounds these vocalists employed. This theory explains that even audiences willing to enjoy harsh sounds from saxophones or guitars often resist when voices make sounds that audiences understand as not-human.

Experimental poetry and scat were combined and transformed in free jazz spaces in the 1960s and 1970s by vocalists like Yoko Ono (in solo work and her work with Ornette Coleman and John Stevens), Jeanne Lee (in her solo work and her work with Archie Shepp and Gunter Hampel), Leon Thomas (in his solo work as well as his work with Pharoah Sanders and Carlos Santana), and Phil Minton and Maggie Nicols (who devoted much of their energy to creating unaccompanied free jazz vocal music). By studying free jazz voice, we can learn important lessons about what we expect from the voice and what happens when those expectations are violated. This book doesn't only trace histories of free jazz voice, it makes an attempt to understand why this story hasn't been told before, with an impressive breadth of scope in terms of the artists covered, drawing on research from the US, Canada, Wales, Scotland, France, the Netherlands, and Japan.

Chris Tonelli is Assistant Professor of History and Theory of Popular Music at University of Groningen in the Netherlands.

Transnational Studies in Jazz

Series Editors
Tony Whyton
Birmingham City University, UK
Nicholas Gebhardt
Birmingham City University, UK

Transnational Studies in Jazz presents cross-disciplinary and global perspectives on the development and history of jazz and explores its many social, political, and cultural meanings.

Jazz Sells
Music, Marketing, and Meaning
Mark Laver

Austral Jazz
The Localization of a Global Music Form in Sydney
Andrew Robson

Jazz Diaspora
New Approaches to Music and Globalisation
Bruce Johnson

Voices Found
Free Jazz and Singing
Chris Tonelli

Remixing European Jazz Culture
Kristin McGee

For more information, please visit: www.routledge.com/music/series/TSJ

VOICES FOUND

Free Jazz and Singing

Chris Tonelli

NEW YORK AND LONDON

First published 2020
by Routledge
52 Vanderbilt Avenue, New York, NY 10017

and by Routledge
2 Park Square, Milton Park, Abingdon, Oxon, OX14 4RN

Routledge is an imprint of the Taylor & Francis Group, an informa business

Library of Congress Cataloging-in-Publication Data
Names: Tonelli, Chris (Chris J.) author.
Title: Voices found : free jazz and singing / Chris Tonelli.
Description: [1.] | New York : Routledge, 2019. | Series: Transnational
  studies in jazz | Includes bibliographical references and index.
Identifiers: LCCN 2019029762 | ISBN 9781138341029 (hardback) |
  ISBN 9781138341036 (paperback) | ISBN 9780429440427 (ebook) |
  ISBN 9780429802980 (adobe pdf) | ISBN 9780429802966 (mobi) |
  ISBN 9780429802973 (epub)
Subjects: LCSH: Vocal improvisation (Music) | Jazz vocals—History and
  criticism. | Free jazz—History and criticism.
Classification: LCC ML3506 .T66 2019 | DDC 782.0165/6—dc23
LC record available at https://lccn.loc.gov/2019029762

ISBN: 978-1-138-34102-9 (hbk)
ISBN: 978-1-138-34103-6 (pbk)
ISBN: 978-0-429-44042-7 (ebk)

Typeset in Bembo
by Apex CoVantage, LLC

CONTENTS

SERIES FOREWORD

Since the 1990s, the study of jazz has changed dramatically, as the field continues to open up to a variety of disciplinary perspectives and critical models. Today, as the music's meaning undergoes profound changes, there is a pressing need to situate jazz within an international research context and to develop theories and methods of investigation that open up new ways of understanding its cultural significance and its place within different historical and social settings.

The Transnational Studies in Jazz Series presents the best research from this important and exciting area of scholarship and features interdisciplinary and international perspectives on the relationships between jazz, society, politics, and culture. The series provides authors with a platform for rethinking the methodologies and concepts used to analyze jazz and will seek to work across disciplinary boundaries, finding different ways of examining the practices, values, and meanings of the music. The series explores the complex cultural and musical exchanges that have shaped the global development and reception of jazz. Contributors will focus on studies of the music that find different ways of telling the story of jazz with or without reference to the United States and will investigate jazz as a medium for negotiating global identities.

Tony Whyton
Nicholas Gebhardt
Series Editors

ACKNOWLEDGEMENTS

This book would not have been possible without the support of the International Institute for Critical Studies in Improvisation (IICSI). The data was collected during my postdoctoral fellowship with IICSI, and afterwards IICSI has continued to provide important support. I am eternally grateful to the whole IICSI team, especially Ellen Waterman, Ajay Heble, Daniel Fischlin, Eric Lewis, Frederique Arroyas, Rachel Collins, Justine Richardson, Elizabeth Jackson, Richelle Forsey, Lauren Michelle Levesque, Kimber Sider, and Kim Thorne.

My deep gratitude also extends to the artists who shared their time, ideas, and sounds and supported the project in other ways. First among these is Paul Dutton, who nurtured my interest in this topic for two decades with all manner of generosity. I could not possibly thank him enough for the mentorship, friendship, and support he has given me. Fifteen years of inspiration and energy from Christine Duncan were also elemental to shaping this project. She is "best kind," and I thank her for the free-flowing generosity over these years. Kindness from Tomomi Adachi for an equally long period has also played a special role in forming this project. I'm glad our paths crossed as many times as they have, and I'm grateful for the kindness he has shown to me. Extraordinary levels of kindness also flowed my way from Phil Minton, Maggie Nicols, David Moss, Trevor Wishart, Jaap Blonk, Gabriel Dharmoo, Ute Wassermann, Michael Edward Edgerton, and W. Mark Sutherland. They all gave more than just their time and ideas to this project, and I am grateful for the ways they have gone above and beyond. I am also sincerely thankful to Richard Armstrong, Theo Bleckmann, Thomas Buckner, Lisa Butel, Viv Corringham, Gary Diggins, Géraldine Eguiluz, Soressa Gardner, Annette Giesriegl, Ayelet Rose Gottlieb, Camille Hesketh, Joane Hétu, Shelley Hirsch, Anna Homler, Christine Jeffrey, Thomas Johannsen, Salome Kammer, Donna Lytle, Dafna Naphtali, Mankwe Ndosi, Helen Pridmore, Carol Sawyer,

Petra van der Schoot, Fay Victor, Veryan Weston, Grace Yuen, Gerard Yun, Pamela Z, and dozens of members of Christine Duncan's Element Choir and DB Boyko's Voice Over Mind Choir, who were all fantastically generous for participating in this research. Another set of artists I am deeply grateful to are all the members of the various Vocal Exploration Choirs I established in Guelph, St John's, and Groningen; we have shared wonderful moments, and I am thankful to have spent time with you all. Special thanks goes to Mack Furlong, Alison Carter, Michael Waterman, Cassondra Murray, and Kati Szego for the extra love you've put into VocalX. Finally, there are too many artists to name whose collaboration has allowed me to joyfully keep up the singing practice that has informed my perspective on this volume's topic. I am grateful to everyone I've sung with over the past twenty years. Some have been mentioned above, but a few others I am especially grateful to are Jude Weirmeir, Fiona Chatwin, Tina Pearson, Paul Bendzsa, Guy Obrecht, and Andrew Staniland.

This project has also benefited from grants from the Bruneau Centre for Excellence in Choral Music. I am grateful to the BCECM for their support, and special thanks goes to Meghan Forsyth and Doug Dunsmore. I also benefited from the collegiality of the board of the Phenomenon of Singing International Symposium; special thanks goes to Ki Adams and Andrea Rose. The Sound Symposium has also helped put wind in the sails of this project, and I thank Kathy Clark-Wherry and the entire Symposium family. This book also benefitted from the editorial assistance and generosity of Rhiannon Bruce, Forrest Kentwell, Aubrey Williams, and Nora Leidinger—I send you all heartfelt thanks.

I am grateful for the collegiality related to this volume of Zeynep Bulut, Jeffers Engelhardt, Gianpaolo Chiriacò, Jeremy Strachan, Dylan Robinson, Estelle Amy de la Bretèque, J. Martin Daughtry, Clara Latham, Eric Porter, Deborah Withers, and Kristin McGee; for the help of the special collections staff at Columbia University Library, the University of Berkeley Library, the British Library, the Louis Armstrong Archive at Queen's Library (Sarah Rose and Ricky Riccardi), The Getty Center in Los Angeles, and the MoMA archives; for the generosity of friends throughout this process, including Aaron Gervais and Stella Kim, Adam and Marla Wilson, Don Scott and Jessica Stuart, Bill and Aimee Bahng Boyer, Claire Wilkshire, Don Nicols and Rebecca Bryant, and Gayle Young and Reinhard Reitzenstein. For many years of continual support and mentorship, I send limitless thanks to Jann Pasler and Jason Stanyek. My deepest thanks go to Michael and Ellen Waterman for the profound and multilayered roles they've played in my life for the past quarter-century, to my parents and family for all their support and love, and to Leslie, who has given me so much.

Finally, my gratitude extends too to Tony Whyton and Nick Gebhardt for their stewardship of the Transnational Studies in Jazz series and Constance Ditzel and Ben Bierman for their contributions to bringing this project to the series.

INTRODUCTION

Extended, Extra-Normal, and Everyday Voices

An Opening Invitation

Encounters with the voice, with the voices of others and with our own never-fully-knowable voices, are what matter most about this book. *Voices Found* has emerged from spaces of encounter. I refer these as free jazz spaces, though others won't agree with my nomenclature (more on that below). Free jazz spaces are often spaces of encounter, spaces of finding. We encounter others there, but we also encounter parts of ourselves and our instruments we didn't know before. The singers this book is about are almost all on lifelong quests of vocal finding. And they'd like you to join them.

Given the importance that encounters with the unfamiliar will have throughout this book, I encourage you, the reader, to begin this book by reflecting upon your own encounters with the voices introduced here. Consider reading the next few sentences and then proceeding to the book's companion webpage—www.improvisationinstitute.ca/research-project/voices-found—for some initial listening and self-reflection. Listen to the "Voices Found Playlist" and take note (literally if you're willing; why not write it down?) of the thoughts and feelings that occur. Take note of *all* your thoughts as you listen, even the ones you find embarrassing or those that seem irrelevant. You may want to focus on the adjectives and associations that enter your mind. You may want to note any feelings or, perhaps, memories that arise. Doing this before you read on may yield the most valuable lessons offered by this book. As you read on, you may want to revisit some thoughts or feelings that arose in this initial listening. Exposure to the histories conveyed in this book may change how you experience free jazz singing, but your record of your initial reactions, especially if you are new to this music, might aid the philosophical objective of *Voices Found*—the exposure and denaturalisation of the cultural filters through which we make sense of and value voices.

Conveying under-examined histories is the other objective in the pages that follow. Your reactions aid that goal as well: they are part of the history of what the sounds of free jazz singing have afforded. Knowing how they are distinct from or similar to the reactions I will discuss in the pages that follow is valuable. We all experience music through the filter of the ideologies society has instilled in us. *Voices Found* attempts to make certain muted ideologies audible in ways that might hold the potential to alter future thought and action. Spending time with the music at the heart of this volume and endeavouring to decipher those ideologies as they manifest through our listening, is in the spirit of *Voices Found*. So it is valuable to begin by listening. It is valuable to begin by reflecting on what the sounds of these singers do when your mind and body meet both them and their invocation and accompaniment of co-present, mediatised, or imagined bodies.

Was It Worth It?

If you've entertained my request, it may have already yielded insights. Hopefully, if it did, those multiply as you read on. What you'll find here in *Voices Found* are reflections on various critical facets of free jazz singing, including: how interdisciplinary or interarts practices have shaped free jazz singing; the ways technologies like tape recorders and samplers have affected free jazz singers and sound poets; the broad range of free jazz and non-free jazz influences on free jazz singing; a theory of why we sometimes feel threatened by unfamiliar vocal sounds; and, finally, an introduction to and reflection on how free jazz singing gave rise to an inclusive improvisational choir movement in recent years. My primary focus will be on the ways the spaces of free jazz have invited vocalists to explore and employ vocal sounds that most forms of Western singing have excluded, sounds sometimes referred to as "extra-normal" forms of singing.[1] The singers prioritised in this volume substantially employ sounds *not* rooted in sung pitches, melody, or normative speech patterns and timbres. In other words, I highlight singers devoted to improvisational work with less conventional abstract vocal sounds. So, more common forms of jazz singing like vocalese, vocal emulations of famous instrumental solos, and even more pitch-centred forms of free jazz singing are not examined in this volume. Throughout the book, I refer to the vocalists I am concerned with examining here as free jazz soundsingers.

"Soundsinging" is a term singer, writer, poet, and improviser Paul Dutton coined in the mid-1990s. He was inspired by a friend of his who, during a discussion they were having about jazz singer Jeanne Lee, realised a connection between Dutton's work and hers, commenting: "She sings sounds too, doesn't she?"[2] He began employing the term as an alternative to *extended vocal technique*, a frequently applied description of his work and one that he detests.[3] His hatred for that term is an appropriate starting point for both the history and the theory offered in this volume. It is appropriate, firstly, because his objection to the term points us to divides within the broader field of vocal arts, and, secondly, because it alludes to the ways Western music discourse often positions the production of "pure" pitches as a privileged practice within the broader category of singing. Indeed, sequences of "pure" pitches are the only types of vocalisation that qualify in some definitions as "singing."

Dutton objects to all three of the words in the phrase "extended vocal technique." "Vocal" is a problem because of the way it misrepresents the physiology of the sounds his work employs. He intends soundsinging "to signal that what is being worked with includes nonvocal sounds such as tongue pops, lip-smacks, tooth grinding, saliva swishing, tooth-rubbing, sucking, lip-flubbing, and a wealth of other totally nonvocal effects."[4] He prefers to think of such "effects" as sounds rather than techniques, stating: "I'm an artist, not a technician."[5] This reflects the substantial role surprise plays in Dutton's practice as well as the improvisatory practices of many free jazz singers.[6] He likes to be surprised by the sounds that emerge as he vocalises, and he has developed methods to help ensure that happens regularly.[7] While "technique" might suit the act of intentionally producing desired vocal sounds, something Dutton undoubtedly does as well, it seems less appropriate for a practice in which one seeks to be surprised by one's body in the course of improvisational music making. Finally, "extended" is the most problematic term, as it implies that the less conventional sounds employed by the singer are an "extension" out and away from the core of their practice, and it positions the Western standard of pure pitch-based singing as a universal core. For singers like Dutton and many, but not all, of the singers we meet in the following chapters, this simply isn't true. This less conventional material with which soundsingers work is often the core of their art. Thinking of these sounds as extensions harmfully misrepresents vocal practices like Dutton's, as it reinforces a false notion that pitch-centred singing is the core of all Western singing.[8]

Though the sounds of soundsinging are often referred to as unfamiliar or "extra-normal," Dutton points out that what is extra-normal is often not the sounds themselves but simply the ways they are being deployed. He writes:

> Fact is, no matter the amazement that people, including me, might feel and express at some of the more extreme or outré sounds that come out of the mouths of oral sound artists, there is little or nothing that any of us working this territory do that is not done every day in equal or lesser degree by every speaking human on the planet. Multiphonics? There isn't a sound in nature, let alone human speech, that is anything else: the only truly pure single frequency ever to occur is an electronically generated sine wave. Overtones? Anyone uttering a vowel is emitting a range of overtone frequencies, known in linguistics as formants, that give that vowel its characteristic sound. Then there is the vast array of expressive non-verbal utterances employed in oral sound art, including grunts, groans, wheezes, gasps, shrieks, screams, whistles, rasps, lip smacking, tongue popping, vocal inhalations, snorts, coughs, gulps, and smooches, to name but a very few, almost

any of which occur universally in the course of a multitude of human activities—physical work, sex, play, eating, sleeping—and emotional states, such as grief, joy, surprise, anger, and so on. The art of sound poetry lies not in making the sounds but in isolating and emphasizing them, and then creatively applying and organizing them (Dutton 2012, 131).

The sounds of soundsinging are at once ordinary and extraordinary, powerful and pedestrian.

The histories *Voices Found* offers unfold alongside a theorisation of the work performed by soundsinging, in particular the effects these singers' less conventional vocal sounds have had on listeners. Recent thinking on music and meaning has moved us far from the dangerous notion that sonic events will have the same effects on every listener. And so, by pointing here to the work performed by specific vocal sounds, I am not suggesting that these sounds have a uniform effect on all listeners or that specific sounds necessarily do specific kinds of work. In this sense, music is most definitely not a universal language. However, categories of sounds have histories; types of events can recur. It can be appropriate to discuss outcomes that tend to happen when listeners who have adopted certain ideological assumptions encounter certain varieties of musical sound. Throughout this volume, my examples of outcomes do undoubtedly emerge from singular, irreducible, bygone contexts of reception. I draw on experiences shared during interviews with dozens of singers, on archival material, and on autoethnographic reflection on my own singing. These stories of encounter will hopefully speak to and against experiences you have had and, in the process, broaden our knowledge about the kinds of work these and other voices have done.

A History and an Argument

Histories always obscure more than they include. The list of free jazz vocalists mentioned only briefly in this volume (getting far less recognition than deserved) is long, but it may well be surpassed by the free jazz vocalists not mentioned at all. The body of work the book does give attention to, on the other hand, is vast; I am confident that it collects together and stands as a substantial and unique contribution (and challenge) to existing histories of free jazz, jazz, and singing. In these pages, you will meet dozens of vocalists whose approaches have challenged dominant notions of who should sing in public and who should not, what kinds of sounds singing should embrace, what kinds of vocal sounds deserve to be referred to as singing (or music), and the methods that lead to socially valuable solitary and collective singing practices. The portion of the history of singing, jazz, and free jazz that this body of work represents prompts us to ask important questions about who and what different forms of singing and music making include and exclude and what they achieve and fail to achieve. My hope is that this, the first book devoted to tracing these histories, will open doors for singers (especially for those previously excluded or alienated from singing) who might, through exposure to the figures and histories to which this book points, feel newly empowered to develop singing practices that feel authentic and relevant to their experience. I hope it helps lead soon-to-be former "non-singers" to find community through their practices and new identities and embodied pleasures as singers.

My core argument, in and around the histories I trace, is that understanding the effects soundsingers have had will also help us understand affordances of more normative singing. However, lessons about the voices deemed most fully human and/or accorded the most respect and privilege will appear mostly as the implied inverse of vocalisation that fails to register as fully human to certain listeners. The vocal practices I chronicle here form a tradition of ignoring the unspoken imperative to restrict our vocalisations to pitch-centric song or normative speech in timbres considered coherent with the ways our bodies have been categorised and coded. The singers in this tradition have embraced vocal (and non-vocal oral) sounds that belong to all of us but are robbed from most of us. Free jazz created a space in which singers have ignored the vocal norms that dominate our lives and embraced pleasures that we are taught as children to leave behind.

Which Singers Are Soundsingers?

Before we progress further, it is important to point out that few singers, including most of the singers discussed in this volume, self-identify as soundsingers. One reason for this may be lack of exposure to the term. However, some singers have absolutely taken notice of the term and have consciously chosen not to identify with it. Singer and poet Jaap Blonk explained to me that the term was not so useful for him:

> because you could also just call it singing and someone like David Moss says, "everything I do is singing." We should widen the definition of music by telling that music is organized sound, and singing is just anything produced by the voice—well not ordinary speech—but anything that is meant to be art or music.[9]

Blonk's comment reflects a consciousness of how terms like "soundsinging" have the potential to marginalise singers who employ unconventional sounds. Few of the singers employing these sounds work exclusively with them; many also sing in pitch-centred ways. As such, identifying with the term soundsinger might be akin to disavowing those elements while limiting listeners' perceptions of their practice. It might also unjustly cause sounds that would be well-served by the honorific associations carried by the term singing to be excluded from that privileged category. It's not surprising that the question of nomenclature prompted Blonk to refer to David Moss, as Moss is an outspoken vocalist who lobbies for himself and other singers who employ less conventional sounds to be understood as singers who sing. Moss explains: "What to call what I do has been an issue for a long time. Now I simply say I sing, as a kind of social-political statement, which is to say that what I do is as much singing as any other form of singing."[10] Experiential associations have accrued to the term singing that exceed technical definitions of the term. Even when working exclusively with non-vocal oral techniques, a soundsinger might still feel like they are singing in the sense that they are committing to a total bodily engagement resulting in sounds that emerge from airflow passing through the inner spaces of the mouth and body without the use of external instruments.

Though I recognise Blonk and Moss's objections, I value the term soundsinging because it helps us speak about the ways different kinds of vocal sound might do different kinds of work in the world. Without a more specific name for the singing tradition in which Moss, Blonk, and Dutton participate, it becomes very difficult to refer to and understand the implications of that tradition. Whether this utility outweighs the term's potential harm is, to me, uncertain. Moss points out the potential damage similar terms cause when he explains:

> Categorisation of the human voice is, first of all, dismissal of anything outside of the category. When you categorise something, you therefore close it off from the outside world and you say "aha, this is what it is, I understand it now." That's the A thing about categorisation. And the B thing about categorisation is once you categorise, you have rules and hierarchies to obey and to live up to, and people have expectations—their expectations are generated by these names.[11]

In other words, a singer like Moss who uses both widespread and less conventional techniques might feel restricted to less conventional techniques at a performance billed a "soundsinging performance." This label might affect audience expectation in ways that might variously be considered advantageous or unwanted.

Despite these dangers, I have chosen to adopt the term here.[12] It is my hope that I can do so without promoting the reductive notions that soundsinging is not singing or that singers that soundsing do or should limit their practices to the employment of less conventional sounds. I would encourage readers to employ the term judiciously; if it's not necessary, use "singing" instead. I will attempt to do so throughout the course of the book, employing the term "singer" more often than "soundsinger." To respect the traditions, practices, and figures involved in the histories I discuss here, it is essential to remember that soundsingers, whether or not they identify with the term, are all also singers. Soundsinging is always singing.

Similarly, I have opted to occupy a middle path in my use of the term "free jazz." Certain musicians in scenes conceptualised as "free improvisation" or "European free improvisation" scenes, for various reasons, reject the terms "jazz" or "free jazz." While I intend no disrespect to these musicians' choices, I opt here to refer to the field they call free improvised music as free jazz throughout this book for two reasons. The first is academic. I seek to claim a space for this music within the field of jazz studies. Much of this book will be concerned with showing the wide-ranging diversity of sources that have fed into free jazz vocal practices. Despite these broad and various sources of origin, it was the jazz tradition that first and foremost generated the practices I write about here. The singers in these pages, and singers in general, have received too little attention in jazz studies; by marking these practices as jazz, I am attempting to claim space for them within that discipline and stimulate more scholarly work on these lineages. Secondly, referring to free improvisation as free jazz can contribute to counteracting what George Lewis refers to as an "attempted erasure or denial of the impact of African-American forms on the real-time work of European and Euro-American composers" (2004, 132). The term "jazz" can contain African-American musicians who have been informed by jazz traditions, marking them as belonging only to those traditions, working to exclude them from other spaces and practices their work intersects with. Jazz can also, conversely, be imagined to exclude certain musics, like free jazz, that are derivations from earlier jazz practices. This book will discuss the work of a number of African-American vocalists but alongside a larger number of non–African-American vocalists. Many of the histories I concentrate on here took place in Europe in scenes that sometimes eschewed the term "jazz" in ways that contribute to the kinds of erasure Lewis theorises. While I do not aim to minimise the distinctness of the cultural and social contexts from which the various singers covered emerge, I do want to point to the ways they have intersected and influenced one another across those contexts and the ways none of the practices I call free jazz singing could have emerged without jazz-associated African-American histories and musicians.

And so, in these pages, I will refer to all "free improvisation" as "free jazz." At a few points I will slip into employing "free improvisation" when my consultants or the musicians discussed tend towards the term in their discourse. The erasure Lewis discusses is complex, and "free improvisers" have an array of diverse spoken and unspoken reasons for identifying with that term instead of "free jazz." Many of these musicians have, of course, worked to make African-American traditions and musicians more audible and well supported, and African-American musicians too have rejected the term "jazz" for various reasons.[13] My choice to use "free jazz" instead of "free improvisation" should not be taken as a dismissal of all of the varied motivations that have led musicians to identify as free improvisers but as a strategic choice that I find suitable for my topic and context. Further, to add one last comment on terminology, I will insist that most of the vocal practices I discuss here fall into the tradition of free jazz, and free jazz amounts to an important thread in the broader category of "experimental music." This is a minor obsession here, which is discussed further in Chapter 1.

Though this book seeks to deal specifically with the history of free jazz, the term "soundsinging" can also, in my estimation, be usefully employed to refer to non-improvisational practices as well. Singers who specialise in less conventional sounds in composed music but who also do not want to position pitch-based singing as their core, or as the core of what constitutes singing, might consider adopting the term for their practice. Many of the social effects I discuss here may emerge in contexts other than free jazz, although the kinds of spaces in which other genres appear, along with the cultural filters through which they are received, can differ drastically. The interdisciplinary blurring that I detail in the following chapters has led to the sounds of free jazz singers manifesting in many kinds of musical and non–music-centred spaces, leading to encounters with many different kinds of listeners. As we theorise and try to account for the social processes vocal sounds help enact, the contexts of sounding, both physical and cultural, seem to matter as much or more than the sounds themselves.

Methods

Arts-based or practice-based research is the foundation on which this project was built. I was a free jazz singer before I became a theorist and researcher. However, bringing my practice into the space of scholarship helped me clarify that it was, in large part, a desire for understanding that attracted me to my musical practice to begin with. I longed to understand why I could hardly breathe, why I was so powerfully affected by my first encounters with live performances by Dutton and Phil Minton, why I felt both invited and compelled to make music in the ways they did, and why my passion for both making and hearing others make that music has lasted. Sustaining a free jazz practice alongside the perceptual filter of the music researcher, though it may have led to certain biases and blindnesses in my work, has also led to embodied and social processes and encounters that non–practice-based research methods would not. I consider some of the performances I have given, particularly the performances I have organised and facilitated with the community-engaged, inclusive improvising choirs I began leading in the postdoctoral phase of my research, to be both research sites and an important, impactful outcome of my research. These free jazz choirs amount, in my conception, to an applied ethnographic research method; they generate events that inform my ongoing research while offering participants access to a community and community-engaged practice that benefits many of them by offering a space for self-examination, discovery, physical activity, and social connection that is sometimes intercultural and profound. It was primarily through a sense of obligation to the legacy of my research consultants' community-engaged practices—my firsthand witnessing of the benefits they have brought to others—that I first felt called to facilitate spaces for others to explore solitary and collective vocal improvisation. A desire to help contribute to the community service and engagement imperatives of the institute funding my postdoctoral work, the International Institute for Critical Studies in Improvisation (IICSI), was another factor motivating my choice to make applied ethnography a part of my artistic/musicological work. It is difficult, of course, to parse out the desire to serve others from the social benefits that accrue to academics and artists that work with applied methods. The cultural and economic capital that this work has helped me and many of the artists I will discuss acquire is undoubtedly another motivating factor for much of this work. However, this kind of work has been a risky path towards capital for everyone I discuss in this book, including myself. Everyone I discuss in these pages has dealt with precariousness of various types in their careers and has sustained their practices through such periods, less because they felt security and comfort was liable to come with persistence and more because they were following eudaemonic and ethical imperatives to continue pursuing the solitary and collective practices they had found. My research methods are inescapably intertwined with such felt imperatives, and I strongly feel that there is a need for ethnographic arts scholarship that comes from this fully engaged place alongside alternate methodologies that gain insight from a more detached observational perspective on arts engagement and communities. Both lead to knowledge the other cannot yield.

Interviews with free jazz vocalists, free jazz choir members, and listeners have been another core research method. The artists generously expressed a rich array of histories and personal reflections, and documenting these has been a central imperative of this project. Preserving these was an obligation. To diminish, slightly, the filter my authorship places on these, I include "In Their Own Words" sections here. To diminish it even more, I have established a webpage in partnership with IICSI (http://improvisationinstitute.ca/research-project/voices-found/), where I include longer interviews. My method has been collaborative; all of my interviewees have been given the chance to read and modify the transcripts. Most have taken the opportunity to do so. Though I was well supported throughout this research and managed to speak to many of the artists whose work is most relevant to this study, time and resources were, as always, limited, and many artists deserving to have their work featured here are not represented. As I've already insisted, all histories are partial, but, nevertheless, I take this opportunity to apologise to all the singers I haven't had the time to study, consult, or consider.

Alongside the ethnographic methods employed in the work, archival research was also a valuable tool underlying this research. I visited public archives in Berkeley, San Diego, Los Angeles, New York City, London, and Paris and was also granted access to the personal archive of Phil Minton. Each of these visits led to discoveries that made the histories I present here richer and more precise.

Structure of the Volume

Voices Found is divided into two parts: Sources and Theories. The emphasis of the first is on elements that gave rise to free jazz soundsinging. The second is primarily concerned with theorisation of sounds, encounters, reception, and ideologies. The first part begins with a chapter that argues that interdisciplinarity was essential to the rise of free jazz soundsinging. I discuss the work of Yoko Ono, Jeanne Lee, Christine Jeffrey, Maggie Nicols, and Annick Nozati and explore how the interdisciplinary crossings between music and poetry, concept art, sculpture, dance, and theatre were essential to shaping the artistic and vocal practices of these five early free jazz singers. I discuss these five women, comparing and contrasting them with one of their male contemporaries and counterparts, Phil Minton, which reveals some distinctions in the ways male and female musicians navigated free jazz cultures in the 1960s and 1970s. Examination of the careers of these six vocalists presents us with an understanding of many of the most important interarts blurrings contributing to free jazz singing. Following the opening chapter are three interview excerpts from three of the figures featured in Chapter 1: Jeffrey, Minton, and Nicols.

Chapter 2 covers some of the ways technologies have shaped singing. The chapter is divided into two halves, the first of which covers the practices of the Ultralettrist poets, a concrete/sound poetry movement that began in France in the 1950s, embraced the tape recorder in ways that had profound implications on the ways poets and, later, singers would use their voices in performance. In the second half of the chapter, I turn to free jazz singers' comments on the ways samplers, sound synthesis, and processing devices have informed free jazz singing and modified the ways we conceptualise the meanings of vocal sounds.

Chapter 3 concludes the first part with a freewheeling tour of a broad range of influences on free jazz singing. I offer perspectives on scat singing, introduce free jazz singers not discussed elsewhere in the book, and reflect on the ways particular recordings and figures have shaped free jazz voice. I consider free jazz singing as a practice that encourages singers to appropriate limitlessly from the dynamisms of the world around them, not for the purposes of capture and control but rather as part of fluid embodied mimetic communion with sounds we long to bring into our bodies and personalise and hybridise.

Part Two begins with a chapter that examines differences between free jazz singing in the 1960s and the 1980s with a focus on the impact of the transnational, transgeneric, and transcultural encounters afforded by free jazz spaces and performed by voice-only free jazz ensemble projects. I focus on the projects of David Moss and offer brief career sketches of several of his contemporaries and collaborators. In so doing, I am able to fill important gaps from Part One and point briefly to other notable institutions and figures. The chapter also begins to focus on the reception of unfamiliar vocal traditions by looking at the ways certain audiences hear soundsinging through assumptions based on the bodies and available biographical details of singers. Following Chapter 4 is the second of the three sets of interview excerpts. This set introduces singers that began their practices in the 1970s or 1980s, including David Moss, Anna Homler, Jaap Blonk, and Paul Dutton.

Chapter 5 forwards a theory of the social functions vocal sounds can serve. This is the chapter that best highlights the productive nature of practice-based research as the theory I offer emerged from an incident that occurred after a performance I gave with Dutton. In this chapter, I explain that listeners often react to soundsinging with attempts to try to "correct" or contain the singers. I argue that these "policing" attempts are reactions to a disturbance of a symbolic order that requires bodies perceived as categorical counterparts to the listener's body to voice only sounds that construct that category as distinct and superior to its Others, the human and non-human bodies these listeners are semi-consciously invested in constructing as lesser or not-as-fully-Human (I use the capital H to indicate these self-privileging hierarchical imaginaries, distinguishing them from a more material definition of what constitutes the human). I argue that this incident is evidence that public sounding of unconventional vocal sounds can pose a challenge to some of the insidious and deHumanising imperatives that pollute the everyday. The chapter also appeals to a second example, radio host Howard Stern's reaction to Yoko Ono's 2014 performance at the Glastonbury Festival, to help expand the theory and its applicability, and to help illustrate certain core ideologies that undergird the practices of many free jazz soundsingers while addressing the ways the gendered, racialised, classed, and normativised body figures into the experience of voice.

Finally, Chapter 6 deals with the ways free jazz vocal practices have led to the development of free jazz community choirs. The literature on choral music and community choirs has seemingly not begun to recognise free jazz and conduction-based improvising choirs as a present and vital methodology for organising collective singing. This chapter seeks to help remedy that problem by tracing a history of these practices. And since these collective practices help illustrate ethical tendencies that run more broadly through free jazz soundsinging, the impulse towards inclusivity that is reflected in these choral practices is appealed to as an illustration of the same impulse fuelling much of free jazz soundsinging at large. Then, in the final "In Their Own Words" section, we meet six singers from the third and fourth generations of free jazz voice: Christine Duncan, Mankwe Ndosi, Tomomi Adachi, Fay Victor, Gabriel Dharmoo, and DB Boyko.

Then, in my conclusion, I end with a short meditation on the political potential of free music that I frame as a kind of prayer. As you'll see throughout this book, free jazz singing has led me to my own sense of what is sacred, my own ways of building community. It has been both a salvation in many senses and a cross I've had to bear, as others sometimes treat it as a threat they must contain or flaw they must correct. And just as I began this introduction with an invitation, I end the book with another—an invitation to make kin with what we don't yet know lies within us and around us: a vocal finding that will make us more socially virtuosic.[14]

Notes

1. Michael Edgerton's significant publication *The 21st Century Voice: Contemporary and Tradition Extra-Normal Voice* notably opts to prominently employ this term.
2. Paul Dutton, email to the author, 20 January 2019.
3. Paul Dutton, email to the author, 8 March 2014.

4. Ibid.
5. Paul Dutton, email to the author, 18 July 2004.
6. Many improvising singers have told me they value this type of vocal finding. Greetje Bijma wrote in her essay "Singing with the Wind": "I find it beautiful to spontaneously discover new facets of my voice, and this is something that is still happening. In fact it recently happened during an orchestra work wherein I shared an improvisation with the concertmaster. The high vibrato that came out in the concert had never been in my voice previously" (2006, 550).
7. For more on Dutton's techniques to heighten his ability to surprise himself during improvisation, see my discussion of his "Imp's Roves" in Tonelli (2016).
8. Resistance to the notion of "extended techniques" in free jazz is not unique to free jazz voice. Saxophonist Jack Wright, for example, when asked about "extended technique" in an interview with John Berndt, commented, "at this point I find players using a more integrated technique, where nothing is "extended" because no technique by itself connotes a radical departure" (Berndt 2018).
9. Jaap Blonk, interview with the author, 8 November 2013.
10. David Moss, interview with the author, 6 July 2013.
11. Ibid.
12. I have been a publicly performing free jazz vocalist since 2000. I have been employing the term "soundsinging" to refer to my practice and identity for much of that time to indicate Dutton's work was an essential influence shaping my practice. Though I sing in other genre contexts and in pitch-centered manners, I have done most of my performing, improvisational and non-improvisational, with less conventional techniques. These "extra-normal" sounds are the core of my work as well, not an extension of a pitch-centred core.
13. For a discussion of some of these motivations, see Schuiling 2019, 64–66.
14. The notion of social virtuosity here comes from and alludes to the work of Maggie Nicols, discussed in Chapters 1 and 6.

PART I
Sources

1

INTERDISCIPLINARY WOMEN AND EXPERIMENTAL VOICE

I do not "sing to pass the time I have left to live." I spent this time singing urgently to live. To find my way of singing, at first I screamed and yelled from the depths of my body, from pain. I made myself dizzy but it was there I found pleasure and peace for the first time in physical, intellectual, and moral form. To listen, be heard, and be in harmony in an environment that accepts you and that you understand, that's what I tasted . . . I chose the voice and improvisation . . . The result is a strange song, composed of various sounds based on different forces . . . Guttural sounds, lyrical sounds, multiphonics, explosive sounds, murmurs, hissings, sounds expressed through extreme tension, sounds that resonate in the body, harmonic sounds, spun sounds, trills, leaps between head voice and chest voice. I sing all these sounds and cultivate a form of expressive research and a musical approach that reflects righteous feelings through a beautiful instrument.

—Annick Nozati 2000[1]

In a 1983 review in the French publication *Jazz Magazine*, Christian Aguetaï enacts a distinction between singing and the performances of Parisian vocalist Annick Nozati by writing: "In the beginning was the word. Then singing. Then Annick Nozati . . . who is neither storyteller nor singer."[2] For Aguetaï, the notion of "singing" was distinct from what he described as the "simple" and powerful "poetry" of "Nozati and her sounds." The passage that opens this chapter demonstrates that Nozati herself did *not* make the same distinction. She identifies her practice as singing, even as she goes on to describe the fundamental role played in her work by a variety of sounds others (like Aguetaï) do not consider singing. For Nozati, allowing herself to work with these particular sounds made it possible to feel she has accessed something essential. These sounds were fundamental to the shaping of her vocal practice into a form she considers moral.

In this opening chapter I proceed from Aguetaï's impulse to recognise the practice of free jazz singers like Nozati, who improvise using sounds many listeners refuse to consider singing, as deserving of attention. At the same time, I follow Nozati's lead. I refuse to mark these practices as non-singing. However, I acknowledge that improvisation that explores body and voice in less conventional ways—whatever that may be in distinct cultural spaces—is often treated differently from normative singing and can give rise to social processes and affective experiences sometimes distinct from those afforded by other forms of singing.

Free jazz vocalists have been largely ignored in jazz studies, voice studies, and experimental music literature. However, free jazz vocal practices have made an important contribution to the body of practices referred to by "singing," by "jazz," and by "experimental music." The term "experimental music" is problematic (it is both a reification and a poor description of many of the practices under its umbrella, which often do not involve "experiment" per se), and it also bestows prestige, more often than not, as we well know, on white male composers and their works. The work of scholars like George Lewis, Ellen Waterman, Fred Moten, and Benjamin Piekut points to the roles race, gender, class, and nation play in excluding musicians and their practices from associations with the privileged category of musical experimentalism.[3] They each have shown how "adventurous jazz" has been left out of dominant accounts of experimental music that work to construct the category as a "white configuration" (Piekut 2011, 4, 10). As these forms of jazz get left out of the category of experimental music, within the borders of "adventurous jazz," vocalists are often marginalised, the voice often being considered too emotional or insufficiently abstract to exemplify the qualities that lead many to privilege "adventurous jazz" itself. Then, in one final layer of marginalisation, within the histories that take jazz voice seriously, ideologies exist that marginalise the unconventional approaches Nozati describes, which here I refer to as free jazz soundsinging.[4] And so, three layers of exclusion exist for vocalists who work improvisationally with unconventional sounds within the contexts of "adventurous jazz."

Each chapter in the first half of *Voices Found* explores a distinct source from which free jazz soundsinging emerged. These begin here with a focus on how it developed largely through the efforts of trailblazing women who crossed interdisciplinary divides to develop a practice of singing they found experientially invaluable. These women championed these methods in the face of efforts that sought (and continue to seek) to invalidate and marginalise it, despite the fact these singers felt it to be honest, healing, and moral.[5] Their collective efforts constitute a chapter in the history of experimental music whose recognition is overdue, a chapter capable of teaching important lessons about the meanings and processes that unfold when the voice is free to conduct the "expressive research" Nozati describes.

Alongside Nozati, this chapter follows four other women—Yoko Ono, Jeanne Lee, Christine Jeffrey, and Maggie Nicols—and one man—Phil Minton—through the contexts that constrained and afforded their work. These six careers do not, of course, tell the entire story of the rise of free jazz voice or even free jazz soundsinging, but they do reflect an important theme: the role interdisciplinarity played in the development of free jazz singing and in the negotiation of how women could participate in jazz performance in a manner that felt authentic and liberatory to them. Each of the five women discussed here crossed disciplinary borders and, in doing so, challenged the limits of acceptable vocal and musical practice. Without the innovations they brought into music from sound poetry, sculpture, experimental theatre, and dance, free jazz vocal practices would be less multidimensional and less critical.[6] This chapter examines this history and attempts to shed light on the gendered musical politics that marginalised these practices and shaped the ways these singers used their voices in the 1960s and 1970s.

In the 1980s, it became more common for free jazz singers to collaborate with one another. A broader consciousness that voice-only free jazz could stand on its own, proceeding without instrumental collaborators, arose. In this chapter, I outline developments leading to this, and I affirm that those largely responsible were female innovators whose experiences, moral compass, convictions, and interdisciplinary practices deserve wider consideration in the face of past marginalisation, dismissal, and ignorance of their work.

From Concept Art and Sound Poetry Into Soundsinging: Yoko Ono and Jeanne Lee

Yoko Ono is the most widely recognisable free jazz singer. Born in 1933 in Tokyo, Ono moved to New York in 1951 and, over the course of the next decade, began to establish herself as a major figure in contemporary music and art. In the decades that followed, exhibitions of her work as a concept, performance, and visual artist appeared in celebrated art institutions around the globe. Her musical work in the fields of art and popular music has been deeply influential, and her status as a pop culture icon from 1968 to the present is unquestionable. However, despite this recognition, writers who have chronicled her career often make short shrift of her work as an improvising vocalist. Since soundsinging itself has received so little attention, it has been difficult for many to make sense of this component of her creative practice. Equally, the striking work she has done in this area and the virulent reaction it often receives have made it difficult for them to completely ignore it. More often than not, their strategy for acknowledging this component of her creative practice involves a quick quotation of a particular passage from a review by Jill Johnston that appeared in *The Village Voice* on December 7, 1961, and an equally quick retreat back into other areas of her history and practice.

Johnston's review describes Ono's November 24, 1961 performance of her piece *AOS for David Tudor* at a concert of her work at Carnegie Recital Hall, and reads: "Yoko Ono, I presume it was Yoko Ono, concluded the work with amplified sighs, breathing, retching, screaming—many tones of pain and pleasure mixed with a jibberish of foreign-sounding language that was no language at all." Writers quoting this passage have often implied it contains everything that needs to be said about Ono's vocal work—she screams, she sighs, some sounds invoke moments when the body is in pain and others are sexually suggestive, and the word, that mark of "civilised" cultural practice, is absent, placing the meaningfulness and value of the performance into question. Though the passage is capable of conveying important aspects of Ono's vocal work, readers of the passage may or may not extrapolate from it that here was a musical performance informed both by feminist performance art and a history of intentional poetic resistance and rejection of the word.

Before the Lettrist poets (discussed further in Chapter 2) refused the semantic in their writing in the 1940s, arguing that words can only alienate poets from the dynamics of their embodied and affective existence, this refusal was also a feature in the 1920s of the work of Dada poets like Tristan Tzara, Hugo Ball, and Kurt Schwitters (Bohn 2001, 260–61). By the early 1960s, there had been decades of precedent for forms of poetry not prioritising the semantic, and at that time in New York, Ono was part of the Fluxus movement, a creative community that was extending these precedents in new ways. In 1960, Jackson Mac Low, a close friend and collaborator of Ono's, began working with a style of performance poetry that had also been used by the Dadaists, which he referred to as simultaneities.[7] Like much of Ono's work, Mac Low's simultaneities thwarted the dominance of semantic meaning and foregrounded the materiality of the voice not by refusing but by obscuring semantic content. Mac Low's simultaneities were poems intended to be read by multiple simultaneous readers who are "asked to read the verbal material at a pace and volume of their own choice" and "generate individual rhythms of articulations" (Kostelanetz 1978, 77). Some involved reading the same texts in different orders, and others involved a palimpsest of multiple different texts. Available recordings of performances of these works confirm Richard Kostelanetz's appraisal that they were often "unrelievedly chaotic" experiences wherein meaning could be subordinated to the effect of a wall of vocal materiality that was abstract by virtue of the fact the overlapping voices often made it nearly impossible to make out the semantic content (Ibid.).[8]

In 1961, Mac Low composed a poem called "Speech." The fact that he provided "directions for reading this poem aloud" is indication that "Speech," like many of Mac Low's poems, was a poem intended to be performed (Mac Low 2008, 95). "Speech" places a demand on the performer to produce unconventional vocal sound in the delivery of its second epigraph. Mac Low instructs the reader to: "Read the first epigraph and perform the second" (Ibid.). This second epigraph is a performance instruction asking the reader to reproduce a version of "The Sea Gull" by Joseph Gould. The instruction reads: "The 'reader' climbs onto a table or chair, flaps his arms wildly, like wings, & screams like a sea gull a good many times, as loudly, and harshly, and shrilly as possible" (Ibid.).[9]

These examples begin to show how abstract unconventional vocality was a part of poetic practice in Ono's New York. Acceptance of abstract vocal sound as poetic content in her community may have played a role in giving Ono the confidence to employ abstract unconventional vocal sound in her own performance and musical work. By positioning this type of work as music rather than poetry, Ono was setting the stage for much of what would come later in the realm of free jazz voice.

1961 was, for Ono, a year heavily oriented towards vocality. This is reflected in a number of her compositions. 1961 was the year she composed her *Voice Piece for Soprano*, a piece that encouraged a basic form of vocal "excess" by inviting the performer to scream in three different ways. This piece, and others I will discuss below, belong to the category of concept art, a practice Ono worked with extensively; Ono printed concept pieces like *Voice Piece for Soprano* for visual display, and a reader's encounter with the instructions and the imaginations and feelings that result can be considered a realisation of the work without any actual sound occurring. Yet at the same time, *Voice Piece for Soprano* and the other pieces I will mention below are indeed pieces Ono has realised through audible vocal performance. They are part of her legacy not only as a conceptual artist but as a vocalist, an improviser, and a composer for voice.

Another such work is her *Cough Piece*, also composed in 1961, whose instruction is: "Keep coughing a year." Though it may be unlikely Ono has ever performed the piece for the duration the instruction suggests, she has performed and recorded a shorter version of the piece. Hanne Beate Ueland describes Ono's 1963 recording of *Cough Piece* by saying: "The work consists of rhythmic coughing into an electronic 'carpet' of sound. At first hearing, the coughing can seem harsh and frightening, yet eventually it weaves itself into a web of sounds that lack variation: it becomes a seductive, meditative warp" (Ueland 2005, 127).

The "first of her word of mouth pieces," *Whisper Piece* (1960) involves an audience passing "on a word to each other in a whisper" (Iles 1997, 17). Though this may seem to involve only conventional speech, abstract vocal materiality was central to the work; Iles writes, "according to Ono," this piece was "about destroying the word" (Ibid.). When we whisper, the noise elements of speech, the sounds of airflow and stoppage as we create fricatives, plosives, and sibilants, are often louder than the voiced elements. When we listen to whispering, the abstract materiality of those noise elements draws attention to itself and often prevents us from clearly hearing semantic content. *Whisper Piece* might, then, be considered to have key elements of a collective participatory soundsinging experience, given the fact that it involves the vocalisation of everyone present at the performance.

These concept works are thoroughly interdisciplinary, blurring the lines between visual art, poetry, musical performance, and theatre. The idea of sound poetry, poetry that is incomplete until it has been sounded, is distinct from the concept work, which can be realised without sound. Yet when the concept work is positioned as music (through sonic realisations or gestures like titling the pieces in a manner conventional in music), audibility and musicality become the frames through which the pieces are experienced. This similarity helps us to see Ono's vocal practice as one that emerged cross-disciplinarily in conjunction with her poetic and concept work.

The language of Johnson's *Village Voice* review, the reference to "jibberish," and the flippant construction "Yoko Ono, I presume it was Yoko Ono," begin to communicate some of the resistance Ono encountered in presenting abstract unconventional vocal work as music. Though this type of work was gaining respect in certain poetry contexts, becoming recognised as a legitimate and athletic poetry of energy and human vitality, it would be some time before a critical mass of others began to develop musical practices sonically similar to Ono's, forming a community of practitioners capable of embodying the idea that this musical practice was emergent, shared, and valid.

Jeanne Lee

In the mid-1960s, another practice Mac Low was engaged in was "electronic poetry." He subjected electronic typewriters to randomisation processes to produce aleatoric electronic poems.[10] He sometimes read these over audio recordings of noise or other earlier performances he had given. Occasionally, these performances included elements we could consider soundsinging. A review of the fourth annual New York Avant Garde Festival in 1966 explained: "Jackson Mac Low spat forth shrieks, and ululations to the accompaniment of electronic feedback and the explosive sounds of the battle of Da Nang" (Garabedian 1966).

Mac Low is a link between Ono and another important early free jazz singer, Jeanne Lee. In the same period that saw Mac Low shrieking at the New York Avant Garde Festival, Lee participated in *A Program of Electronic Music, Electronic Poetry & Live Simultaneities by Jackson Mac Low, Max Neuhaus, James Tenney* at Town Hall in New York. This event, which took place on September 13, 1966, featured five of Mac Low's works, one of which was a duo performance between Lee and Mac Low of one of Mac Low's electronic poems.[11]

Born in 1939 in New York City, Lee is undoubtedly one of the most important vocalists in "adventurous jazz," though her work has been underacknowledged. Most of her early works are angular, harmonically inventive, and interpretively subversive performances of jazz and pop standards but are relatively conventional timbrally.[12] At Bard College, where she was studying literature, psychology, and dance, Lee met Ran Blake, and the two formed a piano-vocal duo that would occupy them for much of the early 1960s (Porter 2013, 90). Little available documentation exists of her work in the period between the early work with Blake and her return to commercial recording in 1969. As such, it is not immediately obvious how she transitioned from timbrally conventional vocal jazz to the timbrally diverse work she became involved with by 1969. However, archival sources reveal that in this period she was actively performing both jazz and sound poetry in a union of traditions that undoubtedly helped catalyse her extra-normal vocal work of the late 1960s.

The period documentation gets sparse roughly coincides with her marriage in 1964 to the poet David Hazelton. The couple moved together to Berkeley and quickly became involved in interdisciplinary artistic communities in the Bay Area. Hazelton was enrolled in a poetry class at San Francisco State University along with two poets, Doug Palmer and Jim Thurber, who would become Hazelton's closest friends and collaborators in this period.[13] Together they attended the first San Francisco Poetry Centre Readings, which featured luminaries like LeRoi Jones, James Wright, and Gary Snyder (Thurber 2008). Thurber explains that the three of them "began having a lot of 'face time' with the various poets around town who were open to mentoring us. The most available ones were Snyder, [Lew] Welch, [Philip] Whalen, [Robin] Blaser, [Robert] Duncan, George Stanley, Jack Spicer, Michael McClure, [Kenneth] Rexroth, and [Allen] Ginsberg when he was in town" (Ibid.). Hazelton went on to become a catalysing figure in the Bay Area poetry community, founding the poetry journal *Synapse* and organising a number of events, including the *First International Concert Reading of Experimental Poetry in the Bay Area* and the *First Exhibition of Experimental Poetry in the Bay Area*.

The venue for these two events was the Open Theater, an important interdisciplinary performance space in Berkeley from its opening in September 1965 to its closing in March 1966. The Open Theater was home to experimental theatre, spontaneous happenings, multi-media performances, jazz and rock concerts, poetry readings, and avant-garde classical music performances and lectures. Ian Underwood, a musician whose credits include playing in Frank Zappa's The Mothers of Invention and alongside Ornette Coleman in 1959 in the Herb Pomeroy Ensemble, acted as one of the music directors of the space. At the time, Underwood led a group called the Jazz Mice which Lee frequently performed with, including in an October 30, 1965, performance that was advertised, in one of the earliest uses of the term, as "psychedelic music."[14]

While continuing to perform separately in their own mediums, Lee (who had been writing poetry since she was eight years old) also collaborated with Hazelton.[15] She was credited as an editorial consultant on both the second and third editions of *Synapse*, and she performed a number of poems on the *First Experimental Concert Reading of Poetry in the Bay Area*. These included: a version of Robert Lax's poem "One Stone," which she performed with Underwood on saxophone; versions of Andrew Rawlinson's "Indeterminate Poem" and "Serial Poems 1 + 2" with Hazelton, Eileen Adams, Reed Cooper, and Ruth Franklin; a version of Mac Low's poem "Second Gatha" with the same team of voices; and a version of Mac Low's poem "Thanks" with Hazelton, Adams, Cooper, Franklin, Jim Wehklage, and music by Charles MacDermid.[16]

Mac Low was an important figure for Hazelton and Lee in this period. "Second Gatha" was both performed at the *First International Concert Reading of Experimental Poetry in the Bay Area* and printed in the program distributed at the event;

Mac Low's poems "The Comet" and "Thankfulness" were included in the third volume of *Synapse*; and, alongside Lee, Hazelton was also one of the readers on Mac Low's 1966 Town Hall concert.[17] Beyond Mac Low, Lax, and Rawlinson, Lee was also engaged with the work of other Fluxus artists and sound poets during this period. In a narrative of her career she prepared before her untimely passing in 2000, she described "composing music for the sound-poetry of Dick Higgins, Alison Knowles, Dieter Rot, Ian Hamilton Finlay and Henri Schaeffer."[18]

Though it was not until 1969 that Lee began appearing frequently again on commercial recordings, an unreleased recording of her appearance at the 1967 Baden-Baden Free Jazz Meeting exists. A description of this performance demonstrates some of the ways her approach to vocality in this period differs from her early work. She appeared at this Free Jazz Meeting with saxophonist Gunter Hampel, trombonist Albert Mangelsdorff, and a rhythm section composed of Buschi Niebergall and Pierre Courbois.[19] The recording documents a five-and-a-half-minute excerpt of their performance that begins with Lee reading the opening section of Robert Lax's poem "Andalusian Proverb" as follows:

> rooster
> rooster
> rooster
> rooster
> with your
> head cut
> off:
> what
> are you
> thinking
> now,
> you rooster,
> what are you
> thinking now
> of the bloody
> morning?

The end of this passage triggers Mangelsdorff to enter with staccato sixteenth notes that oscillate between his opening note and the minor third above. Lee wordlessly mirrors this staccato but with more irregularity and diversity of pitch content. The others then enter and contribute to the non-metric, pointillistic texture established by the voice and trombone. Lee's material stays in this staccato style for roughly forty seconds, at which point she engages in several throaty cries that seem clearly inspired by the crowing of the rooster referenced in Lax's poem. The pointillistic material returns before Lee begins to emit more rooster cries. Here, these transform into an unconventional technique involving rapid oscillatory articulation. She pauses for a few moments and re-enters with several voiced lingual trills. This is followed by some creaky phonation, more lingual trills, tense ultra-high-pitched shrieks, and then, finally, an improvisation using fragments of the opening text alternating with occasional abstract vocal utterances.

This 1967 performance contains many elements that recur throughout the history of soundsinging: a willingness to let the voice take on the timbre and function of other instruments, a willingness to let vocal performances be informed by non-human sound sources, and the influence of poetic forms that use repetition and/or fragmentation of words to underscore the materiality of language instead of its semantics. Her subsequent improvisational use of the opening text and her movement in and out of meaning betray the influence of sound poems intended to break down the semantic and blur the lines between poetry and music. This subsequent transformation of the opening text can be transcribed as follows:

rooster
rooster
rooster
rooster
with your head cut off
What are you thinking now
you
rooster
with your head cut off
what are you
what are you
what are you thinking now
now
now
now
of the bloody mooooooooooooooorning
what are you thinking now of the bloody morning?
mooooooorning
wha ah
wha ah
wha ah ah ah
wha ah ah
ah ah
uh
uh uh uh uh uh
uh uh
uh uh uh
uh uh uh uh uh
uh uh uh uh uh uh

uh uh uh uh uh
HAH
ah
are you thinking now
you rooster
what are you thinking now
of the bloody
morning
moorning
moooooor

Lee uses Lax's poem as a source for improvisation and breaks semantic language down into its non-semantic material components in a manner characteristic of the modular poems of Dick Higgins or Mac Low's gathas. She also transitions from phonemes to abstract unconventional techniques in a manner similar to Mac Low's movement into shrieks and ululations in his electronic poems. The manner in which she allows animal sound to act as a starting point, informing and inspiring the development of her own unconventional vocal techniques, bears resemblance to Mac Low's epigraphical incorporation of Gould's "The Sea Gull." But, distinct from many performances by Higgins or Mac Low, Lee was operating in a context that was unambiguously music rather than poetry centred.[20]

The general permissibility of abstract unconventional vocal sound in the sound poetry world Lee was immersed in between 1964 and 1966 seems to have played a pivotal role in the emergence of the variety of sound she made in 1967 and later. The practices and sound worlds of the free jazz contexts she entered into in 1966 and beyond were certainly a primary and immediate convention affording her the freedom to work with unconventional vocal techniques, particularly the precedent in that world to push your instrument into realms of "extended" technique. However, it is also clear that the choices she made in those free jazz contexts were informed by the experimental poetry practices she worked with in the mid-1960s. Other free jazz vocalists without backgrounds in sound poetry developed quite different strategies for free jazz vocalisation, strategies that often remained pitch-centric and/or word-centric. Like Ono, Lee worked with emergent conventions in experimental poetry and transferred them cross-disciplinarily into musical contexts. In doing so, she realised performances foundational to the broader practice of free jazz soundsinging.[21]

Yoko Ono, Jeanne Lee, and the Mixed Avant-Garde

Beyond her early performances in New York, another important early performance context for Ono was England in the mid- to late 1960s. An invitation to appear as part of the 1966 Destruction in Art symposium attracted her to London. Her initial period there in 1966 led to rich artistic opportunities for her. Vocality remained a part of Ono's practice beyond her initial burst of vocal activity in 1961 and 1962, but the next event of major importance to her practice as a singer, at least from the perspective of the present study, was entry into jazz contexts via her 1968 collaborations with Ornette Coleman, Charlie Haden, David Izenson, and Ed Blackwell. Ono has explained that Coleman attended a Paris show she was involved in and requested to meet her afterwards. During the conversation that unfolded he invited her to perform with him on his upcoming Royal Albert Hall appearance (Denberg 1997). This performance took place February 29, 1968. Perhaps of greater importance, due to their broader dissemination, were the recordings made during the rehearsals for the performance. One such recording was included on the 1970 *Yoko Ono/Plastic Ono Band* album. The track, which was given the title "AOS," documents how Ono's soundsinging frequently manifested as a form of feminist performance art.

"AOS" begins with Ono holding a single note while slightly modifying its timbre by adding and removing breathiness. She begins to oscillate the pitch and add tremolo as Coleman enters on trumpet. She works with this vocal material— gentle tremolos and small interval pitch variations—for the first two minutes. Shortly after the two-minute mark, there is a long pause. The other players wait for Ono to re-enter, and she does so with a series of moans whose looseness contrasts with the breath support demanded by her opening material. Between the moans she loudly voices her inhalations.

Pointing out that these moans seem intended to be sexually suggestive carries a danger. One of the tropes listeners use in attempts to delegitimise soundsingers is the marking of their vocalisations as "sex sounds." This is particularly true of responses to Ono, due largely to the deeply sexist and racist responses generated, in part, as a result of her celebrity. In most cases, these sounds bear little resemblance to the actual sounds of sex. However, Ono's approach to soundsinging is one in which the occasional explicit reference to the non-semantic "indicator" sounds we use in everyday life, including the sounds of sex, plays an intended and important part in her work.[22] In her work, non-semantic but referential sounds like moans and screams serve to invoke reflections on gender, embodiment, and power.

Her intention to explicitly reference sex seems clear in this recording when she begins to incorporate the words "no, not yet" into her moaning. The moaning becomes a regular panting that increases in intensity and climaxes with a violent, tearing scream that immediately alters the mood of the section. The transition might be experienced as a shift from consensual sex to non-consensual rape, a shift from gentle to rough or violent sex, or it might be experienced as a transformation of Ono's voice from a locus of pleasure to a locus of either pain, rage, or threat. Different listeners will interpret this abrupt transition differently, but regardless of their interpretation, the drastic contrast between two very different indicator sounds will almost certainly invoke thoughts of sexual politics and violence. These themes cohere with a broader feminist politics that runs through

Ono's work, and they affirm that her approach to non-semantic vocal improvisation is not devoid of "extra-musical" concerns.

Between the invitation from Coleman and the concert on February 29, 1968, Ono involved herself with other free jazz musicians in London. She was present at the February 18, 1968, recording session of *Karyobin* by John Stevens's Spontaneous Music Ensemble. This was an important connection. Stevens's ideas about improvisation and how the voice should and could be used in free jazz played an important role in shaping Maggie Nicols's vocal practice, and Nicols would go on to develop projects that would fundamentally shape aspects of free jazz vocal practice. Stevens also is a point of connection between Nicols, Ono, and Lee; he worked with Lee in 1967 at the Baden-Baden Free Jazz Meeting and with Ono in 1968 before performing with her in 1969 at the A Natural Music Nothing Doing in London Concert, and it was around this time that Nicols was beginning her work with Stevens. This connection will be discussed more below as we move deeper into Nicols's history. However, it is worth asserting here that Lee and Ono's approaches to the voice, informed by sound poetry and fostered by their movement between Fluxus-oriented and free jazz spaces, could have played a role in shaping how Stevens thought about the free jazz voice as he guided Nicols into the practice.

Both Ono and Lee's movement between jazz and Western art music contexts exemplify Benjamin Piekut's concept of the "mixed avant-garde."[23] Piekut employs this term to counteract the "snipp[ing] away" of certain musical histories "to preserve the cohesion and consistency" of representations of musical experimentalism (2011, 5). The imagined categories such histories help reify play a role in the justification of certain groups' access to cultural or economic capital and, subsequently, the denial of resources to others excluded from these categories. The mixed avant-garde, by contrast, is the messy reality that these artificially bounded categories obscure, a reality that was never contained in the ways these categories suggest. While this book, no doubt, like all histories, snips away histories and figures deserving of inclusion, it certainly does not do this to sustain the privilege of an already institutionally dominant art form and certain of its adherents.

Gender is a powerful force influencing many of the categories Piekut's concept is intended to help undo. The sexuality Ono projects in improvisations like "AOS" can function as a source of threat, and rendering it historically inaudible is the most effective way for a male-dominated avant-garde to contain that threat. The relative invisibility of the soundsinging tradition is undoubtedly a result of it being snipped away repeatedly in histories of experimental music, jazz, and singing. The politics that led the women discussed in this chapter to inaugurate free jazz soundsinging has come to shape both the practice and, we can theorise, the decisions that have left the practice out of so many of the histories well situated to address the tradition.

In his essay "Jeanne Lee's Voice," Eric Porter makes note of the "syncopated rhythmic conception" Lee incorporated into her reading of randomly generated typewriter characters at Town Hall with Mac Low. He notes the ways her black female body operated in moments like her permutation of the typewriter character ",", into the spoken "comma" and then "mama," a signifier Porter acknowledges that, when delivered by a black female body, is capable of evoking the black vernacular tradition of female blues singing. This, Porter argues, operates in conjunction with a deliberate effort Lee made to mark herself as a mother in her public performances. He notes that in her work Lee regularly "asserts her identities as an improvising artist *and* a woman with a child [and] [t]his assertion speaks of the way Lee's work negotiated, if not necessarily transformed, gendered definitions of improvised artistry" (Porter 2013, 99). Just as Ono notably performed her identity as an improviser and a mother, Lee was also claiming space in and performing both artistry and femininity in a musical domain dominated by men.[24] Also like Ono, she simultaneously faced the challenges of these gender politics, made the decision to publicly perform her identity as a mother, and cultivated a performance practice involving substantial use of abstract, unconventional vocal improvisation. For Nozati, abstract unconventional vocal sound was a tool that helped her feel in harmony with a (perhaps partially imagined) world that accepted her. For Lee and Ono, these sounds were part of their broader strategy to refuse to be reduced to the types of gender performances expected of female vocalists. They each made efforts to perform and connect to a more complete acknowledgement of their experiences and identities as women. These gender-informed efforts, fuelled by interdisciplinary innovations, should be acknowledged as a significant part of the mixed avant-garde.

From Sculpture Into Soundsinging: Christine Jeffrey

CHRISTINE JEFFREY: I wasn't a frontline singer.
CHRIS TONELLI: What do you mean by that?
CHRISTINE JEFFREY: I mean when you have a singer who is placed at the centre, everything goes around that, everything circulates around it . . . the beauty and drama of this instrument, and the look . . . I wasn't working like that. I was working more spatially. I was making my sculptures with sound.

(Christine Jeffrey, interview with the author, 6 May 2015)

Christine Jeffrey's presence in improvised music in the early 1970s was important to the development of soundsinging and, as she makes clear in the quotation above, her practice as a sculptor was an essential factor guiding her approach to vocal performance. Born in 1947 in Carlisle, Cumbria, in the Northwest of England, Jeffrey's vocal work differed in a number of ways from Ono and Lee's. The passage above highlights one of these differences—Ono and Lee were both used to being "frontline" singers. Though there were moments in both Ono and Lee's careers when they operated on an equal footing with their instrumental collaborators, these moments oscillated with others in which they willingly took up the normative position of singer as visual and sonic focal point.

Ono and Lee also both frequently worked in formats in which their soundsinging would emerge out of the delivery of spoken or sung lyrics, serving as a solo sandwiched between more normative forms of vocalisation. This was not the case in Jeffrey's practice. Jeffrey was a kind of *total* soundsinger in that she worked exclusively with abstract unconventional sound. Unlike many of Ono and Lee's collaborators, the instrumentalists Jeffrey worked with were never accompanists providing a ground for Jeffrey's solo soundsinging explorations; they all shared the same function, the same role as interacting improvisers who could take up the musical foreground or draw back from it as they saw fit. For these reasons, Jeffrey's presence in European free improvisation provided a unique model for how a singer could negotiate their practice. Though this model could and did inform the practices of both male and female singers, the path out of the front line was an especially important option for women. As the innovative multi-disciplinary American vocalist Fay Victor described to me in a 2013 interview, female singers have to fight "to feel like part of the band instead of just window dressing on top of it."[25]

The path that enabled Jeffrey to develop was discovered through apparently chance events. Describing her earliest experiences as a vocalist Jeffrey said she "was like . . . a found object, like the Duchamp urinal."[26] Indeed, her very first vocal performance was a favour for a friend that led to her being "discovered" by composer and original electronic instrument builder Hugh Davies and incorporated into a number of his projects. From 1965 to 1969, Jeffrey was a student at the Slade School of Art, University College, London. One of her fellow students, Gerald Newman, whose concentration was abstract painting, was examining his conundrums with the fixity of easel painting and decided to enlist a group of friends and create a performance connected with opening up other working possibilities for his painterly objectives of accomplishing totally random marks and events. He created a piece, which Jeffrey described as "really just lots of abstract lines and squiggles on a paper page," and arranged to have his friends interpret this graphic score in an improvised performance as part of an event held at University College London theatre (Ibid.). Jeffrey was asked to participate and gravitated towards using mainly her voice interpreting the score. Others also used voice but more often employed interactive movement, objects, or instruments. She gave a passionate performance, recalling: "I just got carried away. I opened my mouth and people started laughing, not in a derisory way, but in a participatory way, when I started making sound." (Ibid.). Davies happened to be in the audience. He approached Jeffrey and invited her to help realise a piece he was writing for voice and brass.[27] She obliged, and they developed some friendly exchanges. However, after performing Davies's piece Jeffrey felt "at a bit of a loss," wondering "where does this go from here?" (Ibid.).

Hoping to widen her perceptions of possible options, Davies brought her to meet and witness a performance by Cathy Berberian, the figure in contemporary Western art music best known for performance with "extended" vocal techniques. Jeffrey was impressed and at Hugh's behest agreed to perform Berberian's *Stripsody*, a 1966 graphic score consisting of images and onomatopoeic words one might find in a comic strip. Jeffrey recalls it was "on the strength of" her performance of *Stripsody* that Davies invited her to come along and try improvising with his group The Music Improvisation Company, a collective initiated by Derek Bailey, which consisted at the time of Davies and his own uniquely built electronic instruments, and two other leading figures in European free jazz: saxophonist Evan Parker and percussionist Jamie Muir (Ibid.). Free improvisation served as the provisional answer to her question "Where does this go?" For the next several years (spring 1970 to spring 1973), she was a frequent presence in the London free jazz scene. She became a regular member of The Music Improvisation Company and developed close collaborative relationships with Bailey and Muir, often appearing with them in other group configurations. By spring 1973, when she withdrew from music making for approximately seven years, she had worked with a number of other figures and groups in the London scene, amongst others Terry Day, Johnny Dyani, Paul Lytton, Paul Rutherford, Frank Perry, Phil Wachsmann, Georgie Born, Lindsay Cooper, and the group Henry Cow. She began to perform publicly again in 1980, contributing sporadically to events and festivals in the UK and France until 1987, when she again ceased performing.

As I mentioned, Jeffrey's innovation of soundsinging as a musical identity complete in itself, available as an alternative to frontline singing, was an interdisciplinary extension of her practice as a sculptor. Newman's concerns with fixity was an interest Jeffrey shared.[28] She explains:

> I tended to build things up with clay rather than be a carver-out of things, so you touch continually . . . and that reflects some kind of inner process that you're going through . . . Something is going on with your ears; it's like you're listening to the space around that subject . . . [but] I was finding a lack in that way of working . . . It seemed to just rely too much on the visual . . . it wasn't, somehow for me, communicating about this experience I had within my self of actually creating so that space is occupied . . . [or] the idea of time, because when I did the beginning stage of a clay built sculpture, that all became covered up as if that hadn't happened, was somehow disengaged with concluding. I was searching for something much more as a medium, that wasn't so solid . . . So . . . when fortuitously volunteering to help out with Gerald's piece and using my voice, the minute I starting using my voice, that, to me, seemed very much to do with my experiences, dimensionally, of what I'd been engaged with in trying to make sculptural objects, because you'd make a sound . . . and you can't solidify it, so then you don't fall so much into the inevitable grasping when making shape, or

making an object, which can only 'take off' constricted by the elemental, material fact of its life, and somehow fixes itself . . . I felt the more ephemeral aspects of its conception and gestation into form somehow didn't get reflected . . . So it was to do with that and, fortuitously, I found I could use voiced sounds, and then not only that, but using my own body, the producer of my sounds, as another sort of plastic element.

(Ibid.)

Her blurring of the plastic arts, and the more ephemeral act of sounding, solved a problem that she later realised didn't need to be solved quite so literally, as her focus on exploring created forms, material and those only generated in mind through the medium of Buddhist meditation practices and philosophy, began to take precedence over her musical activities in 1973. Despite this shift and despite the relatively short duration of her two periods of public musical activity to date, her vocal sound sculpting was noticed by other figures in the London free jazz music community who would go on to occupy much more prominent positions in that world than Jeffrey.

Phil Minton: From Music to "Music?"

Phil Minton is one of the most internationally prominent improvising vocalists. His consistent presence since the mid-1960s and the depth of his focus on abstract, unconventional vocal work have led him to become one of the best known free jazz singers. Unlike Jeffrey, and like Lee and Ono, Minton's musical identity is not limited to soundsinging. He grew up singing in church choirs, and he sings pitch-centric material on many of his projects.[29] He spent many years as a singer and trumpeter in popular-song-oriented projects. A native of Torquay in South West England born in 1940, Minton dates his impulse to improvise with unconventional vocal sound in professional settings to back before 1966, the year he left the UK for a five-year period playing in dance bands in Sweden, explaining: "I'd been involved in the real early stages of the free jazz or the European free improvising. Friends like Lou Gare from the Mike Westbrook band, they went on to form AMM. This is where I wanted to be, but I was a little bit shy about it. There was no one really using their voice in this sort of way. I didn't know of anybody."[30] His shyness faded somewhat during his time in Sweden. Commercially available evidence of his soundsinging dates back to a recording from 1969 (first released in 1999) of a session with Swedish musicians Lars Göran Ulander (alto sax), Lars Gunnar Gunnarson (bass), and Sten Oberg (drums).[31] This recording and others Minton made in the period immediately following his return from Sweden suggest that soundsinging was something Minton incorporated relatively sparingly into his work in this period.

During his time in Sweden, the London scene had changed. Minton recalls: "while I was in Sweden, I got to hear that there were voice women. Actually,

Maggie [Nicols], who was very young at the time, was experimenting quite early on . . . Christine Jeffrey had done some things with Derek Bailey. I can't think of anyone else, but there were. It was happening. I didn't feel completely alone."[32] This suggests that recognising one's musical practice as shared can make a difference in the decision to pursue the practice. The presence of these "voice women" made Minton feel less alone, and his musical identity gradually shifted over time to one that increasingly resembled the Jeffrey model, though, again, he has remained invested in a variety of distinct vocal forms.

In 1975, Minton recorded a series of solo vocal improvisations at the newly opened South Hill Park Arts Centre in Bracknell.[33] The recordings reflect the increasing commitment Minton was directing towards soundsinging in the mid-1970s. Though it would be six more years until these recordings were released, they would later come to be combined with two sets of solo vocal improvisations he would record in 1980 and release the same year as the album *A Doughnut in Both Hands—Solo Singing*. Knowledge of the existence of female improvisers employing unconventional vocal techniques encouraged Minton to feel less alone and to conceptualise that voice-only free jazz had the strength to stand on its own, without the need for instrumental accompaniment. Jeffrey provided an important model that would later be adopted by others like Minton. Minton built on this model by becoming, it seems, the earliest musical performer to record a full album of solo voice-only free jazz for commercial release. *A Doughnut In Both Hands* offered voice-only free jazz as a musical practice complete in itself and encouraged the next generation of soundsingers by assuring them they weren't alone in their explorations of this marginal but, for all the singers we have discussed in this chapter and this book, essential musical practice.

From Experimental Theatre Into Soundsinging: Maggie Nicols and Annick Nozati

One of the "voice women" Minton came to be aware of in his time in Sweden was Maggie Nicols. Nicols was born in Edinburgh, Scotland, in 1948, but moved to London in 1959 and began the path that would lead her to become, alongside Minton, one of the central figures in free jazz singing. Like Minton, Nicols's centrality is due in part to her consistent presence in free jazz from the late 1960s to the present. Like Ono, Lee, and Minton, Nicols is engaged with a broad array of vocal styles. Soundsinging is a component of her work thanks to the radically inclusive nature of her philosophy of voice and improvisation.

She began her vocal career singing standards in "pubs, hotels, and clubs, at weddings and business functions, with some wonderful British jazz musicians" (Nicols quoted in Cowley 2008, 14). She describes her first encounters listening to free jazz as performances in which the voice was not present but where she "could hear a voice doing that kind of music" (Ibid.). When she shared this thought with others she learned that the percussionist John Stevens was, in fact, making free improvised music that included the voice. She sought him out sometime in late 1967 or early 1968 and attended a performance by Stevens and vocalist Norma Winstone. She found the performance "very inspiring," thinking: "Wow!—I want to do that with my voice" (Ibid.). Winstone was active in jazz from 1965 and remains so. She led her own bands, worked extensively with Stevens and with many of Mike Westbrook's projects, and collaborated with myriad of other musicians. Though her free jazz work in these early years was extensive, this work focused predominantly on pitch-based improvisatory singing. She did colour her work with some unconventional sounds; however, existing documentation suggests that these sounds remained a relatively minor element of her singing.

Nicols made contact with Stevens and his close collaborator Trevor Watts in 1968, and she received an invitation to join them for an improvisation session at the Little Theatre Club.[34] Her first experience improvising with Stevens and Watts was transformative; she says of it, "I had never experienced anything like it. It was an absolute liberation for me" (Ibid.). Part of what made it liberating was Stevens's instructions for how she should approach vocalising in the context. They were performing his structured improvisation piece *Sustain Piece*, which involves sustaining a note of one's choosing for the full length of a breath and repeating this over and over for extended periods. Stevens's instruction was that "it doesn't matter if your voice wavers or wobbles or croaks" (Nicols quoted in Tonelli 2015). Achieving a purity of tone was not a priority. What was a priority was achieving, through repetition, a state beyond self-consciousness. Nicols explains:

> John's pieces seem designed, in the manner of meditation, to take you away from all conscious limitations and preoccupations. My aim when I sing is to tap into the infinite resource of the unconscious mind. If you're coming from the conscious mind you're far more likely to run out of ideas. I do believe there is a shared human experience, whether or not you choose to call it the collective unconscious. That source is unlimited—everything that's ever been is in there and it's always moving. Connecting with that, you're opening out with constant movement and change.
>
> *(Nicols quoted in Cowley 2008, 14)*

Nicols's relation to soundsinging comes less from a conscious desire to explore specific vocal sounds and more from her policy of accepting any direction her body and voice take her when she allows the unconscious mind to guide her improvisations. This is one aspect that leads me to refer to her practice as radically inclusive. When one follows the voice in this way, it will guide us into sounds other than pure tones. It will croak and wobble and wander into multiphonic soundings and timbres that fail to symbolise the genders we've been interpellated into and, often, even our humanness. Challenged to recall how unconventional sounds came to become part of her singing, Nicols replied, "I never set out consciously to do that. Everything happens because I went into the subliminal mind in fact and discovered stuff, discovered what was there."[35]

Also radically inclusive is the fact that Nicols's unique approach to improvisation is not limited to improvising with sound. Within music contexts the "everything" that "happens" in her performances frequently includes dance and forms of restored behaviour which may manifest through song, speech, or movement. Performance theorist Richard Schechner defines restored behaviour as "physical or verbal actions that are not-for-the first time" (Schechner 2002, 22). I employ the term here as a means of referring to Nicols's tendency to shift into displays that may be viewed as more theatrical than musical. Many of her improvisations display behaviours that normally occur exclusively outside of the space of musical performance—Nicols might launch into the behaviour of chastising herself for being sloppy or the behaviour of a teacher pontificating to a student or the behaviour of someone proclaiming their love for toasted cheese and butter or the behaviour of scolding someone for going too long without cleaning their oven, or all four within the space of one improvisation.[36] These sections of her improvisations are frequently autobiographical performances restored from her own everyday experiences as a mother, an activist, a lover, a woman, a Scot, an anarchist, or a frontline singer in a realm of unequal gender roles. In other cases, they display and restore behaviours she has witnessed in others, allowing her to temporarily engage in intersubjective embodiments that also often reveal the dynamics of gender and power in everyday contexts. In all instances, these theatrical displays underscore the performativity of and power dynamics within everyday action.

The incorporation of these theatrical excursions into musical contexts has been an innovative extension of the musical methodology she derived from Stevens. For her, tapping into the resources of the unconscious mind invokes these memories of past behaviours. Rather than police the impulse to restore and display them in favour of retaining a "purely musical" space, Nicols has extended Stevens's philosophy by being true to these impulses and developing an improvisational methodology that blends absolute music and theatrical display.

The choice to do this within musical contexts has required courage. Nicols explains, "there was a lot of hostility to that."[37] She speculates that this hostility was the result of the dominance of an ideology of absolute music in European free jazz communities in the 1970s, arguing: "I think they felt it was a bit vulgar, or it wasn't aesthetically abstract enough . . . I get the sense they felt it was muddying, it was polluting the purity of the music in some way."[38] Since the late eighteenth century, ideologies of musical modernism have argued for the superiority of absolute over programmatic music. Gary Tomlinson notes that "in the decades before 1800 . . . instrumental music—music without words, non-song—posed a new exclusionary category redolent of European spiritual superiority" (2012, 62). These ideologies have persisted to the present day and have played a role in the formation of the ideologies of jazz modernism Nicols encountered. As such, her efforts existed as a courageous challenge to the ideologies that dominated many of the contexts she worked in. These approaches figured prominently in the performances of Nicols's group, the Feminist Improvising Group (active 1977 to 1982), and they were undoubtedly one of the central reasons the group was frequently dismissed as lacking in musical seriousness (alongside the group's belief in mixed-ability ensembles that included performers of varying levels of musical skill).[39]

Nicols's interdisciplinary improvisation is also a result of her movement between musical and theatrical domains. Theatre has been important to Nicols from the beginning of her career. From ages twelve to fifteen, she attended the Italia Conti Academy of Theatre Arts. After this, she became a showgirl at the Windmill Theatre, participating in their "living statue" format of erotic performance.[40] When the Windmill closed in 1964, she began to oscillate between the roles of frontline singer in pubs and strip clubs, dancer, showgirl, and hostess, all of which, of course, involve a degree of theatricality.[41] Theatre became central again after her initiation into free jazz. Looking for a place to rehearse, Nicols's ex-husband and former bandmate Harry Vince negotiated access to the Oval House Theatre in a period in which it was one of the most important venues in the UK for experimental, gay, lesbian, and women's theatre.[42] Nicols has stated that alongside Stevens: "Oval House was my other influence."[43] A 1972 article in *Melody Maker* described how the Oval House "obviously has a great effect on her thinking—mainly because it's exposed her to all sorts of other art forms. As well as music, the centre houses workshops for theatre, dance, mime, and clowns, and Maggie feels that they've all drawn strength and inspiration from each other" (Williams 1972). The same article quoted Nicols describing how at the Oval House, "We watch each other working, and it opens us all out" (Ibid.).

It was in this period of multifaceted involvement with the interdisciplinary environment of the Oval House that Nicols first started incorporating movement, speech, and theatricality into her improvisations. She cited a performance in 1971 with Vince as "the first time I brought other things into an improvised performance" (Nicols quoted in Charlton 1982, 41). She recalls:

> I remember one gig I was doing, this must be about 1971, when the music really wasn't happening . . . it felt so dishonest that at one point I just felt myself compulsively doing a movement and all of a sudden, I couldn't believe it, but out of my mouth came this voice, "I'm lying, I'm LYING!" and I started dancing because it was the only way I could escape, because of course I'd been a dancer, but I'd never thought of connecting it. So through a really frustrating block and unconsciously verbally owning up to that block something new and positive came out and that's something I've actually developed and worked with over the years —being that honest, talking, demystifying, baring it all.
>
> *(Nicols quoted in Scott 1990)*

Though Nicols's interdisciplinary approach to improvisation was informed by her background in experimental, fringe, and other forms of theatre, it is unclear if these environments also explicitly shaped her openness to unconventional sounds. The methods she developed working with Stevens seem to be the primary source of this openness. However, it is also worth acknowledging that Nicols had exposure to both Ono and Lee in her first year as an improvising vocalist. Nicols recalls encountering Lee at the Total Music Meeting in Berlin in November of 1968, where Nicols performed in a quartet version of the Spontaneous Music Ensemble alongside Stevens, Watts, and a second vocalist, Carolann Nichols.[44] Lee appeared at the meeting with Gunter Hampel, and there is evidence to suggest she may also have actually performed with Stevens at the meeting using a soundsinging-style vocal approach; in his book *Innovations in British Jazz, Volume One 1960–1980*, John Wickes wrote: "For the performance of 'Familie' at the 'Total Music Meeting' . . . in 1968, John Stevens used the voice of Jeanne Lee—wife of German multi-instrumentalist Gunter Hampel—a highly individual vocalist who had developed techniques to translate 'natural' sounds with the human voice" (1999, 60).[45] The experience of witnessing a vocalist as respected as Lee "translate 'natural' sounds with the human voice" may have helped reinforce Nicols's sense that unconventional approaches to the voice were a legitimate component of free jazz vocalisation.[46]

The community of practice Minton was lacking in the early 1960s was one Nicols found shortly after first discovering improvised music. A few months after her first work with Stevens, on March 2, 1969, Nicols performed with the Spontaneous Music Ensemble at Cambridge University in A Natural Music Nothing Doing in London Concert, the same concert at which Yoko Ono, John Lennon, John Stevens, and John Tchicai performed an extended improvisation that would later become the track "Cambridge 1969" on Ono & Lennon's album *Unfinished Music No. 2: Life with the Lions*. Again, this close encounter with a leading exponent of extra-normal free jazz singing may have worked on some level to legitimise such sounds for Nicols. Similarly, the work Stevens did with Lee and Ono before meeting Nicols may well have influenced him to assure Nicols: "it doesn't matter if your voice wavers or wobbles or croaks."[47]

Annick Nozati

While the vocal practices of experimental theatre may or may not have influenced Nicols's openness to unconventional vocal sounds, they undoubtedly played a role in Annick Nozati's development as a soundsinger. Born in 1945, Nozati developed as a multi-disciplinary artist in Paris in the 1960s. Her work as an improvising singer began with an invitation in 1967 from French composer Jacques Lasry. Since 1955, Lasry had been performing with a series of sound sculptures created by François and Bernard Baschet. Lasry's invitation to Nozati was for her to come and interact with these sculptures. Though Nozati was not at this point an "improvising singer," she had been working with her voice as an actress in a theatre troupe called Compagnie Grain D'Orge. It is notable that the leader of this troupe was a speech pathologist named François Le Huche. In 1963, Le Huche published *La Voix Sans Larynx* (The Voice without the Larynx), an instructional manual to help post-laryngectomy patients recover speech ability through techniques like the use of esophageal voice. Le Huche's experience with alternative methods of speech production likely contributed to Nozati's interest in alternative forms of vocal production. Though little available documentation of the work of Compagnie Grain D'Orge exists, a partial understanding of the role of unconventional voice in experimental theatre in France in the 1960s can be gained by a discussion of the work of another theatre group Nozati was involved with in the 1960s: the Living Theatre.

The Living Theatre is celebrated today as one of the most important groups in experimental theatre of the 1960s. Though the group was founded in New York City, from September of 1964 until 1968 they were in exile in Europe after a conflict with the U.S. Internal Revenue Service. Though the extent of Nozati's involvement with the Living Theatre during this period of exile is unclear, she stated that she was influenced by their methods.

One of the works the Living Theatre developed and toured in Europe in this period was their *Mysteries and Small Pieces*. Documentation of this piece demonstrates that an extended section of the work called *The Plague* contained at least six minutes of uninterrupted ensemble engagement in improvisatory work with unconventional vocal sounds. Living Theatre founder Julian Beck stated, "the basis of *The Plague* is [Antonin] Artaud's description of the plague in Marseille in the 17th century and the idea is that if we can move the audience physically, that is, if we can make them feel physically revolted, disgusted, pained, agonised, frustrated, if we can break through the doors of feeling, then once beginning to feel something, maybe the other doors of feeling will open up" (Beck quoted in Brockway 1969). Artaud's theatrical methods and efforts also involved attention to unusual vocal timbres and articulation and, like the Ultralettrist poets I will discuss in the following chapter, aspired to find ways to exceed language.

In an interview, Nozati described how "[she] began [her] artistic life as a comedian in 1965 in experimental, non-verbal theatre, such as the Living Theatre" (Nozati quoted in Blackford 1997). It is probable that her first encounter with Lasry was in a theatre context, as Lasry and François Baschet were active as music directors for theatre in France throughout the 1960s. As with Jeffrey and her "discovery" by Davies, Lasry's invitation to Nozati coaxed her across an interdisciplinary divide into music. Like Jeffrey and other free jazz soundsingers who value autodidactic approaches to shaping the voice, Nozati described herself as being "self-taught in music and singing . . . without the classical rudiments of music" (Ibid.).[48] Also like Jeffrey, this distance from the prohibitions and aesthetic hierarchies of dominant music cultures allowed her to confidently use her voice in unconventional ways in improvised music contexts. Forms of vocal pedagogy focused on the production of "pure" tones frequently characterise unconventional timbres and sounds as "unhealthy" in an ideological use of the term that vocal students are often compelled to universalise. Conversely, Nozati's autodidacticism allowed her to form her own approach to vocalisation as well as her own sense of what constitutes vocal health.

Nozati describes how after beginning her explorations with the Baschet sculptures, "[she] also met and worked with improvising musicians, in particular the Art Ensemble Of Chicago who were then living in Paris" (Ibid.). Around 1975, her work shifted from predominantly theatre to a deep devotion to improvised music. She remained active in this field until her death in 2000.

Though Nozati's vocal style was more heavily invested in the production of pitched material than Jeffrey's, she usually wove rapidly between pitch production and complex unpitched sounds. Like Jeffrey, Nozati crossed into music from another discipline, and her embrace of unconventional vocality was fuelled in part by her disconnection from the norms and prescriptions of professional musical communities. Unfortunately, despite her activity throughout the 1970s, commercial recordings of her work do not appear until 1983. Her self-titled debut album features solo improvisations and compositions composed predominantly of nonstandard vocal techniques. Judging from the unconventional quality of that work, her autodidactic approach to voice, and the sonic qualities of the sound sculptures that informed her early practice, it is likely Nozati's early singing was also largely a form of soundsinging.

Conclusion: Interdisciplinary Women and the Mixed Avant-Garde

By 1983, there were a number of voice-only free jazz recordings available. Alongside Nozati's self-titled solo album debut and Minton's *A Doughnut in Both Hands* were Maggie Nicols and Julie Tippetts's 1982 vocal duo record *Sweet and S'ours*, and an extraordinary live record released in 1977 of vocal quartet improvisations, compositions, and structured improvisations by Nicols and Minton with Tippetts and Brian Eley, a participant in Nicols's vocal workshops at the Oval House. This quartet, which, like the recording, was simply titled *Voice*, was an early example of free jazz vocalists working together without instrumentalists present. The project was short-lived but helped prove that voice-only free jazz was possible, while also helping to give rise to the improvisational choir movement I will discuss in Chapter 6. Just a few years later, collaboration between free jazz vocalists on voice-only festivals, evenings, or, equally significant, isolated improvisations on shows that also featured instrumentalists, would become common. These voice-only recordings and performances served to affirm the existence and legitimacy of the new practice of voice-only free jazz.

It was at this point that voice-only free jazz soundsinging had fully emerged. Many soundsingers who began their practices after 1980 describe discovering the practice on their own, without knowledge of other practitioners. However, they also describe discovering quickly that others existed. Though free jazz voice remains relatively marginal and many listeners have not yet experienced free jazz soundsinging, practitioners who began after the early 1980s share the benefit of

knowing they are part of a small transnational community of improvising vocalists, a community in which the first generation of practitioners asserted the legitimacy of their practice and worked to help others understand the ethico-aesthetic
motivations behind their unconventional uses of the voice.

Our understanding of these motivations begins when we acknowledge that free
jazz soundsinging emerged largely from a group composed mostly of women marginalised in various ways—not just because of their gender but often also because
of their race, their sexuality, or their unwillingness to conform to the norms of the
frontline singer—who refused to isolate the various components of their artistic
practices from one another. Each of these women practiced a radical inclusivity
that challenged the norms and borders of artistic disciplines that would have prevented them from cultivating a creative practice uniting important aspects of their
interests and identities. Lee, Ono, and Nicols refused to parse out their identities
as mothers from their identities as artists. Nicols refused to submit to the norms
of jazz modernism and exclude the gendered power dynamics of her everyday
life from her improvisations. And all five of these women refused to keep their
experimental poetry, sculpture, dance, or theatre isolated from their music making.

This chapter may have been more coherent if it dealt just with the histories
of the five early female soundsingers. However, Minton was clearly a contemporary of these women who played an equally significant role in the formation of
soundsinging in the late 1960s and early 1970s, and saving his history for another
chapter would be yet another instance of historical revisionism in the service
of an oversimplified narrative that privileges particular groups by obscuring the
more complex realities represented by Piekut's concept of the mixed-avant-garde.
On the other hand, there are many ways that Minton does not fit in with the five
women discussed here. The shyness that kept Minton from vocalising more in his
early experiences improvising in London must be understood in connection to
the fact that Minton was accepted and respected as a trumpeter in those communities. We can contrast this fact with Nicols's comments on how she came to
be a free jazz vocalist and not an instrumentalist in the late 1960s. She describes
how she "had a hunger, [she] loved John Coltrane, [she] was obsessed with Bill
Evans," but rather than taking up Coltrane's instrument, the saxophone, or Evans's
piano, she felt her only entry point to this music she loved was the voice, because,
as she has stated, "I didn't see any women playing instruments, I just assumed
that we were biologically not meant to play instruments. I know, it's sad, right?
But, it's really how I felt" (Nicols quoted in Tonelli 2015). Other male singers
who, like Minton, gravitated to vocal improvisation from another instrument have
described how their community of musical collaborators often strongly rejected
this choice. American vocalist David Moss, for instance, describes how when he
began using his voice in his improvisations alongside his drumming:

> I felt then that the rest of the New York scene was not at all interested in
> the singing voice and tolerated my voice because I was drumming in an

interesting way. And so I held my voice back, forced myself to stop singing; and there were complete gigs where I wouldn't make a single sound
with my voice. I felt like I had a hand clamped across my mouth. I knew
I was being silent for a good reason. It seemed clear to me that, in this
abstract noise scene, if I started opening my mouth and singing what I felt,
I wouldn't be asked back.[49]

Moss's comments help us understand that Minton's shyness may have been connected to the fact that his soundsinging may have put his acceptance as an improvising trumpeter at risk. Nicols's notion that women simply had no option of
being accepted as instrumentalists reveals that acceptance in this musical community was (and still often is) radically different depending on one's gender.
While Moss and Minton's vocalisation may have threatened their acceptance as
instrumentalists in their musical communities, many women entered those communities knowing that these varieties of acceptance were out of reach for them.
Though all of these women's experiences were different, none of them were in
the position Minton was in. They were all in the very different position of knowing their acceptance within these communities was constrained in ways distinct
from their male counterparts. Yet by the late 1960s, second-wave feminism had
a foothold in America and Europe, and the notion that women could "listen, be
heard, and be in harmony in an environment that accepts" all aspects of their
identities and aspirations was informing women's visions of their creative practices
as well as their visions for a new social order.[50]

Nicols recounts that at the Oval House one day she found a copy of the feminist text *The Female Eunuch* by Germaine Greer. She recalls how Greer's chapter
"Hate: Loathing and Disgust" "spoke clearly" (Nicols quoted in McKay 2002) to
her about various forms of mistreatment she experienced in and beyond the jazz
scene. The book helped her understand how this treatment was part of "a pattern
of oppression, a socially built culture of patriarchy" (Ibid.). The result of this new
understanding was, as she describes: "I stopped worrying obsessively about male
approval" (Ibid.).

It was in this new era of feminist thought and action that these five women
and one man looked differently at their options and made bold choices to cross
disciplinary boundaries and cultivate a creative practice that, as Nozati suggested
in the opening epigraph above, was "physical, intellectual, and moral" in form and
capable of yielding "pleasure and peace" by radically including sounds, divergent
practices, and modes of expression that felt true to these singers. The new practices they innovated offered Ono, Lee, Nicols, Jeffrey, and Nozati ways of integrating various dimensions of their practices and identities into a new and satisfying
unity. For Minton, the interdisciplinary excursions of these women provided him
with a community of practitioners that emboldened him to risk losing the acceptance he had achieved as an instrumentalist and fully embrace a practice that he
had long felt drawn to but that feminised him and that made his musical life and

status more precarious and uncertain. For Minton too, soundsinging offered a way of integrating parts of himself that the gender politics of jazz modernism and the broader social order functioned to keep separate or deny him. Explaining his choice to employ unconventional vocal sound, Minton explains:

> I think humanity has been duped somehow or other. In Western Christian society, we've been told: "this is what the voice does." Think how politicians and priests talk, they're giving this information over and over about right and wrong. Vocal oppression I would say ... We've been sanitised vocally ... I think the human voice has been suppressed and I like to think that I'm part of the liberation, the vocal liberation movement.[51]

The social forces that legitimise male instrumental expression in the free jazz domain and discourage male vocal expression are one and the same with those that make it difficult for women to be accepted as instrumentalists in that same domain. These are also the same forces that have left soundsinging out of histories of musical experimentalism. These are all dimensions of the gender politics and values that extend from a still-dominant musical modernism that the concept of the mixed avant-garde can help to counteract. The free jazz soundsinging innovated, in part, by these five women and one man deserves a space in jazz history, free jazz history, and the broader history of this mixed avant-garde; we all deserve the opportunity to understand what this "vocal liberation movement" can offer us, and what we can gain from this "form of expressive research ... that reflects righteous feelings through a beautiful instrument."

Notes

1. My translation of Nozati's French.
2. My translation of Aguetaï's French.
3. See Lewis 1996; Waterman (forthcoming); Piekut 2011; Moten 2003.
4. See the introduction for a discussion of this term.
5. See Chapter 5 for a theorisation of efforts to correct and contain less conventional vocal sounds.
6. Here I use "critical" in the sense of "critical theory," Max Horkheimer's notion of theory that seeks to diminish suffering and inequity.
7. See Ades 2006 for examples of Dada's simultaneous poetries. Ades includes, for example, a letter from Hugo Ball describing Tristan Tzara's organisation of a three-voice simultaneous reading of poems by Henri Barzun and Fernand Divoire as well as a three-voice reading of poems by Tzara himself (Ball 1916). There is also an explanation by Tzara of how Barzun was the first to suggest this method but how Tzara's intention differed in that Barzun sought a polyrhythmic quality which Tzara was not interested in (Tzara 1916). Tzara explains his intention, the creation of events wherein each individual listener would attend to different components of the dense presentation and create their own unique work. This theme of empowering the creativity of the audience will be explored in Chapter 5 in relation to Ono's Fluxist ideologies and the ways soundsinging often shares this participatory emphasis.

8. Recordings of simultaneities are available as part of the Jackson Mac Low Papers at the University of California, San Diego. There are also examples online on Concordia University's *SpokenWeb* archive.

9. Gould's performance of this poem is documented in Mitchell 1942. Mitchell quotes Francis Lambert McCrudden, the head of a poetry society called the Raven Poetry Circle, describing how at their "nature-poetry night [Gould] begged to recite a poem entitled "The Sea Gull." I gave him permission, and he jumped out of his chair and began to wave his arms and leap and scream, 'Scree-eek! Scree-eek!' It was upsetting. We are serious poets and we don't approve of that sort of behavior."

10. In his article "Jeanne Lee's Voice," Eric Porter explains that Mac Low created his piece *The text on the opposite page may be used in any way as a score for solo or group readings, musical or dramatic performances, looking, smelling, anything else &/or nothing at all* by "assigning two-digit numbers to the keys of typewriter and then depressing the keys in an order determined by the occurrence of random-digit couplets in the RAND Corporation's table *A Million Random Digits with 100,000 Normal Deviates*" (2013, 102–3).

11. A commercial recording of this was released in 1977 by New Wilderness Audiographics. Mac Low described the performance in the liner notes of this recording. See these notes or Porter (2013), which reproduces parts of Mac Low's description. Mac Low subsequently performed the piece with a recording of the Town Hall performance playing in the background. One such performance was given at Sir George Williams University in 1971. In his spoken introduction to this 1971 performance, Mac Low states that Lee, who he refers to as "a very fine blues singer," was "in the various works that were performed on that concert," implying that she performed on more than just the duo piece. It is probable that she also participated in the realisation of the pieces "4th Gatha," "The Long Hot Summer (new Summer 1966 version)" and/or "Asymmetries, Gathas, and Sounds from Everywhere," all of which involved indeterminate simultaneities of multiple voices, readers, or poems. The program for the concert can be found in the Jackson Mac Low papers at the University of California, San Diego. The recording was reissued in 2018 on the album Jackson Mac Low *Poetry and Music.*

12. A case could be made that the ornaments she employs and her breathiness on her early recordings amount to a unique approach to timbre. However, such devices are subtle compared to the wide-ranging timbral exploration she employed later. The work is not short, however, of being subversive, as it contains imminent critiques of the gender politics of the standards she performs. For more on this aspect of her early work, see Eric Lewis's forthcoming research on Lee.

13. The class was taught by Mark Linenthal.

14. 24 October 1965 edition of the *Oakland Tribune*. At the time of writing, a scan of the listing was available online at http://thinkerumgatherum.blogspot.ca/2009/07/birth-of-psychedelic-music.html. Accessed 20 January 2019.

15. Lee discusses her history as a poet in an interview with Lona Foote published in *Ear Magazine* in May 1988, saying: "I started writing poetry when I was eight, and all through high school, where I was poetry editor of the yearbook. In college, and after that, poetry became a kind of journal. It was the way I moved through the world, my environment, making sense of it to myself" (28).

16. Evidence that Lee performed these works comes from the discography that comprises part III of Christian Scholz's *Untersuchungen Zur Geschichte Und Typologie Der Lautpoesie* (*Studies on the History and Typology of Sound Poetry*), available online at www.engeler.de/lautpoesiediskographie.pdf. This discography also states that on the concert Hazelton read Ernst Jandl's poems "Ode Auf N," "Schmerz Durch Reibung," "Schützengraben," "sehnsucht," "Restaurant," and "Reich Der Toten." It also indicates that the performance of "Thanks" also featured music by Charles MacDermid.

17. Evidence of this comes from www.engeler.de/maclow.html.

18. Lee quoted in Porter 2013 from an unpublished "Narrative of Career" in Porter's possession.
19. Lee first met Hampel in 1966. The two were working together frequently by 1967 and later married.
20. It is worth noting that Mac Low was, in addition to being a poet, a musical composer and performer. As such, he too operated in contexts that were unambiguously musical. However, the simultaneities and other pieces I am discussing here as precursors to soundsinging were likely to be received most often as poetry, poetic performance art, or between music and poetry. Fluxus artists often framed as music activities that would not traditionally be considered music, even activities that contained little or no sound. Blurring the lines between traditional artistic domains and fostering individualistic reception through means like encouraging others to attend to the musical qualities of visual events was a substantial concern to many artists in the Fluxus movement. However, these forms of blurring do not entirely erase the fact that Lee's Free Jazz Meeting performance was at a music festival and that she was part of a group of performers that understood themselves to be musicians exploring a musical genre. Even if Mac Low understood his simultaneities as music, audiences would not necessarily experience it this way because of the context. Lee as an accomplished jazz vocalist taking techniques of sound poetry into a jazz context was distinct from Mac Low. Audiences experiencing her work in this jazz context would have been likely to understand her work as, first and foremost, music.
21. In the years that followed, Lee used conventional speech, conventional singing, fragmented speech that weaved in and out of meaning, and soundsinging in her work in nearly equal measure. Some highlights of her exploration of soundsinging can be found on the track "Maliperos Midnight Theatre" on Marion Brown's 1969 album *In Sommerhausen*, "Crepscule" from Gunter Hampel's *The 8th of July 1969*, her contributions to Marion Brown's 1970 *Afternoon of a Georgia Faun*, the entirety of her 1972 *Familie* recording, and "JJ&A" from her 1979 album *Nuba*.
22. Trevor Wishart defines indicator sounds as "acoustic utterances [that] may be taken to indicate the state of the organism, but are not necessarily voluntary emissions" (1996, 246). When soundsingers employ screams, moans, coughs, gasps, etc., these sounds are not actual indicator sounds, but they reference actual indicator sounds.
23. Lee's appearance at *A Program of Electronic Music, Electronic Poetry & Live Simultaneities by Jackson Mac Low, Max Neuhaus, James Tenney* at Town Hall, her composition of music for the sound poetry of Fluxus artists like Higgins and Knowles, and her involvement in events like John Cage's 1976 realisation of his *Renga With Apartment House 1776* all speak to the "mixed" aspects of her career.
24. Ono performed her identity as an improviser and mother in works like her "Don't Worry Kyoko (Mummy's Only Looking for her Hand in the Snow)," a piece in which Ono improvises with the words of the title in a modular manner resembling Lee's version of "Andalusian Proverb." Performances of "Don't Worry Kyoko" often proceed from repetition of elements of the song's title, which then break down semantically, transforming into extended abstract vocalisation.
25. Fay Victor, interview with the author, 8 November 2013.
26. Christine Jeffrey, interview with the author, 6 May 2015.
27. This piece was realised with six brass players and Jeffrey's vocal improvisation.
28. Indeed, this shared concern was a dominant trend in British art at the time. In the introductory essay in a catalogue for a retrospective entitled *1965–1972—When Attitudes Became Form*, curator Hilary Gresty writes: "Within seven years, the 'new' changed from static, coloured, abstract sculpture which fulfilled the criteria outlined by William Tucker of being floor-based, of human scale, having completeness of form which could be immediately comprehended, using materials in a controlled and determined way and was totally abstract, to being applicable to something which crossed the boundaries

of many disciplines, which asked questions, not only about its own means, but also about knowledge itself" (1984, 5).

29. Notable examples include the sung portions of *Songs from a Prison Diary* (1989), an evening-length work by Minton and the pianist Veryan Weston based on the writings of Ho Chi Minh, and Minton's vocal work in Mike Westbrook's settings of the writings of William Blake, which they have been performing together sporadically from 1971 to the present. Minton's singing on these projects adopts the clear tones of the Western classical vocal ideal. On other projects, like the work he did in Westbrook's rock project Solid Gold Cadillac, Minton adopts a grittier blues-influenced timbre.

30. Phil Minton, interview with the author, 24 June 2014.

31. Phil Minton Quartet 1999 (1969). For more on Minton's work on this record see Chapter 3.

32. Phil Minton, interview with the author, 24 June 2014.

33. Minton's use of South Hill Park Arts Centre to record in 1975 followed his involvement in Theatre at The Park in South Hill Park as a member of Mike Westbrook's All Star Brass Band. The band performed a live soundtrack to a production of Ben Jonson's *Bartholomew Fair* from August 5 to 9, 1975. Minton's recording session was on 15 August 1975. Westbrook's projects were featured at a number of South Hill Park events around this time, including the Bracknell Jazz Festival at South Hill Park in July 1975. The theatrical and interdisciplinary performance work Minton was a part of both within and beyond his involvement with Mike Westbrook's bands is, of course, relevant as well to the core theme of this chapter.

34. Keeping with the theme of interdisciplinarity underscoring this chapter, it is worth noting that the Little Theatre Club was a venue for live theatre but also accommodated musical performances often in the late evening after the evening's theatrical performance had concluded or on Sunday afternoons when no other performance was occurring. Stevens was responsible for establishing the venue as a site for musical performances, and he made music there nearly every week from 1966 to 1974. Nicols performed regularly with Stevens's Spontaneous Music Ensemble in and beyond the Little Theatre Club for approximately six months, from fall 1968 to spring 1969. Later in her career she frequently collaborated with Stevens through the co-teaching of music workshops for the Jazz Centre Society and in other contexts. I discuss this in more detail in Chapter 6.

35. Maggie Nicols, interview with the author, 25 June 2014.

36. These particular examples were all taken from a single improvisation that occurred 25 March 1982 by Nicols, Joëlle Léandre, and Lindsay Cooper at l'Ancienne Gare de la Bastille. See "Heads Will Roll" on the album *Live at the Bastille*.

37. Maggie Nicols, interview with the author, 25 June 2014.

38. Ibid.

39. Nicols emphasises technically virtuosic musicians often lack social virtuosity, which might be defined as the ability to be deeply aware of and respectful of others and their needs. For her, social and musico-technical virtuosity are both skills that lead to valuable experiences for improvisers and audiences of improvisation.

40. The "living statues" method was a way of evading censorship. Representatives successfully argued to the London theatrical censor that since nude statues were not considered obscene, if the "Windmill Girls" were merely posed in tableaux and not moving that this too should not be considered obscene.

41. Between 1964 and 1968, Nicols often travelled for work, working in Manchester, Greece, Iran, and at the Moulin Rouge in Paris. She also worked at a wide variety of performance spaces in London.

42. Maggie Nicols, interview with the author, 25 June 2014.

43. Ibid. For more on her involvement with the Oval House and its role in the rise of free jazz choral music see Chapter 6.

44. Maggie Nicols, interview with the author, 25 June 2014.
45. Lee and Stevens were also both participants in the 1967 Free Jazz Meeting in Baden-Baden.
46. Nicols has described to me how she "loved Jeanne Lee" and how she compared herself to her for some time, wishing she had some of the qualities of Lee's style. However, she made no reference to Lee's work with less conventional sounds. Rather, it was the "understated" quality of some of Lee's performances that she admired. My speculation that Lee's excursions into soundsinging helped create a sense in Nicols that unconventional sounds were acceptable seems plausible but remains speculation. Again, Nicols does not emphasise the unconventional sounds she uses as particularly important parts of her work, she employs them and accepts them but does not underscore them in the manner I am engaged in here.
47. Ono was present at the 18 February 1968 recording session of John Stevens's album *Karyobin*. Recording that day were John Stevens, Evan Parker, Derek Bailey, Kenny Wheeler, and Dave Holland. This meeting led to a concert by Stevens, Bailey, Parker, and Ono at the Arts Lab in London on 21 April 1968.
48. For more on autodidacticism in free jazz singing, see Chapter 3.
49. David Moss, interview with the author, 6–7 July 2013.
50. See chapter epigraph.
51. Phil Minton, interview with the author, 24 June 2014.

In Their Own Words I

IN HER OWN WORDS—CHRISTINE JEFFREY[1]

CJ: I went to the Slade school of Art. It's part of University College, London . . . I found it sort of difficult and took refuge in the sculpture department. I think that's when I really started to find out where I was going . . . That's when I did the first vocal pieces . . . That's when Gerald [Newman] (he was an abstract painter . . . at that time interested in randomness and also in John Cage) . . . decided to write a . . . score . . . I volunteered to do it when asked if I would help out with it by a fellow student and friend, sculptor John Davies, along with a few other people . . . It wasn't really about voice . . . we weren't singers. It wasn't about a musical result . . . but through that, what happened was I started making sounds using voice. I became interested in my own right in what was happening, as relating to what I was doing which was in the sculpture realm, and had basically so far been a lot of work from life . . . life sculpture. What I was becoming more and more interested in was the problem of things, having been stated or made, were as if just stuck in time and didn't continue being fluid, and also the idea that if you have an object you have to go around it rather than being in it, in a space . . . Hugh Davies had come to the UCL theatre and he saw the piece . . . and asked me then to do a piece which he was writing . . . So I did that . . . I'd opened something in myself which was really important in terms of what I was doing sculpturally.

Hugh was a really kind person, a very gentle, very nice man. He said that Cathy Berberian was in London and he thought I should go see what she was doing and meet her. So we did. That was impressive. And then I did *Stripsody* at the UCL theatre, and then on the strength of that, when Hugh was playing together with Derek Bailey and Jamie Muir and Evan Parker, as a group together, he invited me to come along and sing some sets with them at a gig one night at one of the London colleges, City College I think it was . . . A few people said to me "Oh, you're like Yoko Ono screaming" but I'd never actually heard her so I didn't know how she worked vocally. Derek [Bailey], mentioned her too; I think he'd worked with her in a gallery performance context[2] . . . Anyway, the gig went great with us all and I was invited to be part of them whenever there was a future gig for that particular grouping . . . Probably what was happening was that I wasn't relating from any kind of musical clichés, because I didn't know any. So, maybe that was refreshing for them . . .

CT: So Hugh said you should check out Cathy Berberian? Could you tell me about going to do that?

CJ: She was performing at Royal Festival Hall . . . She was a friend of his.

CT: Oh, really? Did you meet her then?

CJ: Yes. We went to see her and then we went around the backstage . . .

CT: What were your thoughts that night about the way she used her voice and how it might have been different or similar to what you were starting to explore?

CJ: I thought she was like a "proper" singer, even if she was doing unusual things . . . She was obviously coming at it from a different place than I was coming at it. I used to feel I'd landed in this wonderful place by default, but, okay, it's interesting . . . I didn't feel, to begin with, the later insecurities of not having "proper" musical training . . .

CT: Did Berberian perform *Stripsody* that night?

CJ: She might have. I can't remember. Probably she did. Probably that's why Hugh took me.

CT: And then you sought out the score yourself and decided to perform it?

CJ: Hugh gave me the score and I just went and did my own thing with it. I practiced it a lot . . . Hugh was very astute like that. He wasn't trying to turn me into a singer, so to speak . . . I felt a bit of a fraud as a "musician."[3]

CT: Why?

CJ: Because I didn't really know what they were talking about technically, musically, and I was doing what I was doing instinctively and from another kind of platform I suppose, though obviously it was music. When I was at one of the Chantenay festivals Alan Hacker, a clarinet player . . . asked me to come do a gig with him in Paris. His wife Karen Evans was a classical pianist and was giving a solo performance there too . . . I went to Paris with them, but it turned out to be a great trial of my self-confidence, that kind of formal world of musical performance. Where I was coming from then was more like an exploration, an interaction with existing soundscapes that were already there . . . When it's a given form that you follow, when you do that, you have fall back a lot on learned techniques . . . It's like you're repeating. It's not like you're totally new, pristine. It's like snow that's been walked on a lot . . . if it's clear unmarked snow, you find your own way, pretty much, which was the way I was working. That's the way it works. It's not to say that the other way is no good, it's great for some people, but it's not what I was going for . . .

Alan invited me after Chantenay to come meet and stay with his friend Harrison Birtwhistle further down south in France with him, but I didn't go. I was caught in a process of real assessment about it . . . I can't say that I decided to stop doing it. I didn't. I just moved, following personal creative truths, and that world, everybody who was engaged with it, seemed to recede of itself, like naturally fading echoes . . . Then when I came here [to the monastery] and began to study meditation in earnest, then I began to see that it fell away, that need to externalise things all the time, to be looking by making marks, sounds, reactivity. It became very, very rich, and I didn't need to do all those things as a means . . .

CT: I'm curious about this feeling that you're doing something you already did.

CJ: If it's not fresh, alive, it doesn't have a quality of revelation. It's the same thing all over again . . . if somebody asks you to do it, you can do it, but then there's this feeling that you can't waste any time, life's short, you mustn't waste any time. It's like when people say "Oh, do that joke again you always do." It's that level. So there's a reluctance to engage in that way, because also, if you do you're going down the path leading towards creating a fixed identity—that's who I am, that's what I do—that's not such a skilful thing to do if you're very interested in trying to find out what's the essence of being, your essence of being . . . I feel it's somewhat dangerous in a way, because it's very easy to get seduced by all that certainty, very, very easy . . .

CT: How did you find your sounds and what do you think they might have meant to you?

CJ: I wouldn't think what they meant. They just seemed to be right. It was also to do with where in the body the sound is coming from. It wasn't just that you need your stomach to make a deep, low sound, but if you're making it from there, that communicates something to somebody on another level. It wasn't like I want to make that kind of sound, so let's get it down in there. I think it was to have to do with, again, getting back to the roots of being a sculptor, it had to do with the body as a defined form of a kind, and the sounds that it made. And at the same time . . . you just play around with what comes from where. It's playfulness as well—what comes from where—and sometimes it's humour. It's sort of like, no sounds were ever off limits . . .

CT: How did you find the sounds you used? Did you see anyone else doing them?

CJ: No. I just did it.

CT: You just discovered them all on your own?

CJ: Just listen now [we were speaking outdoors at dusk and the birds and insects were particularly noisy]. It's all there. The spaciousness of how it all comes to you. It's not flat. The body is not flat, inner sounds, outer sounds, everything.

CT: Did you have an active practice of listening to environmental sounds and trying to vocalise them?

CJ: No. I don't think I did, because I didn't use to go around practicing in that way, but at a further point on I did start to think: "Oh, I better get a good voice now."

CT: What made you think that?

CJ: This was a sort of insecurity which developed spending so much creative time amongst accomplished musicians and starting to feel I was expected to have a "good" voice. I was probably making it all up, possibly due to my roots in a totally different tool area, but I think also because I had concern people may not understand where I was coming from. Instead of just seeing what it simply was, they'd be judging my voice as an instrument of beauty, of not beauty, musical capabilities . . . it all changed somehow. I couldn't find the openings for spontaneous mutuality, flow through the moment, when I was working later on. I didn't have any compensatory musical language skills in common. In fact, it seemed to be destructive towards the meditation aspect of what I was increasingly focusing on, that whole flow . . .

I had reserved a sort of horror about what I called ladies singing from their bums and tits. I mean, I'm not being mean about women who do that. I can appreciate and enjoy it, watch it. But I didn't want to get into that. It was like you are this isolated female object at the front of the stage with, inevitably, a group or band of people blowing their raised trumpets, whatever. It's a form and it's sometimes a beautiful form and people do amazing stuff like that, but I never saw myself like that.

CT: Was there ever any pressure to move in that direction?

CJ: No, it wasn't what I was about and I thought it was about time that things weren't just about that as well.

CT: You had found your vocal practice.

CJ: I think it was after a Chantenay gig in France that somebody said to me: "You should train your voice. You'd have a really good coloratura. Have you thought about training?" And I thought: "This is an issue." It was this problem.

CT: Why was it an issue?

CJ: This thing about layers of convention and definition of what music or the voice is. Why can't it be just what it is?

CT: You felt that way about the voice when someone turned to you and said you should train classically?

CJ: Yes. It made me doubt that what I was offering could hold up, that it wasn't of much contributory value. Perhaps that what I was doing was seen as just some things I was playing about with. But I wasn't playing at it. I certainly didn't want to get insistent or strident about it though, and get diverted. What appears in the clearest focus is the pressing issue of personal integrity on a creative journey, the spiritual journey, life's journey. That was always paramount for me.

Christine Jeffrey interview excerpts appear with the permission of Christine Jeffrey condensed from a longer interview conducted by the author.

IN HIS OWN WORDS—PHIL MINTON[4]

CT: I've read that when you were young you often would imitate your family members.

PM: Yeah . . . My family had very, very rich voices. My father was a baritone singer and my mother was a soprano. The family was always singing . . . I was a boy soprano as well . . . I did it more for entertainment for people. Like, I used to do Jimmy

Durante, an American show biz singer. He was also called "Schnozzle Durante." He had a very large nose. He used to sound like [*does a raspy Durante impression*]. My parents always had very, very clear voices, very pure voices and I used to entertain the family by impersonating these people that, actually, I realise, were often people that had something pathologically wrong with their voices, people like Schnozzle Durante; he used to talk like that all the time. Like Louis Armstrong [*does brief Armstrong impression*]. I found that quite easy to find . . .

CT: Do you have a theory about why you were attracted to those kinds of voices?

PM: I think it probably had a lot to do with the fact that my parents and all these voices around me were all these very clear, pure voices . . .

CT: You've said you had a private practice of vocal improvisation your whole life, but was it after you left England that this private practice first began to become public or was it before that?

PM: In 1950s Britain, there were education establishments called art schools. Some of my friends in Devon were pupils at art schools, training to be artists. At the time I wished I'd been one, but could not draw, or do anything with my hands; handwriting was also a problem. One of these friends, Mike Tolliday, introduced me to Jackson Pollock and we decided that jazz should sound like an action painting. I would play some finger-wiggling trumpet and Mike would throw paint on the walls of his studio the size of a big cupboard. I think these days were very influential on later events when I moved to London in 1963 and met other musician art students like Keith Rowe and Stan Willis who likewise had interest in the more "abstract" areas of music. Let's face it, American Black jazz at this time was truly awesome—Coltrane, Dolphy, Mingus, Coleman, Booker Little—and it seemed almost like sacrilege to attempt to emulate them. And, of course, it was also very fucking difficult to play their music. I could do the "Brit fake blues singing" that was popular at the time, but could not take that music seriously; I loved the real Black American blues as much as the contemporary jazz. I'd come out to London in 1963. I came to join the Mike Westbrook band as a trumpet player and also I did a jam session with John Surman and some other guys locally in the area where I lived in Devon and I used to do a very mean impersonation of Jimmy Rushing in those days. I loved all the blues singers, the blues voices. Jimmy Rushing was one I could do very convincingly. There was a lot of this going around in the early 1960s with the blues boom that happened, especially in England, in London. Again, it was from Voice of America, I think, when they were promoting the sounds of American Black music in Europe. That's where a lot of the rock music singers came from. I could do that quite easily. I could impersonate a fifty-year-old blues singer, being a nineteen-year-old clean-living white boy. I could get a [*demonstrates a throaty blues timbre*]. I don't even want to use that but I used to. I could fix it. But it absolutely wasn't me at all. I was never really comfortable with it . . .

CT: I like to use Paul Dutton's term soundsinging . . . I think you have used it in past interviews yourself. Is this also your preferred term?

PM: I've always called it singing.

CT: Yes. There's a politics to not parsing it out. There's also a utility to having a term to use to refer to more timbrally diverse forms of singing. If we were going to use a term other than singing, what would your preferred term be?

PM: Shall we say soundsinging?

CT: Okay, so you don't mind if we use soundsinging occasionally as a short form. That specific side of your singing, it appears on the *Up Umeå* album.

PM: Yes, Umeå refers to a river, also a town where little jazz sessions used to happen in the 1960s.

CT: More free jazz oriented?

PM: Yeah. I was involved with some of the players up there. That was completely separate to the dance band work that I used to do.

CT: Was that context the first place you performed soundsinging in public?

PM: I think that was it. Yeah. We didn't have many gigs, I must say. I was still working with the dance band as well . . .

CT: What motivated you to leave Sweden and come back to London?

PM: There were a lot of reasons. I wasn't particularly happy with this job, although I was quite comfortably paid. I didn't feel I was part of the scene. The scene was going on in London and I wanted to be back . . .

CT: Were there any other influences, vocally, when you started bringing this out publicly? Any other soundsingers that might have helped legitimise the practice for you or made you feel like it was okay to do it?

PM: Yeah, first hearing the sound poets. Bob Cobbing and people like that.

CT: So, you had discovered Bob Cobbing by that point in the late 1960s?

PM: I think probably this would have been in the 1970s. I didn't know about Bob in the 1960s. But, Bob Cobbing, Clive Fencott, there were a few. There was this whole sound poet scene in London that was quite separate to the improvised music. I sort of knew about them . . . I was working with these theatre groups like IOU and Welfare State and most of the people were pretty open. It was an experimental period of all sorts, visually. Everything seemed like it was okay. So I was quite happy. People welcomed me . . .

CT: In 1975, you recorded the first part of what would become *A Doughnut in Both Hands*. Can you tell me about the context of that recording?

PM: They were live improvisations recorded, and then I went back and listened to them afterwards and selected the pieces that I liked.

CT: Am I right to think it was recorded at the South Hill Park Arts Centre in Bracknell?

PM: I did a lot of recordings there, yeah.

CT: So, it was in a studio then, not in front of an audience.

PM: Yes. It was in a very nice acoustic recital room.

CT: Had you been doing solo vocal improvisation performances prior to that?

PM: I don't think I had, actually.

CT: What motivated you to record solo vocal improvisations?

PM: I thought it needed to be done. Someone's got to do it.

CT: By that point, had you heard anything similar? You said you had heard the sound poets in the early 1970s, when you got back. Was there anyone in music doing solo vocal work of that kind? Had you discovered Demetrio Stratos, for instance, by then? His first solo vocal recordings were after yours, of course.

PM: Working with Mike, we were on the same bill as Demetrio Stratos at an Italian gig. That was the first time I came across him.

CT: When was that?

PM: I think it would've been around 1977. We were working in an Italian festival. This was with a Westbrook band that wasn't Solid Gold Cadillac.

CT: The Westbrook Brass Band?

PM: Yes, the Brass Band. And together with Henry Cow we had a group called The Orckestra and we were on the same bill as Demetrio. We got on actually, we were backstage jamming together actually. I remember we were talking about overtone singing. I didn't know how to do it and he was just discovering it himself. He showed me the technique. He was at the beginning stages of doing it as well and I was also working on multiphonics. We were jamming together with overtone singing and multiphonics and we said we must do something together and then sadly he went off to America, I think. We exchanged addresses, in those days when you had to write to people, we never got around to doing anything and, sadly, he died. He was working in a parallel world . . .

CT: Was the 1975 portion of *A Doughnut in Both Hands* released in any form before 1981?

PM: No.

CT: When you released it in 1981, how did that change your life as a musician?

PM: It got a very good review in America. I was quite surprised. I don't think it got many good reviews, but it got one. I'm trying to remember the magazine. I started to get offers of work as an improvising vocalist.

CT: Did that lead to you putting down the trumpet completely?

PM: It was already on the way down. I'd already decided that this wasn't for me. I was working exclusively as a singer . . .

CT: Let's shift to talking a bit about the Feral Choir. You were asked to do the first workshop in the late eighties in the music centre in Stockholm. But I read that you had been leading vocal workshops prior to that?

PM: No, I don't think I had. I didn't want to do a voice workshop. There's a recording with Lol Coxhill and Welfare State Theatre Group where it's a song that Lol wrote, I think it's called "Song of the Evening," and I suggested to Lol that we have a background of voices using some of the musicians that were present and some of the actors from Welfare State. I suggested this soundscape of voices to go behind this quite classical-sounding melody. I think this is probably the earliest manifestation of my idea of what may be called feral choral music. People have called me a feral singer. I always rather liked that idea. Then I was asked to do this thing in Stockholm and I thought I'd try to extend the idea of these vocal soundscapes, not particularly doing voice workshops. It was done as an experiment. I'd say, "you guys go [*he turns to his left and models a steady dental-labial rhythm, then turns to his right*] and you guys go [*he models a saliva swishing sound and then turns dead centre*] and you guys go [*he models fast arcing sibilants*]" and we'd put these things together. It was a one-off thing at the time. I did it and then I think someone else heard about it. It evolved. I was doing it once in France with some people that weren't sort of experienced, it was like a community workshop on a housing estate somewhere in the suburbs. There were lots of people; they weren't singers. They were just people who wanted to come out and use their voices. It was quite hard work I remember. But, afterwards a husband of one of the women that had been involved in it—who I actually had spotted and I was thinking she hadn't been all that happy with it all because all she seemed to be doing was going "la la la la la"—came up to me and said: "Phil, she was so happy to be in this group." She was there as well and she came over and said it was one of the best experiences of her life and all this sort of stuff. The whole group was so warm towards me and I thought: "this is something else that I'm doing here." I started to get into it then and would offer it out as something I did. This is probably ten years after. So, I was reluctant. I would always think "Oh God, I've got one of these choir things coming." I didn't realise that I was on to something . . .

CT: So, prior to that experience the groups you were working with were exclusively singers?

PM: They were musicians, yeah. But, when I was with people with no experience of jazz or experimental music, this was what turned me. I got more and more into working out the different timbres that could be used and started to really think compositionally about the pieces, although the people are improvising . . .

CT: Since then have you gone out of your way to work with the kinds of communities that you worked with in France?

PM: I always say it's open to absolutely anybody. I don't want it to be just like people that do experimental vocal work. I've done it in music colleges, which I'm not too keen on, with singing students. I don't want it to be part of any curriculum in music colleges; people are reluctant to come along, you know violin players saying [*he imitates a reluctant violinist*] "oh, voice," trombone players. It's gotten easier. There seems to be a whole constituency of people now that are really into it and they know what they're coming for: people want to use their voices, non-singers and non-musicians.

Phil Minton interview excerpts appear with the permission of Phil Minton condensed from a longer interview conducted by the author. More information on Minton can be found at www.philminton.co.uk.

IN HER OWN WORDS—MAGGIE NICOLS[5]

CT: Can you tell me about your family and the environment you grew up in?

MN: I was born in Scotland, in Edinburgh. My dad's from the Isle of Skye, which is the Highlands. My mother grew up in Marseille. She's half French, half Berber, Algerian Berber. My mum ran away from home to go onstage . . . My mum is an amazing improviser. When I was a child she would talk in tongues to me . . . it would be like improvised dialogue really . . . I moved to London when I was ten or eleven . . . I then found out about the stage school, Italia Conti . . . It was quite an extraordinary school and I learned acting, singing, dancing . . . Then I left school very young . . . I walked into the Windmill Theatre, which was a kind of vaudeville, semi-nude revue show. I got myself an audition, even though I was underage . . . I was there the year it closed. I didn't get to do any singing. It was all chorus line stuff, dancing, five shows. It was hard work . . . When the Windmill closed down . . . some agents came around and they had a job going in Manchester in a strip club for a singer. I had not sung in any way, because I didn't get a chance to sing in the Windmill, even though some girls did. I always wanted to sing . . . so this was a wonderful opportunity. So there I was in this strip club in Manchester . . . singing cabaret . . . There was a good piano player there. So I started learning. Basically, that's how I started singing . . .

CT: So you went down to the Little Theatre Club and heard the voice in a free jazz context for the first time?

MN: That's right, free improvisation with Norma Winstone . . . The first time I went up there was Norma, I think Derek Bailey was playing, Kenny Wheeler, I can't remember if Evan was, Trevor Watts, Pete Lemer, and I remember thinking, "Oh, my goodness, what's this? It's amazing. How do they do this? Wow." And, of course, Norma, she was very influenced by it, but she didn't fall in love with it. She preferred carrying on with standards. I mean, I love singing songs, I love standards, but I fell in love with improvisation . . .

CT: Can you give me a sense of how the more unconventional or textural techniques became a part of your vocal language?

MN: I never set out consciously to do that. Everything happens because I went into the subliminal mind, in fact, and discovered stuff, discovered what was there. Because it's all in there . . . I was practicing in quite a conventional way—I practice more unconventionally now—trying to do, I think, a scale, and I got up and my voice was tired and this freak note came out and it was like "Wow." I think if I had been a classical singer I would have gone, "Oh no! What's happening?" But it was like "What's that? Oh my god, it's wonderful!" And I suddenly started trying to recreate it, asking, "What part of my voice did that come from?" So, in that sense, when I discovered it by accident then I cultivated it. That's the way things have gone for me. Through discovery. Through going deep. And then going, "All right, now I'll craft it. Now, I'll develop it. Now, I'll see where I can go with that." So I never sat down to see what I could discover in my voice. It was just something would happen and I'd say "Oh, I like that. Oh, that's unusual." And then build on it.

CT: I was wondering about others' reactions. When you started using more unconventional techniques, how did the others you were collaborating with react?

MN: Well, I suppose, it was more when I started using things other than sound that I got the biggest reactions, really. Because Christine Jeffrey was doing that as well. Christine Jeffrey, who worked a lot with Derek Bailey. There was already a sort of acceptance of altered voice in free improvisation anyway . . . I think I was quite a pioneer in some of those techniques. But, as I say, I didn't realise I was . . .

The biggest negative reactions would be to the more theatrical side. I remember the first time that happened . . . I was doing a gig with Harry [Vince] and a couple of people and I remember struggling with it. And that struggling was coming into my body and a thought jumped into my head and it was: "I'm lying." I suddenly found myself saying it aloud and that's where that reputation I got for confessional came from. Again, an accident. I didn't intend to be confessional. I just suddenly found that I couldn't bear it. And I was very young still, so I didn't know how to just stop and wait until I was inspired again, which might have been a more creative option. However, because I didn't do that, something else happened. Because I said that, something shifted. Once I acknowledged and owned what was happening, it cleared a space and I started to dance. Being a dancer, why had I never danced? I never danced. And I suddenly was dancing. And because I'd used the words I was like: "Oh, my goodness, I can use words." Now, there was a lot of hostility to that. Not with everyone. Some people found it fine. Other people did not like it at all.

CT: Do you know why they were opposed to it?

MN: It made them uncomfortable. I think they felt it was a bit vulgar, or it wasn't aesthetically abstract enough. I don't know. I get the sense they felt it was muddying, it was polluting the purity of the music in some way . . . Once I got a taste of it, it felt so real, it felt, "Oh, wow, this is in free improvisation, it's all part of the shapeshifting, it's part of being an improviser." And I got to really explore it, of course, with F.I.G. [Feminist Improvising Group], with other women, and that's where I took it to a whole other level because I certainly didn't feel so anxious, because there was a supportive environment . . .

CT: Could you tell me a bit more about Christine Jeffrey? . . .

MN: She sang with Derek Bailey and she probably was a lot more abstract, really. I remember meeting Christine. I never knew her well, but I remember her saying to me—because critics compare and make artists vulnerable, it's a horrible divide-and-rule thing, I don't really like that—but Christine always used to say to me, and I shared this with her, she said, "I always used to think I wasn't a proper singer." I said, "Well, I always thought that I was too much of a singer." She'd either be praised or damned for using unconventional sounds, very little actual conventional voice. And I'd always be praised or damned for moving from actual sung content to abstract sound.

CT: Another singer that used unconventional techniques early on was Yoko Ono. You, I believe, were at an event with her in 1968, the Natural Music Festival.

MN: In Cambridge, I think it was.

CT: Yes.

MN: I'm realising now that John Stevens had obviously been exposed to Yoko. And I think he, again, like the magpie that he was, took that and altered it and put it in his own form. I'm not quite sure how he knew about Yoko, but I think he was quite influenced by her.

CT: How so?

MN: I don't know, because I never really spoke to him about it. I think Yoko had been working with these techniques . . . As you know, she got John Lennon and they did this duo. It was just incredible. When you think about what people are doing now, noise music, that's what her and John were doing. It was really powerful . . .

CT: Do you remember your first encounter with Jeanne Lee's work?

MN: I loved Jeanne Lee. But, again, because we are so used to comparing ourselves to each other, I used to think I wish I could be as understated as her . . .

I did meet Jeanne Lee . . . She was with Gunter [Hampel] in Berlin. It was the Total Music Meeting, when I was with John, Trevor, and this other singer Carolann Nichols . . . And that's how I met Julie—she was still Julie Driscoll then—because she came to the Total Music Meeting and she was totally blown away by it. And John was like "Wow, Julie Driscoll," and then of course Julie went on and sang with the SME [Spontaneous Music Ensemble] . . .

CT: Can you tell me how the group Voice started?

MN: Yes. Brian Eley came to my workshops at the Oval House. I started running workshops in 1969 at the Oval House. Julie used to come to my workshops as well . . . I think I approached Julie first and then maybe Phil and then Brian . . . I loved Voice because we did everything from pieces, like Phil's *Louis Kappa*, to one of the pieces I use in the workshop, more abstract pieces, and we did a lot of free improvisation. But we also did chants, all sorts of stuff. It was an amazing group . . .

CT: On the liner notes to the *Voice* album, it talks about how the voice is something you don't see as much in free improvisation and so this group is very special. Was that the first time you had seen a free improvising vocal group?

MN: Apart from the workshops, yes. I did a lot of performances with the workshops, right from the beginning. So maybe that's where I had the idea to take it out on the road . . .

CT: When did the idea that free improvisation could just exist as voice emerge?

MN: I really think it was from me doing the workshops. Definitely. Because before I had done the workshops I was mainly with instrumentalists. When I first started doing the workshops it was all instrumentalists and a couple of singers, like Julie, coming. But then when I started doing the voice workshops, actually, specifically, voice, that's when I thought wow. It was stunning. And I think that's why I approached Julie and Phil and wanted to do something . . .

Improvisation is a mass music. I'm just realising just how passionate I felt about this for so long and how important it is, because it belongs to everybody. That's why I do The Gathering. Because I want anybody off the street to go . . . To me, to see people who do not consider themselves to be creative and to say "Come, come, it's open to anybody, anybody can come," and it's complete chaos, but trusting it and honouring whoever comes is, I feel, the revolutionary power of this music to me, because I don't want to live in a capitalist system anymore. I really don't. If this music can contribute even if it's in a small way, it's still significant. It really is . . . If people are excluded, it's because there's status. Status is so damaging . . .

CT: I feel very similarly and that's one of the reasons I'm drawn to talk with you, you're so eloquent about it. I feel strongly about your support of mixed-ability ensembles.

MN: John [Stevens] was the master of mixed ability. Thank you, John. I have to give him credit, because John changed my life. John showed me that. He was the master of mixed ability. He could take someone that had been playing for sixty years and someone who had never played and his pieces created excellence. And it wasn't patronising. It was always the professional musicians who often didn't grasp his pieces at all. I've done the *Click Piece* with people with learning differences and they often get it so much better than musicians and they have fun with it. It's so democratic, isn't it? And isn't that beautiful? And it is what I call social virtuosity. It's something I feel very passionate about. And that is John. I can see why it's threatening. If you've studied for years and years and years you probably think, "Oh, my goodness. This person's coming along and they've not done all these years of study." But it doesn't negate that study. It's just different. It's not that one is better than the other. My God, I used to think if I hadn't been a single mum, how wonderful to do eight hours of practice a day. I would have loved to have known what that was like, but I was doing practice while I was hanging out nappies or whatever. I'd love to have more time to devote to practice. But, in the end, your life is your practice as well. It's all valuable.

Words/opinions of Maggie Nicols appear in this volume excerpted and condensed from a longer interview conducted by the author.

Notes

1. This interview took place over 6 & 7 May and 29 August 2015 in Eskdalemuir, Scotland. Jeffrey reviewed and revised the transcript.
2. Ono performed with Bailey, John Stevens, and Evan Parker at the Arts Lab in London on 21 April 1968.
3. Here, Jeffrey made scare quotes with her hands.
4. This interview took place 24 June 2014 in Guelph, Ontario.
5. This interview took place in two parts on 25 June 2014 in Guelph, Ontario and 4 May 2015 in Drefach Felindre, Carmarthenshire, Wales. Nicols reviewed and edited the transcript prior to publication.

2

MUSIC TECHNOLOGIES AND VOCAL FINDING

As the recording was made with the minimum of technological additives, (just myself singing and moving within one space) you may want to adjust levels between tracks.

—*Minton,* A Doughnut in One Hand *1998*

The epigraph above is from the liner notes of Phil Minton's second solo vocal recording, *A Doughnut in One Hand*. Similar comments appear on other voice-only free jazz recordings. On the back cover of Paul Dutton's *Mouth Pieces: Solo Soundsinging*, Dutton introduces the album: "Mouth Pieces. No electronic effects or processing, no feedback, overdubs, or fades. Twenty-one acoustic oral solos, working at the outer reaches of the technical and expressive potential of human utterance, fashioned from sounds, textures, and even a few words." These kinds of comments correct listeners who doubt that certain sounds on the album could be made simultaneously by a single unprocessed human voice. They seem to hint that free jazz singing is an anti-technological form of music making. And, indeed, there is some truth to this; free jazz singers are often interested in finding timbral complexity without resorting to the assistance of electronic sound processing technologies.[1] However, when one scratches deeper into the history of the tradition, it becomes clear that one reason these vocalists can eschew electronic processing is that machines have already made major contributions to shaping the way free jazz singers sing.

This chapter focuses on the roles technologies have played informing free jazz soundsinging and other vocal arts. I will discuss the significant role tape recorders, samplers, and other recorded sound reproduction devices (like turntables and cassette players) and electronic sound synthesis and processing devices have had on the sounds of free jazz voice.

Singing is often thought of as a "natural" activity, though it is clear that technologies like the microphone and electric amplification were responsible for profound changes in the way many vocalists sing. Meditating on the ways technologies have shaped singing helps counter this reductive notion of singing. This chapter seeks to provide this corrective while introducing significant figures, practices, and processes important to the development of free jazz voice.

The Cries of the Ultralettrists

Poet and literary historian Steve McCaffery has pointed out that "[s]ound poetry prior to the developments of the 1950s [was] still largely a word bound thing" (1978, n.p.). He signals that while early sound poetry, like the work of Kurt Schwitters (1887–1948) and Hugo Ball (1886–1927), celebrated the materiality of language by indulging in combinations of phonemes free from semantic content, these combinations "nevertheless persisted in a morphological patterning that still suggested the presence of the word" (Ibid.). McCaffery credits the poet François Dufrêne with first going beyond the morphological signature of language and "investigating the full expressive range of predenotative form: grunts, howls, shrieks, etc" (Ibid.).

Dufrêne was born in Paris in 1930, and by the age of sixteen, after hearing "a few *lettries* on the radio," he became a member of Isidore Isou's Lettrist group (Acquaviva 2010, 10). Isou, in typical modernist fashion, positioned his movement as the logical and necessary synthesis of the poetic developments that preceded it. He saw a linear progression in poetry from concern with the phrase (in the work of Verlaine) to concern with the word (in the work of Rimbaud) to concern with the nonsemantic in the work of Dadaists like Schwitters and Ball (Bohn 2001, 258). Like his Dadaist predecessors, Isou was interested in rejecting semantic meaning. He argued words were a tool of the bourgeois that disenfranchise the poet and alienate them from their feelings and expressive potential (Ibid., 260–61). Whereas the Dadaists sought to destroy meaning, Isou sought to build up a new ur-language based on the letter, the smallest unit of language, a unit that does not usually, in itself, carry semantic meaning. By combining letters/phonemes into sequences without meaning, like the Dadaists, the Lettrists could revel in "the qualities of the voice, the intonation, the speed, the silences, the noises added (laughing, crying), the facial expressions, body gestures and postures, the touch, the odor, the situation in the environment" that make up so much of linguistic communication, without the purportedly alienating semantic component (Jean-Paul Curtay quoted in Ibid., 263). Isou saw his movement as building upon the power of the letter. The classic Latin alphabet provided the basic material for Lettrist poetry, but Lettrism went further and "[a]s early as 1947, Isou expanded their repertoire to include nineteen new sounds, which he designated by a series of Greek letters. In addition to growls, sighs, and hiccups, many poems employ kissing noises, belches, and the sound of snoring" (Ibid., 265). Thus, Isou's focus was not just on rejection but on building a new system for non-semantic expression.

As their name suggests, the Ultralettrists (Dufrêne along with Jean-Louis Brau and Gil J. Wolman) also employed a modernist logic, viewing their movement as one step beyond Lettrism. By the early 1950s, Dufrêne had concluded Isou's methods did not go far enough. He saw Isou as reliant on a system of notation that could not signify "the striking diversity which even one of these 'letters' can encompass" in terms of duration, pitch, loudness, tempo, and timbre (Dufrêne 1966, n.p.).[2] For Dufrêne, the utility of the letter was undermined by the new commercial availability of recording technology.

In a manifesto Dufrêne wrote in 1953, he articulated his desire to create phonetic poems by recording them directly to tape rather than notating them on the page.[3] These poems, which he referred to as Crirythmes (Cry Rhythms), were essentially improvisations (structured or free) composed entirely of abstract vocal techniques. Rather than pieces of improvised music, Dufrêne understood these recordings to be poems "beyond any concept of writing." Yet when the rhythmic is foregrounded in the absence of the semantic the poetry/music divide is particularly blurry (Dufrêne 1966). To listen to these recordings now with knowledge of some of the ways free jazz vocal music has manifested, they can easily be heard as related. And, undoubtedly, the work of Dufrêne and his fellow Ultralettrists resonated into free jazz via intermediary paths like the Jackson Mac Low–Jeanne Lee–Yoko Ono connection discussed in Chapter 1 and the music/poetry blurring of Bob Cobbing and The Four Horsemen I discuss below.[4]

Given that tape recording devices generated Dufrêne's Crirythme method, it makes sense that many of these poems were disseminated as recorded media. Dufrêne began creating this work at least as early as 1952, when he provided a wordless vocal soundtrack to Isou's film *Traité de Bave et d'Eternité*. Three recordings he made in 1958, "Batteries Vocales," "Paix En Algérie," and "Ténu-Ténu," were made available in 1965 on a record that accompanied volume 23/24 of Henri Chopin's journal *Revue OU*.

These 1958 recordings document a practice which was masterful in terms of the diversity of vocal sounds Dufrêne was employing and contrasting structures and methods he used to create with these sounds. "Batteries Vocales" contains no semantic content and is composed entirely of vocal and non-vocal oral sounds recorded to live tape, including percussive sequences of plosives, affricates, sibilants, lingual and labial clicks and pops, and rapid lingual modifications of unlunged airflow velocity. His rapid alternation between these various percussive techniques produces a constantly changing flow of related but distinct timbres and accents and thus shares characteristics with other rapid solo percussion pieces. "Paix En Algérie" differs in that it is not constructed from a single live voice performance. Rather, Dufrêne engages in layering, vocalising over previously recorded vocal samples which he replays while manipulating their speed.

These contrasting examples display that he was interested both in composed, layered works built from the sounds afforded by tape manipulation in combination with unmanipulated or live vocal performance and in live-to-tape improvisations performed by a single voice.[5]

The other Ultralettrists developed their own independent methods of improvising pre-structured or unstructured abstract sounds live or live to tape. In a 1972 interview with Charles Amirkhanian, Henri Chopin cited a 1951 performance by Gil J. Wolman at Le Musée de l'Homme in Paris as the earliest sound poetry performance.[6] Wolman had begun to perform his particular brand of sound poetry at least a year earlier than the performance Chopin cited. A recital by Dufrêne at the Maison des Lettres was reportedly what attracted Wolman to join the Lettrist movement and begin his own work with wordless voice and body sound (Acquaviva 2010, 11).[7] After joining the Lettrists in 1950, Wolman developed a poetic method he called Mégapneumies. This translates as Mega-breath, indicating that many of these poems explore the sounds of inhalation and exhalation. Like Crirythmes, poems exploring asemantic breath sounds also break dramatically from both the phoneme and the morphology of the word into the domain of abstract, extra-normal vocal improvisation.[8]

Though Wolman and Dufrêne had different names for their methods, they shared many of the same techniques, and both were devoted to working improvisationally with abstract, unconventional vocal and non-vocal oral sound. Jean-Louis Brau first met Wolman in 1949. They went together to Dufrêne's recital at the Maison des Lettres and got involved with Lettrism together. Brau called his method *Instrumentations Verbales*. Like Dufrêne, he worked both with live vocal performances and concrete works composed from tape manipulations of his vocal improvisations. Recorded documentation of his work is sparser than Wolman and Dufrêne, but several recordings exist.[9]

Other sound poetry recordings disseminated by *Revue OU* in the 1960s stand as evidence that, like Dufrêne, Wolman, and Brau, a wide variety of sound poets worked improvisationally with less conventional abstract vocal sounds. Most did not go as far as the Ultralettrists in breaking from the word or its morphology or blurring poetry and music, but the Ultralettrists were not the only notable contributors to this method. The first *Revue OU* recording contained work by Bernard Heidsieck ("Poème-partition D4P, or Art Poétique"), Brion Gysin ("I Am" and "Pistol Poem"), and Henri Chopin ("Vibrespace"). Chopin's piece comes the closest to the methods of Dufrêne, Wolman, and Brau. Throughout the piece, we hear recognisable breath sounds, labial popping, the sound of the tongue pressing against and being pulled off the palette, and sibilants. Yet rather than giving the impression of being an exploration into unconventional abstract uses of the voice, the work seems to be focused almost exclusively on technological defamiliarisation of ordinary vocal sounds, namely the incidental sounds of speech and breath. We hear the recognisable vocal sounds only for short durations before they are transformed by various forms of tape manipulation into sounds that become less and less recognisable as voices. This mechanical defamiliarisation is central to "Vibrespace" and to much of Chopin's work. Chopin often produced certain live unconventional vocal sounds in performances alongside his concrete tape pieces, but the wide-ranging exploration of the potential of unconventional vocality was not the central focus of his work in the same way it was for Dufrêne, Wolman, and Brau.

With their inclusion in *Revue OU* and the appearance of the Ultralettrists at a number of French and international sound poetry festivals in the 1960s, the work that they began in the 1950s became part of a broader sound poetry movement. Sound poetry performances and festivals became regular occurrences in many cities around the world in the late 1960s and throughout the 1970s. Then, in turn, the practices of these performance poets later informed vocal work in free jazz contexts. This was all afforded by the tape recorder's commercial availability.

Borderblur in the 1970s: Poetry Into Free Jazz

Describing his 1964 series of poems *ABC in Sound* in 1972, Bob Cobbing said, "I was deliberately using sound for the first time." In a later interview he states, "I think what really started me off was a visit from France by Henri Chopin and Bernard Heidsieck. They did performances at the London Institute of Contemporary Arts (the ICA). I'd been toying with the idea of doing something along those lines myself, but that visit prompted me to work on my *ABC in Sound*" (Cobbing quoted in Thomas 2012, 212).[10] In a later interview, Cobbing pointed out he "certainly learned a great deal from what Heidsieck, Chopin and especially, François Dufrêne, were doing" (Cobbing quoted in Sutherland 2001). Indeed, Cobbing developed a diverse poetic practice, a sizable portion of which followed Dufrêne into work based in non-semantic unconventional vocal sound.

In an essay from 1969, Cobbing wrote: "MY USE of 'vocal-microparticles' as Henri Chopin calls the elements with which we now compose sound poetry, retains, indeed emphasises, the natural quality of the human voice, more perhaps than does Chopin's poetry" (1978, 39). Indeed, the live-voice-plus-tape-layering process that Cobbing experimented with and that Chopin devoted most of his career to was eschewed in much of Cobbing's work in favour of a layering of multiple voices in performance, along the lines of Jackson Mac Low's work, but only after the influence of the Ultralettrists had already informed the ways sound poets were using their voices acoustically. In Cobbing's multi-voice performances multiple readers often distinguished themselves by employing unconventional timbres. Cobbing too, in his solo performances, often distinguished sections of his works in similar ways, changing his timbre dramatically. The vocal elements of these collaborative improvisational performances began increasingly to be heard as musical, and musicians and musical instruments increasingly became part of these collaborations.

Michael Chant, who was a member of Cornelius Cardew's Scratch Orchestra, and Cobbing began to collaborate frequently by 1969. Cobbing and Chant formed a trio with the poet Paula Claire called Konkrete Canticle, in which

Chant's organ playing was often part of the texture. Following this, Cobbing began to collaborate with figures from the London free jazz/improvisation community. By 1973, he formed a group called abAna with musicians David Toop and Paul Burwell. In fall of 1976, Cobbing made several London appearances in Eddie Prévost's band, which featured Prévost on drums, Geoff Hawkins on tenor saxophone, Gerry Gold on trumpet, and Marcio Mattos on bass. Later in his career, he would form the celebrated project Birdyak with multi-instrumentalist Hugh Metcalfe, often also including Jennifer Pike and Lol Coxhill.[11]

This path from poetic spaces and practices towards music was also a feature of the histories of Paul Dutton and The Four Horsemen, a poetry ensemble consisting of Dutton, bpNichol, Steve McCaffery, and Rafael Barreto-Rivera. Nichol used British poet Dom Sylvester Houédard's term borderblur to refer to the ways his visual and performance poetry often exist in a space between poetry and other mediums.[12] The Four Horsemen did, indeed, blur the lines between music and poetry both by creating sound poetry work that could be heard as either/both and by moving into the social and cultural spaces normally occupied by musicians. The group CCMC has been an institution in the Toronto free jazz community since the early 1970s. The membership of the group has changed at various points, reflecting the group's system of allowing potential collaborators to occupy residencies with the group. A residency McCaffery had with the group in the late 1970s led to the idea of collaborative performances between CCMC and The Four Horsemen. Dutton explains:

> Free improvisation became a more dominant feature of The Four Horsemen's performances in the '80s, catalysed by our occasional work with the free-improvising band, CCMC. Throughout The Horsemen's final five years (we decided not to continue as a trio after the untimely death of member bpNichol in 1988), we operated virtually as a free-improv vocal quartet—although we did cheat a little by including pre-written text to be incorporated spontaneously on individual initiative.
>
> *(1992, 15)*

Listening to the recorded documents of their work prior to their collaborations with CCMC, the 1973 album *Canadada* (also released as *Nada Canadada*) and the 1977 release *Live in the West*, the importance of rhythm, timbre, and even, at times, melody and harmony are immediately apparent. *Live in the West* documents performances from three readings given in February of 1974. It begins with a steady pulse pounded with a hammer on the head of a short log. After 8 beats, a single voice enters sustaining the vowel [ɛ], before shifting to an [i] articulation.[13] On both vowels, the voice executes a tremolo and before the vowel shift noise is added to the vowel's pure pitch. The [i] is held for a moment before it rises an octave and the tremolo becomes more dramatic then tenses into a shout that ends the phrase. This is repeated three times before a second vocalist enters with a sustained [ʉ] that underpins the opening phrase as it repeats. The [ʉ] modulates pitch in semitone intervals, providing a harmonic backdrop, first for the opening phrase and then for a speaker that enters after the fifth iteration of the opening phrase. When the speaker enters, the singer of the opening phrase reduces the phrase to an iteration of its opening sound that marks beats 1 and 3 in time with the pounding. The pounding then drops out and a voice begins marking beats 2 and 4 with the [i] from the opening phrase. This a cappella vocal trio continues in this manner until the fourth voice (who presumably was the percussionist before the hammering dropped out) shouts "Mayakovsky!" the surname of Russian poet Vladmir Mayakovsky, and the opening voice alters his part again and begins an unconventional egressive and ingressive panting in a steady eighth-note rhythm. The voice that shouted "Mayakovsky" transitions into explorations of the phonemes of the name and the speaker and the [ʉ] voice transition into a dynamic repeating melody sung by both voices. The piece ends after a few rounds of this new melody with another shout of "Mayakovsky."

In performance poems like "Mayakovsky" and many others found on *Live in the West*, unconventional abstract vocalisations bear equal weight to the spoken and sung elements, and the performances are as musical as they are literary. The same can be said of the pieces on The Four Horsemen's 1987 recording *2 Nights*, which was from the period after they had begun to collaborate with CCMC, recorded during two nights of performances at the Music Gallery, a venue for music in Toronto founded in 1976 by Peter Anson and Al Mattes, two members of CCMC.[14] The range and mastery of The Four Horsemen's unconventional vocal practices had expanded in the thirteen years since *Live in the West* was recorded. In the first few moments of *2 Nights*, we hear labial and lingual clicks and pops, snorts, high-pitched oscillations, controlled strained screeches, ingressive multiphonics, rapid phrases of mouth percussion, and parabuccals that did not appear in their earlier recordings. The structures they were working with are also distinct; they had abandoned pre-formed structures and entered their period of near-total improvisation. Compared to *Live in the West* there are much longer stretches where semantic language and sounds derived from language do not appear. This, however, does not necessarily make this work less literary and more musical; sound poetry, as Dutton reminds us, is "meant as much to denote a poetic (figuratively speaking) use of sound as a sonic (literally speaking) use of poetry" (Ibid., 11). From such a perspective, we can hear normative speech rhythms as musical and non-semantic vocal utterances as poetic material.

Dutton and Nichol began attending CCMC's regular sessions as individuals more regularly in 1987. After Nichol's passing in 1988, Dutton continued attending the CCMC sessions and in 1989 was invited to become a full member of the group. In the subsequent decades, he has continued to work as a poet and soundsinger, has consistently remained an active member of CCMC, and has performed both as a solo soundsinger and with a wide variety of other improvising musicians, including a quintet with Blonk, Moss, Minton, and Makigami called Five Men Singing.

However, years before he joined CCMC, Dutton was already framing some of his solo work as improvised music and some as an indistinguishable blend of music and poetry. He released a split LP in 1980 with the musically referential title *Blues, Roots, Legends, Shouts & Hollers*. It featured four recordings by Dutton, made between 1978 and 1980, and four by P.C. Fencott. Only one of the track descriptions refers to the work as a poem ("Time"), and the general description of the content of the album in the liner notes reads: "The blues of Paul Dutton are rooted in the legends of language, shouted, hollered & otherwise vocalized in a unique blend of musico-literary borderblur . . . Call them poems, call them songs, call them tonsilorous acrobatics, the pieces remain beyond categorisation—works of art composed for, created by and broadening the horizons of the human voice" (Dutton 1980). Despite the reference to composition in this description, the track description for "Blue Reed's (for Jimmy Reed)" marks the track, a voice duet with trumpeter Mike Malone, as "a searing, confluent explosion of voice & musical instrument improvising" (Ibid.) "Imp's Rove" is a structured improvisation Dutton often performs in which he strives to begin by surprising himself rather than pre-conceptualising how he will begin, and "Mondrian Boogie Woogie" is a sonic realisation of one of Dutton's visual concrete poems, created by a "chance-generated" (Ibid.) set of images produced with a typewriter, that emerges from an improvisational approach akin to a free jazz interpretation of a graphic score.

Dutton, The Four Horsemen, and Cobbing all moved more fluidly between musical and literary spaces than the poets that came before them, but all of these poets cultivated a borderblur that began in large part with the Ultralettrist interest in tape. Dutton's decades spent performing work formed in literary contexts in musical contexts and vice versa, his contribution to borderblur, his established place in the history of free jazz voice and his influence on how many later free jazz singers have used their voice are all, in part, thanks to magnetic tape.

Part II—Samplers, Synthesizers, and Singing

> I denied it for a long time; but I had to admit that I used to say, back in the early '80s, that I could make any sound a fucking computer could make. So there's no denying that I was indeed influenced by electroacoustic sounds.
> —*Paul Dutton, interview with the author, 11 & 12 August 2014*

Phil Minton describes how in his vocal exploration, "changing the actual timbre of the voice . . . is what [he] wanted to do" and "the nearest thing was people who were playing with electronics."[15] He goes further and explains, "I think that was kind of an influence on me . . . or gave me confidence, actually."[16] Confidence is a fundamental component in free jazz soundsinging; the singers I have interviewed for this book have described social resistance to singers who use their voice in unconventional ways. Minton, attesting that the sounds of electronic music allowed him to legitimise his desire to use his voice in less conventional ways, indicates another way technologies have been responsible, in part, for altering the practice of singing.

The sounds of electronic music have guided many free jazz vocalists into exploration of new kinds of acoustic vocal sounds. Canadian multi-musical vocalist and improvising choir conductor DB Boyko describes such a process. In much of her early work with the ensemble Hextremities, she concentrated on processing her voice with "delays and harmonizers and all that stuff."[17] But she reached a point where she decided "I'm going to leave that aside and I just want to work with the raw voice."[18] However, ceasing to employ the technology did not really mean leaving the technology aside entirely; as she explains, her period concentrating on electronic music "was really good because it allowed me to kind of think vocally in a different way . . . that . . . gave me the impetus to think about the voice even more in an exploratory way."[19]

Montréal-based singer, composer, saxophonist, and free jazz choir leader Joane Hétu tells a similar story. She describes her early work in ensembles Wondeur Brass and Justine, explaining how the electronic instruments in the ensemble shaped the ways she sings:

> The way I found my own voice was because of Wondeur Brass and Justine of course, and in these groups Diane Labrosse was playing synthesizer and later sampler and I played with her for so long that I'm really used to playing with the sampler and these kinds of sounds and at the time I started to imitate the sounds. Also with Martin Tétreault on turntables.[20]

Dutch free jazz singer and performance poet Jaap Blonk points us to how electronic instrument design has also shaped singing. He describes that:

> the activity of sitting at home in my home studio and listening to something, pushing the fader or turning the knob a bit . . . came back to my vocal practice . . . I got interested in changing timbres very gradually . . . It's very similar for instance to having a filter and turning it, trying to change the sound gradually a little bit.[21]

In this story it is less the sounds themselves than interface design and the ways electronic instruments shape sounds over time that informed Blonk's work.

Even the failure of electronic instruments has shaped the vocal practices of these singers. As he explains in the following story, the destruction of an electronic component of David Moss's solo percussion and electronic rig was a major influence in the development of his vocal vocabulary:

> I proceeded to practice solo music for almost two years . . . I began to add objects to my drum set. My drum set grew bigger and bigger as I wanted

more sound sources. I needed to bring in a deep, resonating tone. I needed to have high attacks. I need to have a low pitch, a drone. And suddenly I needed to have sustained sounds . . . So I went over to the house of my guitarist friend, Baird Hersey. And he had the first tape loop machine . . . So, I borrowed it. I plugged a microphone into it, I began to sing into it so I could make a drone and I began, for the first time, to use loops. And it was a radical moment for me back then in 1973. The voice became a *bed of sound*, which I could sustain and I didn't have to devote a hand or two hands to make that sustaining sound. So, my first time using electronics was for my voice. Aha, I remember: it was called the Echoplex. Then something interesting thing happened. I saw an ad at Bennington College: "Drummer wanted to accompany dance classes, Washington University, St Louis, Missouri." So, I answered. And, the head of the dance department said to me, "Well, actually we found someone, but you sound interesting. Why don't you come and give a concert next spring? Bring your group." And I said, "I have no group." And she said, "Well then, come play alone. We have five hundred dollars." Five hundred dollars! This was 1973, and that was a huge amount of money. I said, "Sure no problem, I'm coming." So, suddenly I was committed to playing a solo concert, which I had never done before, at Washington University. And I spent about six months practicing in my drum-room with the gongs, and the tam-tam, and everything I had there, plus that Echoplex. And almost without deciding, I had developed personal loops, drones and all these layers of sound, and I was building a solo performance simply because I had to play a solo! Then something fateful happened: There was a thunderstorm one night and a huge bolt of lightning hit near the farmhouse and shorted out the electricity and blew up the Echoplex. I mean, fried it, smoke coming out . . . I couldn't afford to buy a new one. So, I said okay, I have to make those sounds acoustically. I had to sing that strongly and that continuously without the Echoplex. I had to do it *live* all the time. This was an amazing moment for me . . . I had the feeling I would get real information, I would get skills and shapes from this leap to being able to create it all from and with my own body. And this informed my work for many years: everything that I would do with electronics I imagined how I could do it acoustically. So, electronically generated sound would become information for my physical and musical development. Things that normally couldn't be done acoustically, I would attempt to do.[22]

No matter how similar vocal sounds are to electronic instrument sounds, awareness of the voice as the source of the sound, when it is present, will factor into the ways those sounds afford meaning. Hétu points to this when she explains, "When the turntable does this same sound it's nice for [audiences], but when I make it they ask 'why are you doing this kind of sound with your voice?' . . . I don't know why with samplers, electric guitars, with a lot of instruments you can do really heavy sounds, but with voice people turn away."[23] The voice is caught up in processes of signification distinct in many ways from all other musical instruments. However, those processes of signification are themselves shaped by technoscapes and by the presence of particular music technologies.

Another of the transitions in David Moss's career offers us insight into such processes. The invention of the sampler and its adoption in the Downtown New York jazz scene Moss was a part of in the late 1970s and 1980s had a substantial effect on the acceptance of his vocal contributions within that scene and on the ways his fellow musicians made sense of and valued his vocal sounds. The anecdote above centres on Moss as a percussionist who gradually added vocal and electronic elements to his performances. Moss was an accomplished percussionist when he began incorporating voice into his work in 1972. Eventually, nearly two decades later, Moss would devote himself entirely to the voice. His description of his vocal technique in percussion vocabulary evidences the way his percussion informed the vocal techniques he developed; it is reflective of the way the voice often served as an extension of his percussion in his percussion performances and the way free jazz creates a space for vocal sound to be shaped by sounds other than human voices.

After he began to use his voice alongside his percussion in 1972, his choice to do so caused tension between him and the other musicians he was collaborating with. Moss was part of an ensemble of musicians and dancers in the mid-1970s, and incorporating his voice caused considerable tension in the group. He describes how "At a certain point in 1974 or 1975 . . . Basically, they told me, if you're going to sing we can't play together."[24] At the time, this pushed Moss further into the realm of solo practice and performance.

By the late 1970s, Moss was again playing collaboratively after a few years of mostly solo performance. Now in the Downtown New York jazz scene, he again encountered this attitude. He explains that:

> The improvised music scene looked upon voice as an *emotional, body-connected* element. This "pure improvisation" that I worked with after leaving Bill [Dixon] and then into the late 1970s (it was around 78 or 79 when John Zorn and I met and started playing together) had no desire at all for emotional sources, or statements, in music. They wanted fast changing, *abstract*, non-genre related, noise-connected, attack-oriented movement. No emotion please! No story-telling. No connection to anything outside the sounds themselves, and certainly nothing like a song. So, every time I opened my mouth, over or with my drumming, my colleagues, even my friends, were bothered. They heard the voice as an annoyance, as extraneous material, not as a sound source. And I wasn't screaming emotionally or doing what you could call clear emotional references. I was doing pretty sonically abstract sound things. But they couldn't get past their own prejudice, their training, and their own new rules.[25]

What began to change this attitude and make the voice a more welcome element in this scene was the increasing use of cassettes, turntables, and samplers as musical instruments and the attitudes applied to sample-based improvisation. Moss describes how:

> I felt then that the rest of the New York scene was not at all interested in the singing voice and tolerated my voice because I was drumming in an interesting way. And so I held my voice back, forced myself to stop singing; and there were complete gigs where I wouldn't make a single sound with my voice. I felt like I had a hand clamped across my mouth. I knew I was being silent for a good reason. It seemed clear to me that, in this abstract noise scene, if I started opening my mouth and singing what I felt, I wouldn't be asked back. Because human voices with all their messiness and connotations and emotional resonances weren't acceptable yet, until somehow the idea of quotation jumped into our music, around 1983. When quotation came in, it entered via cassettes. Mark Kramer played cassettes, pre-DJ, and he would play these fragmentary voices, words, speeches, and quotations of songs. And that was more easily acceptable, even funny and cool, because it wasn't a person doing it. It wasn't alive . . . This was just before Christian [Marclay] came into the scene with his turntables and hand-made records. So, with the cassettes, and then Christian, suddenly a new level of acceptance was reached for the human voice, and I could actually join in with my vocal ideas. The use of quotation and samples allowed my voice to re-enter . . . And that gave an opening for Shelley Hirsch. She joined that scene and did a huge amount with quotation of songs and genres . . . And then other voices from other parts of the world came into the scene. Sussan Deyhim came into the scene, and one by one new voices came.[26]

Given the fact that this was occurring in New York in 1983, the influence of the pastiche-based aesthetic of the New Wave and No Wave movements and the sample-based aesthetic of hip-hop should be acknowledged as influences on the changing norms Moss describes. Both of those developments were also due, in part, to the creative use and misuse of technologies like the turntable. Because of the presence of these technologies in the Downtown New York scene, the hand Moss felt was clamped across his mouth came off.

Conclusion: The Machines That Made Us

Although many free jazz singers do enjoy electronically processing their vocal sounds, often the joy of free jazz soundsinging comes from the celebration and exploration of the diverse ranges of sounds our voices and non-vocal oral apparatuses can achieve on their own, without the aid of anything external to the human body. However, the histories traced here in this chapter reveal that this does not mean that technologies have not played important roles in informing or shaping these explorations. Even when processing is eschewed by free jazz soundsingers, a variety of technologies are invisibly present in and through the ways they have shaped the choices and sounds vocalists have made.

Notes

1. Dutton told me "I'm still constantly surprising myself with some of the sounds that come out of me. That's why I don't do electronics, because I still haven't exhausted the acoustic capacities of utterance" (interview with the author, 11 & 12 August 2014).
2. Here I employ the translation of Dufrêne's original French that appears in Cobbing and Mayer (2014).
3. Here I refer to "Fausse Route: Demi-Tour Gauche Pour Un Cri Automatique," originally published in *Soulevement de la Jeunesse* in March 1953.
4. Dufrêne performed alongside Mac Low at the 1969 "1ra. Audicion de Poesia Fonica" at the Teatro Millington Drake in Montevideo, Uruguay and the 1976 "Posie Sonore-Posie Action" panorama in Paris (Wolman, Brau, and Ono also appeared).
5. Other Crirythmes created through tape manipulation include "U 47" (composed in 1962) and "Haut Satur" (composed in December 1967). Both are available on the CD accompanying *ArchiMade*, a 2005 collection of Dufrêne's work.
6. Here Chopin uses a rather idiosyncratic definition of sound poetry, as it does not include the Dada poets. It was likely a Mégapneumie, a poetic form I discuss ahead, that Chopin witnessed in 1951.
7. Acquaviva refers to recitals in the 1950s at the clubs Tabou and La Rose Rouge where Wolman performed early physical poetry work.
8. *Revue OU* published a 1967 recording of one Mégapneumie entitled "La Mémoire" in 1968. An earlier Mégapneumie recording, simply entitled "Mégapneumies," from 1963, was published in 1965 as part of a record accompanying the book *Poésie Physique*.
9. These include "Ataloche Roche" from 1961 and "Instrumentation Verbale" and "Cantate pour l'interdiction de Mandrake" from 1963. "Ataloche Roche" consists largely of phrases that share the morphological signature of speech, but played back at an increased tape speed that masks semantic content. Alongside these are sped-up passages of Brau exploring sibilant sounds, vocal fry, rapid inhalation/exhalation, saliva swishing, lingual clicks, and other unconventional techniques. "Cantate pour l'interdiction de Mandrake" makes use of thick slapback. It begins with semantic speech and moves into abstract sounds. "Instrumentalisation Verbale" employs tape manipulation, breath sounds, ingressive multiphonics, rhythmic nasal exhalation, and vocal fry. It was recorded in September 1963 and included in the same book and record collection as Wolman's recording "Mégapneumies." Frédéric Acquaviva speculates that the collection, *Poésie Physique*, released in 1965, was "probably a way of recording their precedence, countering their absence from Henri Chopin's . . . multimedia magazine *Ou*, the first issue of which, complete with disk, came out in 1964" (2010, 28). However, as mentioned above, *Revue OU* would include Dufrêne in the same year *Poésie Physique* appeared and Wolman several years later.
10. Here Thomas is quoting from a 1996 interview with Cobbing by Rolf Ahmann.
11. Saxophonist Lol Coxhill and dancer Jennifer Pike also later became part of Birdyak and other musicians and poets appeared occasionally with the group.
12. Paul Dutton, email to the author, 10 March 2019.
13. For the sake of accuracy, I employ here vowel symbols from the International Phonetic Alphabet.
14. At time of writing *Live in the West, 2 Nights*, and selections from *Canadada* were all available on the Penn Sound webpage. See www.writing.upenn.edu/pennsound/x/4-Horsemen.html.

15. Phil Minton, interview with the author, 24 June 2014.
16. Ibid.
17. DB Boyko, interview with the author, 18, 21 & 22 March 2015.
18. Ibid.
19. Ibid.
20. Joane Hétu, interview with the author, 30 October 2013.
21. Jaap Blonk, interview with the author, 8 November 2013.
22. David Moss, interview with the author, 6 & 7 July 2013.
23. Joane Hétu, interview with the author, 30 October 2013.
24. Ibid.
25. Ibid.
26. Ibid. "Pre-DJ" here of course refers to the period before turntablists began appearing in the Downtown New York jazz scene, not the period before the rise of DJ cultures and practices.

3

SCAT TO SUMAC TO SANDERS

Materialities and Sources in Soundsinging

> I was also intrigued by one particular sound. It was John Coltrane and Pharoah
> Sanders I think, *Live at the Village Vanguard*, around 1965, and Pharoah Sand-
> ers was doing these multiphonics and the hair used to stand up on my neck.
> I wanted to know how you could do that with the voice.
> —*Phil Minton, interview with the author, 24 June 2014*

Free jazz recordings like the one Minton is referring to above, a 1966 recording by John Coltrane and Pharoah Sanders entitled *Live at the Village Vanguard
Again!*, have been materially important in the history of free jazz voice. Minton's
desire to produce a vocal variation of this "one particular sound"—Sanders's multiphonics on this specific recording—was afforded by the recording itself, and so
this recording is an irreducible part of the history of free jazz voice. Jaap Blonk
recounts a similar story of an encounter with another free jazz recording, positioning it as essential to a key "breakthrough" moment in the development of the
free jazz vocal side of his work:

> When I started performing I didn't know any other people who were doing
> this. It just happened to me while listening to a free jazz record from the
> '60s. I was playing saxophone and I drifted into free improv trying to make
> all the noises the instrument can do. I also had started performing sound
> poetry, like Schwitters and Hugo Ball and so on. But, I hadn't improvised
> with the voice, but then all of a sudden while I was sitting in my living
> room, listening to this record, I think it was this live recording of Archie
> Shepp with Roswell Rudd on trombone, so it was a very high energy piece
> and I went along and I [*bursts into sound*] just spontaneously. And I found

myself doing that long after the record had ended. That was the start for me. It was very abrupt.[1]

The Shepp-Rudd recording Blonk mentions here (which was the 1966 release *Three for a Quarter, One for a Dime*), also has an irreducible place in the history of free jazz voice, as do the material processes that made it possible for Blonk to possess and listen to a copy of the album in The Netherlands in the early 1980s and for Minton to hear Coltrane's recording in the 1960s.

In this third chapter, I point to a dizzying variety of irreducible sources contributing to free jazz voice. Starting with these examples of specific free jazz recordings that shaped the practices of two influential free jazz vocalists, I pay tribute to how the sounds of instrumental free jazz are undoubtedly, of course, one of the fundamental sources of free jazz voice. However, this chapter will show that instrumental free jazz is one musical source among many nourishing free jazz vocal practices. My goal in this chapter will be to give an impression of the breadth of the sources that have informed free jazz soundsinging. I cycle from free jazz instrumental music to scat, popular music, Western art music, environmental sound, global folk and art music, and back to free jazz to provide an impressionistic glimpse at the complexity of the tributaries feeding free jazz singing. I introduce an array of singers not discussed in previous chapters and, like all histories, I leave many more of them unmentioned, offering a rich but partial, problematic, and personal bushwhacking through an unknowable past.

As I weave through some of these histories—particularly those related to scat singing, the most obvious precursor of free jazz soundsinging—I will pause to consider how the idea of soundsinging might help us think differently about the significance and meanings of certain bygone but sometimes recorded soundings. These theorisations employ the notions of "capital S" Singing, which indicates a conception of certain kinds of singing as non-Singing, and the "capital-H" Human, which indicates a self-privileging worldview that sees one's own categorical subset of humanity as somehow more-fully-Human than others. My theoretical approach suggests that certain human vocal sounds are heard as evidence of Humanness while others are as heard as less-than-Human. Since this capital-H Humanness indicates a worldview that refuses to accept the humanity of certain bodies and voices that are materially human, capital-H Humanness always means a perception of unequal degrees of Humanness, a privileging of some forms of humanness as more-fully-Human. My core argument throughout this book is that vocalists who embrace human vocal sounds that others Other as non-Human play some role in challenging or disturbing such pernicious, self-privileging worldviews. As I trace various nodes in the network that led to free jazz voice, I will begin to discuss the ways this role manifested in some of free jazz voice's precursors, foreshadowing the more detailed theorisation of these processes that will take place in Chapter 5.

While free jazz vocalists have been shaped by their encounters in private spaces with recorded music, they have also been shaped by their encounters with the dynamisms of a wide variety of sounding bodies, both human and non-human. Free jazz singing offers a rare public space where we can allow our bodies and voices to be informed by the speeds and slownesses, the timbres and tempos of a broadened range of the dynamisms in the world around us. Whereas in daily life we usually restrict our voices to utterances that echo the normative vocalisations of other bodies that we perceive as our categorical counterparts, in the space of free jazz singers often allow their voices and embodiment to be informed by other sources. Alongside a discussion of the ways recorded music from a broad variety of musical traditions has informed particular singers' approach to free jazz, in this chapter, I trace certain material histories of free jazz singers' vocal encounters with the sounds of machines, animals, and other non-human sound sources. While the process of allowing the dynamisms we encounter to shape our vocalisation and embodiment can entail risk, it can also lead to reward. This method of allowing more of the outside world to inform our embodiment can lead us to new pleasures and a reclamation of enlivening methods of experiencing our most precious possession, our bodies.

Hillbilly Yodels, Tarzan Calls, and *The Music of the Ba-Benzélé Pygmies*

Phil Minton was, naturally, not the only free jazz vocalist affected by Pharoah Sanders in the 1960s. Leon Thomas worked intensively with Sanders throughout the late 1960s and early 1970s, performing live and collaborating on Sanders's albums *Karma* (1969), *Jewels of Thought* (1969), and *Iphizo Zam* (1973). In the same period, Thomas was also the leader of his own projects.[2] His early vocal style was a rather normative jazz croon, but in the late 1960s he developed a highly idiosyncratic style of abstract vocal improvisation, one he referred to as Soularfone. Steven Feld described the style as "a modified rapid alternation yodel technique with a kind of vocabalic scat singing that sounded more glottal than the dominant King Pleasure or Eddie Jefferson male jazz scat style typical of the era" (Feld 1996, 7). Thomas's narrative of the origin of his unconventional practice relates it back to an injury he sustained in the late 1960s as well as to the demands of performing in Sanders's ensembles. While practicing a yogic headstand he collapsed onto his face, and his teeth bit into his bottom lip.[3] He received eight stitches in his mouth for the injury, and when he met with Sanders before their next performance together, a "benefit for a group of anti-police activists" that was to take place at a church in New York, Sanders insisted he needed to sing on the gig despite his injury (Perrone). Thomas describes what happened next by explaining:

> I couldn't smile. I could hardly open my mouth . . . but I went along anyhow. I got up on the stage and when it came time for me to scat, this sound

just came out. It shocked me. I didn't know where it was coming from . . . I realised it was me and I realised that the ancestors had arrived. Pharoah, standing beside me on stage raised his eyebrows at me. The ancestors had given me what we call throat articulation and they said to me. 'You will sing like this with your mouth CLOSED.' And that was the first time it presented itself to me, in a church. My God! Thank you . . . It surprises me, it does everything of its own volition. I call it Soularfone. The pygmies call it *Umbo Weti* . . . The voice is not me, my voice is ancient. This person you see before you is controlled by ego but my voice is egoless.[4]

Narratives of spontaneous arrival at a soundsinging practice are not unusual. Thomas's story bears similarities to Blonk's story of spontaneously coming to his practice while listening to *Three for a Quarter, One for a Dime*. However, the narrative Thomas used to frame Soularfone is distinct. His moment of discovery occurred in the context of the Afrocentric turn in post-bop jazz of the late 1960s. Tsitsi Ella Jaji describes this turn in her book *Africa in Stereo: Modernism, Music, and Pan-African Solidarity* as inaugurated by "a generation of musicians, including John Coltrane, Pharoah Sanders, and Randy Weston, who took a keen interest in African and other non-Western musics and saw their approach to timbre as reflecting African musical aesthetics" (2014, 176). The experiential dimension and narrative framing of these sounds as the voice of ancestors, a voice that also sounds in African traditional music, is coherent with the Afrocentric practices of many of Thomas's collaborators. We can acknowledge this ancestral visitation and the role it played in framing the reception of Thomas's vocal improvisation while also pointing to sources that seem to have aided this visitation process. Gianpaolo Chiriacò's work on Thomas points to Thomas's encounter in the mid-1960s with recordings of Pygmy music, introduced to him by a percussionist and Swahili teacher based in Harlem called Louis Brown. In particular, it seems to have been the 1966 compilation *The Music of the Ba-Benzélé Pygmies* (compiled by Simha Arom and Geneviève Taurelle) that, as Thomas puts it, "blew [his] mind" in this initial encounter and seemed to inform his approach. Chiriacò also notes, however, that Thomas had encounters with other forms of yodelling that may also have informed Soularfone. He discusses Thomas's awareness of country yodelling and Thomas's history of imitating the call of the transmedially omnipresent and colonially problematic character Tarzan, which was, during the mid-twentieth century, "one of Hollywood's most recognizable and iconic sound bites" (Demain 2012). Johnny Weissmuller starred in twelve Tarzan films between 1932 and 1948 and developed his iconic version of Tarzan's call "inspired by the yodelling of his German neighbours" (Ibid.).[5] Chiriacò writes Thomas cited imitation of the Tarzan call as "his first attempt to yodel" and "among his friends, he was the most skilled imitator of it" (2014).

If we view Thomas's Soularfone as the result of the intersections of free jazz, the rise of commercial availability of recordings of traditional musics from around the world, vocal ephemera from popular music and media, and the legacy of scat vocalisation in jazz, we possess a vocal practice capable of symbolising the complexity and wide range of sources nourishing free jazz soundsinging. These four areas are all deserving of further attention, and all will be addressed later in the chapter. First, however, I will turn to another vocalist whose free jazz work it is essential to acknowledge in a history of free jazz soundsinging and who was also helped along by involvement with Sanders: Linda Sharrock. Sharrock's first professional work was in ensembles with Sanders in New York in the mid-1960s (Wilmer 1977). She then met, married, performed with, and recorded an extraordinary series of albums with another member of Sanders's mid-1960s ensembles, the guitarist Sonny Sharrock. On recordings like the 1969 album *Black Woman*, she improvises in a style that can reasonably be compared to Ono's early free jazz work, often employing sung pitches, but sung pitches that aren't always strongly supported by her breath or clearly consonant with the pitch content of other instruments, as well as sung pitches that develop into extra-normal vibratos, tremolos, or screams.[6] Like Ono's work, this style might convey an irreverent resistance to the authority of vocal normativity—a solidarity with vocal sounds Othered as valueless or not worthy of audition—and/or evoke "indicator" sounds (like the involuntary sounds of pain or pleasure) along with the gender politics evoked by artistic employment of such sounds. However, Abbey Lincoln's screams in Max Roach's *We Insist!* (also known as *The Freedom Now Suite*), which are often mentioned in relation to Sharrock's work, remind us that some of the abstract sounds Sharrock employs in her early work will have been interpreted in their original post–civil rights context as shouts against racial injustice. Sharrock's choice to use weakly supported sounds and unstable and detuned pitches might have struck some listeners as unintentional or the result of a lack of vocal skill rather than an act of solidarity with or true interest in the sounds she uses. However, in both live performance contexts and on her early albums, she offered these kinds of improvisations alongside performances that displayed her competence in more normative vocal styles in ways likely to work against interpretations of this as unintentional.[7] The control she performs elsewhere suggests she is also exercising control when she uses weakly supported sounds and that she is also displaying her sense of the value of such sounds and her affinity with them. On subsequent albums, like the 1970 recording *Monkey Pockie Boo*, her improvisations became even more timbrally diverse, adding to her previous style elements of vocal fry, multiphonics, and a more pronounced multivocality wherein her timbre and tone shift more dramatically at frequent intervals. In this she diverges from the standard norm that a singer should craft a coherent timbral identity for themselves, shifting in tone and timbre only in subtle ways in the context of a given performance and thus performing identificatory stability and intrasubjective oneness.[8] Sharrock's work signalled early in its history that free jazz could be a space of multivocality, a space where maintenance of a stable vocal timbre is not a requirement.

Some of the Sounds of Scat

Initially for Thomas, Soularfone was a solution to the question of how one can scat without being able to fully open their mouth. Scat, of course, is the early answer to the question of how a vocalist can contribute abstract improvisational solos to jazz. As such, it is a clear predecessor to all abstract free jazz singing. Considering scat from the perspective of the present volume therefore entails considering how scat has manifested as soundsinging in the philosophical sense (vocal performances listeners perceive as non or less-than-Singing) and the literal sense (how scat did not merely consist of purely pitched melody-focused vocables).

Thomas described his early encounters with scat recordings, recounting, "What really did it for me was when my younger brother brought home a record by Dizzy Gillespie that featured Joe Carroll, a kind of scat singing blues man" (quoted in Stewart-Baxter 1970). Recordings of Carroll's vocal duets with Gillespie exist as some of the most striking examples of the ways scat performers extended scat technique beyond pitch-based melodic singing. Take, for example, the 1961 recording of "Ool Ya Koo" from The Dizzy Gillespie Big Band's live *Carnegie Hall Concert* album. The vocal element of the performance begins with Carroll and Gillespie's duo delivery of the head melody in a rather normative scat style (keeping in mind scat as a whole was, perhaps still is to some ears, often heard as soundsinging in the philosophical sense). After the head, the two vocalists begin to trade. The broad range of scat styles they employ as they alternate is remarkable, and as the song goes on they begin to include sounds that diverge from the pitch-centred and melodic, though they largely remain related to the song's metrical structure. At 1:26, Carroll pauses for two full measures before sounding a sustained, thin squeal that gets a laugh from the audience, likely due to (1) its divergence from everything that preceded it and/or (2) an understanding that this sound falls outside of what is expected of the singer, and/or (3) its uncanny evocation of a trumpet, and/or (4) an accompanying visual element we miss listening to the audio recording. This is immediately followed by a one measure pause and then an unconventional sustained tremolo lasting three measures. At 3:54 Carroll injects a growl and an ingressive gasp, and at 4:25 he sounds two low growls followed by a repeating tense multiphonic in his upper range. These moments are brief but striking, and they stand as early explorations of some of the sounds free jazz soundsingers would allow themselves the pleasure of working with later in a more sustained manner, apart from the demands of metrical structure and melodic imperative.

In a 1961 article on Carroll in *Metronome*, Dan Morgenstern explains "Joe's idol was the late Leo Watson, the first great pioneer scat singer" (1961, 21). The choice to call Watson "the first great pioneer" is an interesting snub of Louis Armstrong, the singer most commonly associated with the rise of scat. The story most often offered as the tale of the birth of scat is one of Armstrong in the recording studio with his Hot Five in 1926 dropping his lyric sheet during the recording of Boyd Atkins's song "Heebie Jeebies" and providing an abstract vocal solo in place of the lyrics that had fallen. This narrative has been famously contested by Jelly Roll Morton, who claimed the "first man that ever did a scat number in the history of this country was a man from Vicksburg Mississippi, by the name of Joe Sims, an old comedian. And from that, Tony Jackson and myself, and several more grabbed it in New Orleans" (Morton 1938).[9] Though Morton's claim isn't backed up by recorded evidence, audio recordings do exist of vocalists like Gene Greene, Aileen Stanley, and Don Redman performing scat-like solos or fills prior to 1926. Armstrong himself, contradicting the "Heebie Jeebies" myth, told stories of scatting pre-1926, when he was a younger musician forced to perform requests he didn't know the lyrics to. In an interview published in *Cadence* magazine, he was asked about the origins of scat and replied: "In New Orleans we're liable to be out on the lake, playin a little gig. These cats get drunk that hired us, ask us, 'Can you play "(blah, blah)"?' 'Oh, sure, we know everything.' And at the same time we don't know the song. Then we start scattin' and he don't know the difference . . . Started when I was a kid, scat singing" (Armstrong quoted in Rusch 1986, 6).

While pushing the boundaries of scat norms via timbral exploration was one of the ways certain scat singers thrilled and disturbed audiences, the more common subversive element in the music seems to lie in scat's resistance to semantic meaning. Like the Dada and Lettrist poets discussed in Chapter 2, scat singers offered performances capable of being felt as a rejection of the rational order via a refusal of the semantic elements of language while aspects of its morphology were retained. Written accounts of some of the original contexts in which early scat was performed live strongly suggest that scat's refusal of semantics could produce a powerful emotional charge for certain listeners. In his memoir *Harlem Jazz Adventures*, Timme Rosenkrantz describes visits he made to the New York jazz club Onyx when Leo Watson was performing with the Spirits of Rhythm. His manner of describing the performances—"no living soul had ever heard this language sung in such a scalp-tingling way" and "scat-singing those riffs in a stream of unconscious language nobody quite understood but everybody was crazy about"—point to the reception of scat as language-like and to the powerful effect of this language "nobody quite understood," language without semantics (2012, 30). While the two- to three-minute recordings available of vocalists like Watson from the 1930s and 1940s likely differ drastically from the kinds of live performances they would offer in spaces like the Onyx, they do capture some key elements of this work. Recordings like Watson's 1938 performance of "Tutti Frutti" with Gene Krupa and his Orchestra document the ways vocalists in this tradition substituted words that may be experienced as either slang or as asemantic expressions amidst otherwise semantic passages. In the case of "Tutti Frutti" for example, Watson sings "Why should you be *slootay*?" Testimonies like Rosenkrantz's suggest this "slanguage" was capable of producing the kind of felt subversion to the rational order Roland Barthes referred to as significance.[10] Scat singers like Watson and Slim Gaillard, whose seemingly asemantic language

"Vout-O-Reenee" was suggested to be semantic slang when he published *Slim Gaillard's Vout-O-Reenee Dictionary* in 1946, posed a challenge to the authority of the Word, whether through creating alternative insider semantics or resistance to the semantic.

Alongside this hollowing of the semantic, deviations from timbral norms are documented on early recordings of scat. On the 1939 recording of "It's the Tune That Counts" by Watson and his Orchestra, we hear vocal sounds comparable to the Gillespie–Carroll duet; the multiphonic articulation of a descending glissando at 2:03 or the lingual trills that follow at 2:06 stand as snippets of soundsinging in both the literal and, possibly, as Rosenkrantz suggests, the philosophical sense of the term.

Abandonment of semantics and of vocal styles associated by dominant culture with refinement, beauty, and articulateness was, and still often is, risky for singers racialised as black. For those singers often Othered as belonging to racial categories articulated with less-than-Human status, embracing vocal sounds that dominant culture Others as less-than-Human meant and means, producing sounds that some self-privileging listeners will hear as vocal evidence of the correctness of their sense of racial superiority. The asemantic will be heard by some as inarticulate rather than resistant, and the vocally unconventional will be heard by some as incapable rather than agentic, and the effect of those valuations will differ depending on the corresponding valuation of the singer's body. Perhaps, however, a failure to embrace the sounds dominant culture Others as less-than-Human poses what might be a greater risk by helping to reinforce the aesthetic logic of the symbolic order that naturalises these racial hierarchies.

From this perspective, we might rethink two problematic artefacts from Louis Armstrong's career: his 1932 performances in the Paramount short *A Rhapsody in Black and Blue* and in the semi-animated Paramount cartoon *I'll Be Glad When You're Dead, You Rascal You*. As much as he is revered, Armstrong is also reviled for the ways certain of his performances reinforced notions of white superiority. *A Rhapsody in Black and Blue* and *I'll Be Glad When You're Dead, You Rascal You* undoubtedly functioned in this way as they trafficked in primitivist and emasculating representations of the black body. Armstrong appears in *A Rhapsody* in a fantasy sequence clad semi-nude and cloaked in leopard skin as he entertains the King of Jazzland (an African American Armstrong fan who is positioned as the dreamer of the fantasy). In *I'll Be Glad* Armstrong is equated with a spear-wielding cannibal, his filmed likeness transforming to and from an animated cannibal figure. Both films feature Armstrong performing similar renditions of the song "I'll Be Glad When You're Dead, You Rascal You," a song ostensibly about the emotional aftermath of a cuckolding. About *A Rhapsody*, Phyl Garland wrote, "It readily demonstrates why so many blacks came to regard Armstrong with shame rather than the respect he deserved. Here the clown all but obscures the artist" (1980). Rather than explaining this in reference to the visual primitivism of the clip or the mugging Armstrong is often criticised for, Garland criticises the vocal performance, writing, "Guttural cackles predominate, and the fleeting sound of Armstrong's golden horn is buried in the ignominy of minstrelsy" (Ibid.). His invocation of minstrelsy may be meant to imply the leopard-skin outfit or the mugging, but the only element directly negatively invoked is Armstrong's "guttural cackles." From one interpretive perspective, the abstract vocalisations in these two filmic performances read as no different than the leopard-skin garb, as divergences from Armstrong's normal style meant to pair with the garb and help Armstrong perform "African primitive" and embody the blackface minstrel tradition's construction of black laughter as grotesque. On the other hand, laughter makes up only a portion of his vocal performance, and the rest consists of a dynamic abstract vocal improvisation Armstrong shapes in real time that is as capable of conveying a critique of the role containing Armstrong in these films as it is of conveying the vile notion black bodies belong to some imaginary less-than-Human-primitive category.

To understand the critical potential of his abstract sounds, we can appeal to another figure that factors as an influence on free jazz soundsinging, Screamin' Jay Hawkins. Beginning in the early 1950s, Hawkins based a large part of his career on playing a version of the "African primitive" character Armstrong plays in *A Rhapsody*. His substantial history of including passages of abstract unconventional vocal improvisation in his performances is well documented and alluded to in his stage name. When asked in a 1990 interview to name what makes him scream, he began with: "Being black, prejudice" (quoted in Cohen 1990). As Bryan Wagner argues in his book *Disturbing the Peace: Black Culture and the Police Power After Slavery*, the wordless "growling and stuttering" in histories of African American vocal performance can manifest as a form of speech for individuals denied the right to speak or to self-define (2009, 232). Listeners can hear Armstrong's or Hawkins's wordless vocalisations as nonsense, but they might also hear them as the material presence of a consciousness that has otherwise been silenced or deHumanised. Wagner refers to this as "a musical strategy that has been called overvocalizing," a strategy "based on choral embellishments such as melisma" that can "interrupt the prearranged lines of identification in a given composition" (Ibid.).

Overvocalisation provides Armstrong with a means of critique amidst the broader racist frame in which the film contains him alongside the potential counter-reading of the lyrics of "I'll Be Glad When You're Dead" as a statement of protest against a racist establishment.[11] While Garland reduces Armstrong's entire vocal performance to "guttural cackles," distinct listeners hear various other associations. One YouTube commenter responding to *I'll Be Glad* notes, to him, "Louis Armstrong sounds down syndrome like."[12] One way to hear Armstrong's vocalisations is as an embrace of an array of sounds that dominant culture has Othered and devalued (though the YouTube comment does not clearly value or devalue the vocalisations he associates with Down syndrome, it is problematically frequent for certain vocal sounds made by individuals with Down syndrome to be associated with disability rather than ability). With Armstrong contained in a frame that deHumanises him, he can be heard as agentively, if perhaps only semi-consciously, vocally expressing a solidarity with an array of sounds that are also devalued, including vocal sounds heard as disabled. Garland hears Armstrong's instrumental virtuosity as the only way to transcend the racist frame; however, solidarity with the vocal sounds others have Othered may represent a more sustainable strategy in the long run (if not a riskier strategy in the short term) than performing belong-ingness to the category of Human via virtuosity on the "golden horn," as that route contributes to the maintenance of a divide between the Human and the human in the musical domain. Virtuosity on his horn certainly won Armstrong and, by extension, blackness a higher rank in that hierarchy. That higher rank led conversely to both a diminishing of the notion that blackness belonged to some less-than-Human category and an increased desire to contain the threat of a perceived-to-be ascending not-fully-Human black culture. It also importantly led to African American pride in Armstrong's accomplishments. However, we see from Garland's comments that this all comes at the expense of the Othering of the "non-golden" and thus, on some level, assists in the maintenance of a hierarchical symbolic order that divides Human from human. Given the stakes and the domi-nant perception of Armstrong's vocals in these contexts, Garland's impulse makes strategic sense. But clowning and minstrel-style caricature are not the only ways to read Armstrong's abstract vocalisations in these performances. They are capable of being appreciated in themselves as non-representational but aesthetically valu-able abstract vocal improvisation, as an overvocalising that protests the racist frame, as a palpable rejection of the authority of the Word, and/or as a performance of solidarity with sounds that dominant culture has devalued and Othered. From the perspective of soundsinging, we can't reduce Armstrong's vocal exploration in these performances to the "cackles" he sounds and their representational or associ-ative dimensions; these performances were not merely composed of laughter-like sounds. We are compelled from this perspective to also consider how the com-promising primitivist frame of these films allowed Armstrong to explore and emit vocal sounds that the more usual frames that contained his public performances didn't afford him. These vocal performances indeed caused social harm, and reducing their meaning to that harm effect is understandable. However, it remains reduction, as it is possible to also read agency, protest, and/or solidarity with the Othered into these vocalisations.

Soundsinging and Popular Music

Though Screamin' Jay Hawkins's "jungle primitive" persona resembled Arm-strong's character in *A Rhapsody* in many regards, the frame containing the two differed substantially. Hawkins's portrayal of this character was a multi-decades-long affair, and it involved many opportunities to point to the agentive and criti-cal dimensions of his adoption of this trope. Sonically, the two differed as well, of course, though both involved a variety of abstract vocal improvisations framed by the ironic conceit they are the vocal outbursts of an "African primitive." Hawkins's work often made it clear that his intention was to direct critical attention to the history of white desire to view black bodies as primitive; the clearest expression of this was, perhaps, his choice to title his tenth album *Black Music for White People* (with the title displayed alongside a cover image of him in one of his exoticist costumes holding an unconscious white, blonde woman in a white dress). Naturally, his explicitness about his critical intention was not enough to ensure that intention was perceptible to everyone encountering his act.

Hawkins is one of many vocalists in the history of popular music that have had a demonstrable influence on free jazz singing. Paul Dutton opens his 1992 essay "Beyond Doo Wop, or, How I Came to Realize That Hank Williams Is Avant-Garde" with a discussion of the effect Hawkins's recording of his song "I Put a Spell on You" had on him. He writes "I memorized every mutter, scream, snort, howl, and demonic laugh on it, delighting not so much in its humour (it's not, actually, all that funny) as in what I then experienced as its audacity—an uninhibited, outrageous, delicious flouting of convention" (9). Dutton immediately signals the way hearing Hawkins's vocalic body denaturalised the "careful enunciation and rounded tone" that Dutton "had been trained in (or chained in) since age seven, at the boys' choir school" he attended (Ibid.). Armstrong's music performed the same function for Phil Minton. After a discussion of how he would imitate Armstrong and others with raspy voices as a child, I asked Minton why he felt he was attracted to these kinds of voices and he answered: "I think it probably had a lot to do with the fact that my parents and all these voices around me were all these very clear, pure voices."[13] Recordings by Armstrong and Hawkins showed Minton and Dutton ways they could use their voices to resist the traditions they were being interpellated into and the vocal restrictions those traditions entailed. Minton and Dutton's cross-racial mimetic encounters with these recordings factor significantly into their own narratives of their path as young white men developing vocal affinities that would later feed into their free jazz performances.

Dutton's essay also mentions "Little Richard's screams, the falsetto wah-wahhhs of Fats Domino in his early recordings, Muddy Waters' vowel-twisting, consonant-punching vocals, and the slack-mouthed nearly incomprehensible dialect of Jimmy Reed" as well as the "inhaled singing" of Clarence "Frogman" Henry and Hank Williams's "diphonic" singing (1992, 9, 17). He also pays tribute to, while disclaiming any influence from, Janis Joplin's "virtuosic multiphonics . . . on display in her singing on the *Cheap Thrills* album by Big Brother and the Holding Company," and the univocal chording "in early blues and black gospel of the mid 20th century."[14] Similarly, David Moss describes how he "thought of James Brown, Sly Stone, and Aretha Franklin as 'extended vocalists.'"[15] For Christine Duncan "the kind of channelling sound" Yma Sumac made with her voice on the album *Voice of the Xtabay* "awakened a voracious hunger" in her against the backdrop of her "very strict Christian environment" where "all the music in the house was very Christian."[16] And for Mankwe Ndosi it was the "richness . . . expressiveness . . . and the different vocal percussion" of Miriam Makeba that helped her "think about" her "voice as an instrument and that there really wasn't any one way to sing."[17]

The list of popular singers whose recordings have affected free jazz soundsingers is inexhaustible, and it is impossible to uncover them all. However, it is clear many popular vocalists and their recordings have helped free jazz soundsingers shape the ways they developed their vocal practices.

The Extended-Vocal Turn and Western Art Music's Intersections With Free Jazz Voice

Istvan Anhalt's book *Alternative Voices: Essays on Contemporary Vocal and Choral Composition* offers one history of the use of extended vocal techniques in Western art music. He begins with Arnold Schoenberg and Pierre Boulez's use of sprechstimme, then moves to Karlheinz Stockhausen's use of electronic manipulation of recorded voices in the tape piece *Gesang der Junglinge* (1955–1956), a piece created at roughly the same time Dufrêne was making his discoveries with tape (see Chapter 2). This is followed by Cage's *Solo for Voice I* (1958), which he includes on the basis that it affords the vocalist an opportunity to improvise, and Mauricio Kagel's *Anagrama* (1957–1958), a piece that instructed singers to employ a specific and diverse range of extended techniques.

Compositions employing such methods became more widespread in the mid-1960s, with the voice pieces of Luciano Berio cited often as exemplars of this work. We have already encountered Berio and Cathy Berberian collaborations informing the history of free jazz soundsinging in Chapter 1. Alongside Berberian, another composer-performer who had a major impact on free jazz soundsinging via work in new music spaces was Demetrio Stratos. It was around 1970 when Stratos, who had been a vocalist and instrumentalist in various popular music projects since 1962 and who had studied music as a child in the Conservatoire National d'Athenes, began exploring unconventional vocal techniques. Stratos's wife Daniela Ronconi noted it was his infant daughter's impressive vocal capacities that first inspired this work, explaining "he kept asking himself the reason why people lose this interesting capacity while they grow up" (Ronconi paraphrased in Ceolin, Tisato, and Zattra 2011). A significant portion of his research involved studying diverse vocal techniques from various traditional and art music forms from around the world. In 1974, he toured festivals in France, Portugal, Switzerland, and Cuba and collaborated with Juan Hidalgo, Walter Marchetti, and Gianni-Emilio Simonetti, members of the group Zaj, an experimental music and performance group based in Madrid. Stratos's first publicly available recording in a non-popular music idiom was a performance of an excerpt from John Cage's *Sixty-Two Mesostics Re Merce Cunningham* on a 1974 album also containing performances of Cage's works by Hidalgo, Marchetti, and Simonetti. This recording led to a series of collaborations between Cage and Stratos in 1978, the year before Stratos died prematurely at the age of thirty-four.[18] The recording also displayed the command he had gained between 1970 and 1974 of a wide variety of self-developed and cross-culturally appropriated vocal techniques. Following this recording, Stratos recorded and released three highly influential albums of soundsinging compositions: *Metrodora* (1976), *Cantare La Voce* (1978), and a live duo performance with Lucio Fabbri on violin, recorded in 1978 and released in 1980 called *Recitarcantando*. Though he died tragically young, these early recordings continue to be highly influential for a number of free jazz singers.

Stratos's interest in preserving or re-discovering the vocal capacities of the infant voice recall one of the major concerns of another body of vocalists that have intersected at various points with the members and spaces of free jazz communities, the students and the students of students of Alfred Wolfsohn and Roy Hart. Wolfsohn was a vocal teacher who served as a stretcher bearer in World War I. In the cries of pain he heard from the soldiers he carried on stretchers, he came to realise the adult human voice was capable of a range of sounds beyond what vocal instructors normally train students to produce. He came up with his idea of training the "eight-octave voice," or "the unchained human voice" utilising pitch ranges beyond those wherein individual singers can produce stable, "pure" pitches without multiphonic noise (Pikes 2004, XIII, 2).[19] For Wolfsohn and his star pupil, Rueben Hartstein, later Roy Hart, the expressive potential of vocal sounds in these extremes of the upper or lower end of a vocalist's voice were not to be ignored just because the pitches that sound may not sound in a "pure" manner.

Some students of the unconventional vocal pedagogy of the Roy Hart Theatre have worked in free jazz contexts. Anna Homler, for example, (who will be introduced in more detail in Chapter 4) has benefitted from time spent studying in the Roy Hart tradition. Conversely, some free jazz vocalists have rejected aspects of the Hart Theatre model.[20] Though free jazz soundsinging has, at times, been taught in exchange for monetary compensation, many free jazz vocalists have thrived via an approach to vocal development that is autodidactic, and they bristle at the idea of letting a pedagogue suggest what kinds of sounds one should or should not pursue and at the notion of becoming such a pedagogue themselves.[21] The Hart Theatre and its offshoots, like many other schools of voice, leans in this direction, but unlike most other schools of voice, the Hart method has often manifested as both a vocal pedagogical and a therapeutic environment. The differing degrees of hierarchy and aesthetic differences seem to have somewhat limited blurring between the Roy Hart tradition and free jazz soundsinging, but some crossover has occurred. The limit I point to here might be expressed best via Phil Minton's recollection of encountering the Hart School fairly early in his career in London. He describes: "I had come across Roy Hart about 1972. I read a small advert in *Time Out* magazine in London about experimental voice classes. I thought: I think I'd be quite interested in that. I think I made a phone call and it was so expensive that I never got in."[22]

Though Berberian, Wolfsohn, and Hart are some of the best-known figures in the history of extended classical vocal music, they share that identity with a long list of vocalists. Many of these figures have been extensively discussed elsewhere and for that reason I will avoid exploring this list further here. One final set of names from this list, however, that I will mention due to certain notable encounters they have had with free jazz vocalists are the members of the Extended Vocal Techniques Ensemble (EVTE) at the University of California, San Diego (UCSD). The ensemble formed in 1972 at the Center for Music Experiment at UCSD and was composed of Ed Harkins, Phil Larson, Deborah Kavasch, and Linda Vickerman. The EVTE gave a number of influential performances and workshops between 1972 and the early 1980s and created one of the existing extended vocal techniques manuals. Paul Dutton recalls encountering the ensemble in the late 1970s, and Trevor Wishart cites them as an indirect early influence on his work via the composer Warren Burt, who worked with EVTE at UCSD from 1973 and 1975 and who piqued Wishart's interest in "new vocal possibilities" (Wishart quoted in Vassilandonakis 2009, 13).[23]

Wishart is one of a number of singers who are active both as free jazz soundsingers and as contemporary composers of Western art music.[24] He developed an interest in free jazz singing while completing his doctoral work in composition at the University of York. His compositional practices were drastically affected by the passing of his father. Wishart came from a working-class background, and his father was a factory worker in Leeds. When his father died, Wishart felt a "sense of disconnectedness from his world" and decided to buy a tape recorder and go "around factories and power-stations in Nottingham and Leeds, recording the sounds of industrial machinery, with some vague notion of making a piece for him" (Wishart quoted in Milani and Placidi 2009). Prior to this, Wishart had been "writing complex instrumental music (7 tone rows with different intervallic structures + random number tables)" (Ibid.). But his environmental recording sent him on a different compositional path. He explains: "[i]n the studio I discovered that many of my presumptions about composition were challenged in this new medium. Sounds had a life of their own which had to be respected. Preconceived absolute notions of musical proportions and musical relationships were challenged by the concrete reality of the sounds themselves" (Ibid.). Part of his recognition of the essential difference between the environmental sounds and the proportions of instrumental music involved a recognition of the complexity of the voice. He theorises:

> the voice is much more than a musical instrument. Through speech it connects us to the social world, and thence to traditions of poetry, drama, comedy, etc. It reveals much about the speaker, from gender, age, and health to attitude, mood and intention, and it also connects us with our Primate relatives. The listener recognizes a voice even when it is minimally indicated, or vastly transformed, just as we recognize faces from very few cues. And the average listener will be affected by e.g. a vocal multiphonic, an immediate

empathic or guttural link, in a way which they will not be affected by a clarinet multiphonic.

(Ibid.)

For Wishart, the voice belongs in his category of "real-world sounds" (Ibid.), which were the sounds he chose to devote much of his compositional career to.

Wind, Water, and Washing Machines: The Mimetic Dimensions of Free Jazz Voice

Much of Wishart's work explores what is shared between vocal sound and the sounds of machines and the natural world. He has completed deep research into and has designed technologies for sound morphing, often realising, in works like his *Red Bird* or his *Vox 5*, morphing between human vocal and various natural sounds. However, alongside those technological explorations, he continues to come back to "the only resource which has the timbral flexibility and transformational potential of the electronic studio without the price tag: my own voice." Wishart's compositional interest in morphing goes hand in hand with the mimetic approach followed by many free jazz soundsingers. Jaap Blonk provides one example of this, describing a

> tram in Amsterdam, in this place where I lived. Every three or four minutes I would hear the squeaky sound and I started working on that. Noticing that I could develop inhaling high register, sort of strange extra high register, that came because of that imitation. Same thing for the low register, trying to imitate low machine sounds and also maybe musical instruments that go much lower than the human voice like the tuba or some notes on the trombone.[25]

Mankwe Ndosi recalls vocally exploring the sounds of "washing machines to the white noise from the computer and the hum of the refrigerator and, you know, the tires" and she recounted imitating a neighbour's cat "so well that it would react as though there was a cat around."[26] Paul Dutton wrote that after he'd bought his first car, "a little Spider Flat . . . I was embarrassed to realize afterward that the sounds I'd been making that particular evening certainly had a sports-car quality to them" (Dutton quoted in Doherty 2003).

The embarrassment Dutton mentions comes from the fact that while free jazz singers allow a broad range of sounds, dynamisms, and textures to inform their vocalisations, only very rarely are they interested in direct imitation of a recognisable sound source in the course of their performances. Recognisable imitation does manifest on rare occasions to add humour, and some forms of channelling can slip into recognisability on occasion in the manner Dutton describes, but for the most part, established free jazz singers have avoided recognisable imitation. Free jazz soundsingers have largely tended towards hybridisation of appropriated sounds into personalised sounds that no longer clearly signify external sources singers may have mimetically engaged within private spaces. Gabriel Dharmoo, for instance, describes being inspired by "vocal traditions around the world" but also thinking of them as musics he "would not imitate" but would hybridise "like this is a kind of Vietnamese melody . . . then the phonemes will be more, I don't know, Arabic or Tamil."[27] Christine Duncan sees this hybridisation process as an inevitable part of improvisational singing, saying: "it's like the data comes in and the data comes out, but it gets combined with all the other data and then the new form is created. The hybrid form is created."[28] And so appropriation in soundsinging is not usually a form of capture and display or a performance of a mastery of the cultural property of the Other, it is embodied curiosity and engagement with the timbres and textures we encounter in the world, engagement in which we sensually commune with sounds that make us curious, where we introduce the ways our bodies reshape those sounds into fluid combination with the other sounds we have met and invited into bodies.

Conclusion: Back to the Head

On the only commercially available recording of Phil Minton's free jazz vocal work in the 1960s, an album called *Up Umeå* recorded in 1969 at a Swedish national television studio in Umeå, the opening track, "Day," starts with Lars Göran Ulander's saxophone offering a wavering tone with subtle but noticeable multiphonic content. Minton enters with his voice in a manner that clearly emerges out of the saxophone timbre; his voice is barely noticeable at first because it blends nearly seamlessly with that timbre. As the saxophone bends in pitch, Minton follows, until something shifts and he takes the lead, building towards an unconventional tremolo. At five and a half minutes into the track, the whole band drops out and Minton re-enters with a sustained moan that is melodic at first and then moves deeper into the throat, becoming a gargle. He pauses and then lets out a scream that prompts the rest of the group to re-enter. They all play energetically before letting the texture become sparse. Ulander then enters with a sustained, frail, ultra-high pitch, which Minton again matches with a strained whistle tone.

The material processes that put Minton's listening body into proximity with Ulander's saxophone (and vice versa) are as much a part of free jazz singing's history as the processes that put Minton's listening body into contact with a record player sounding *Live at the Village Vanguard Again!*. Both allowed non-vocal sounds to inform singing. This chapter and the first part of this book have just begun to scratch the surface of the material encounters that have mattered in the history of free jazz singing. But if you yourself start to sing this scratching, we'll move even closer to knowing this unknowable history.

Notes

1. Jaap Blonk, interview with author, 18 June 2004.
2. In 1969, he released the album *Spirits Known and Unknown,* followed in 1970 by *The Leon Thomas Album* and *SNCC's Rap.* These were followed by live albums *Gold Sunrise on Magic Mountain* and *Leon Thomas in Berlin With Oliver Nelson* in 1971, the album *Blues and the Soulful Truth* in 1972, and *Full Circle* in 1973.
3. Thomas explained the reason for his collapse was that he had "transcended. I was in one place and my body was another. I dropped to the floor, right on my face and my teeth went into my bottom lip" (Thomas quoted in Lazarius 1995).
4. Ibid.
5. Demain's article also cites claims by MGM studio, claims disputed by Weissmuller, that the call was as much a studio hybrid of sounds as a live utterance by Weissmuller. The lists of sources Demain states MGM claims they employed seems rather excessive when compared to the audio content of the films (including a second track of Weissmuller's voice, a hyena howl played backwards, a speed-modified note by a female soprano, a dog's growl, a camel's bleat, and a raspy bowing of a violin), but there seems to be some truth to the claim that the call was a carefully shaped post-production hybrid.
6. See tracks like "Portrait of Linda in Three Colors, All Black."
7. This is particularly clear on recordings like the track "Soon" from the album *Monkey Pockie Boo.*
8. See, for example, her work on the track "27th Day."
9. See disc 3, track 10, "The Anamule Dance, continued."
10. See "The Third Meaning" in Barthes 1977. For Barthes, signifiance is a layer of meaning experienced in encounters with artworks. It does not emerge from the semantic or symbolic, but via an emotional charge experienced by the person encountering the artwork when they perceive the material qualities of the artwork, the signifier itself, to exist in an emancipatory relation to the normativity of other existing signifiers.
11. It is clear from Armstrong's history that these lyrics were heard as such by certain listeners, including Armstrong himself, who once dedicated a performance of the song to the Memphis police after they unjustly arrested him and members of his band. See Brothers 2014.
12. See www.youtube.com/watch?v=KU86IlIf8Q4. Accessed 20 January 2019.
13. Phil Minton, interview with author, 24 June 2014.
14. Paul Dutton, email to the author, 11 March 2019.
15. David Moss, interview with the author, 6 and 7 July 2013.
16. Christine Duncan, interview with the author, 11 August 2014.
17. Mankwe Ndosi, interview with the author, 26 September 2013.
18. The Merce Cunningham Archive at the New York Public Library holds documentation of one of their collaborations, a performance in March 1978 in New York with the Roundabout Theatre Company.
19. In the forward to Pikes's book by Jay Livernois, he describes how Wolfsohn employed the term "the unchained human voice" (XIII). Pikes discusses the "eight-octave" concept in his opening chapter (2).
20. In my interview with Homler, she referred to her study of the Roy Hart technique as "life-changing." Anna Homler, interview with the author, 23 July 2013.
21. See, for example, Paul Dutton's comments on training in his interview excerpt.
22. Phil Minton, interview with author, 24 June 2014.
23. Paul Dutton, interview with the author, 11 and 12 August 2014.
24. We should acknowledge the compositional output of many free jazz soundsingers. Ono, Lee, Minton, Nicols, and Nozati all composed music at points in their career. Wishart, however, is better known as a composer than as an improviser, and he is deeply

integrated into the institutions of contemporary art music in a way other early free jazz vocalists are not. He is seemingly the earliest free jazz vocalist to strike this kind of balance in his practice, but more recently a variety of other vocalist/composers, including Michael Edward Edgerton, Ken Ueno, and Gabriel Dharmoo, have negotiated somewhat similar profiles.

25. Jaap Blonk, interview with the author, 8 November 2013.
26. Mankwe Ndosi, interview with the author, 26 September 2013.
27. Gabriel Dharmoo, interview with the author, 28 October 2013.
28. Christine Duncan, interview with the author, 11 August 2014.

PART II
Theories

4

VOCAL VILLAGE

The Rise of a New Transnational Vocal Jazz Community

I can only speak about how it began. That was in 1968 . . . What was happening then in France and around the world moved me deeply. A lot of questions came to me and one of them was very strong and very strange: "What is my dream?" I was quite surprised with the answer: "I want to sing." I was not expecting that at all. In fact it was an old dream I had completely forgotten. I realised I could hear a certain kind of music in myself. I was sure some people were doing that music somewhere and I looked for them. I didn't find them. I began to improvise long *melopees*. I had to go very deep in a very unknown part of myself. It sometimes frightened me, but it was a vital necessity.

—*Tamia quoted in Tuynman 1986*

In the June 1981 issue of the French journal *Jazz Magazine*, there is a listing for the three-day *Actual Music Festival of Improvisation* that outlines seven dancers, four actors, eight musicians, and nine singers that would be featured at the festival. The French vocalist Tamia was one of the nine singers, as were Maggie Nicols, Phil Minton, and Julie Tippetts, three of the most established free jazz vocalists in the London scene at the time, the versatile American composer-performer Alvin Curran, and Trevor Wishart, who was based in the northeast of England.[1] If in 1968 Tamia felt she could not find others making the music she heard inside herself, by 1981 she would likely have felt differently, as she was participating in a transnational scene where free jazz soundsinging was becoming a regular presence. This 1981 free jazz festival where the singers outnumbered the instrumental musicians was just one of the many signs that free jazz voice was entering a new phase in the 1980s.

Ensemble and solo voice–only free jazz was starting to appear on records in the late 1970s and early 1980s such as Nicols, Minton, Tippetts, and Brian Eley's 1977 quartet record *Voice*, Paul Dutton's 1980 *Blues, Roots, Legends, Shouts & Hollers*, and Minton's 1981 solo recording *A Doughnut in Both Hands*. Such recordings, and booking practices like that of the 1981 Actual Festival, helped to spread the idea that free jazz vocalisation without instrumental accompaniment was an available expressive practice. Because of this, throughout the 1980s numbers of practitioners expanded significantly.

The focus of this chapter will be to introduce some of the free jazz vocalists whose practices emerged in this period and to explore the milieus that fostered their practices. This exploration offers some sense of the broad range of scenes, organisations, practices, and projects that fed into and helped shape the vocal practices of the second generation of free jazz singers. What seems to me most distinct about this period is the increased audibility and accessibility of free jazz singing in and through the expansion of transnational and transcultural collaborations between free jazz singers. The 1980s and 1990s saw the rise of a number of voice-only free jazz ensembles composed of singers from multiple countries. The varying national origins of the singers were often foregrounded in advertisements for their events; this pointed to free jazz voice's transnational mobility, its widespread nature, and the desire of free jazz singers to work across national and cultural divides.

The extensive number of collaborations that have arisen in the 1980s and beyond outstripped the resources I have had to investigate. However, I will discuss some of the transnational and transcultural collaborations of this period by focusing on David Moss. Moss has been a particularly dynamic, ambitious, and visionary contributor to the free jazz vocal world for the past four decades. By tracing just a few of his many collaborative projects we quickly get introduced to a wide swath of the most active figures in the transnational free jazz vocal scene. This is not surprising given the fact that his very presence as a free jazz singer is due largely to the importance he places on the social dimensions of being a musician. As I discussed in Chapter 2, Moss began his musical life as a percussionist. He reflects on one aspect of his life as a percussionist, explaining:

> For a single concert with my percussion set, six hours of my day would be involved with the non-performative aspect of getting it ready and taking it apart. For the forty-five minute or one hour event in which I would be playing, it took six hours (and I'm not including travel-time), getting everything ready in the room, putting all the stuff onstage, set-up, sound-check, warming up, doing all that work ... in the '90s, when I travelled to give a *vocal* event, I began to realise, to feel, how much more time I had to talk with people, to think about ideas, to rest my body, to summon up my energy, to imagine new beginnings and endings. And of course, I couldn't plan projects with people, or hang out and have those needed bonding talks and collegial moments when I was ALONE on the road setting up my instrument for hours. Now I had chances to talk about playful

possibilities with other colleagues, because I had the time to sit down and have a meal together and to share ideas and actually brainstorm. It feels a bit weird to say this now, but with the drums, the physicality, the physicality of carrying them, packing them, opening them, setting them up, caring for them, concentrating on them, compressed my ability to meet, to be a social performer/person.[2]

His desire to heighten the social dimensions of his music-making caused him to leave the drums behind and devote himself primarily to voice. This aligns with the desire he has demonstrated to bring singers together across cultural, geographic, stylistic borders. By looking at the ways he has approached these collaborations, we can begin to understand key features of the ways the second generation of free jazz voice took shape and meet several key players who contributed to the activities of this era.

Moss's career not only provides us an understanding of the increasingly widespread, transcultural, and transnational dimensions of the free jazz singing in this period, it also helps us deepen our understanding of the commitment of many free jazz singers to fostering autodidactic practices or idiosyncratically self-designed vocal pedagogies. While we will begin this chapter looking at Moss's collaborative voice-centred ensembles, we will complete the chapter looking at one of his most ambitious initiatives, the Institute for Living Voice (ILV).

Overall, the emphasis of the chapter will be on the ways Moss's projects embody the changed status of free jazz singing in the 1980s, 1990s, and, via the ILV, into the 2000s, but I will also touch on certain difficulties Moss and his collaborators encountered fostering transcultural voice-only free jazz and some of his suggested solutions for these problems. Moss helped to make free jazz singers far more audible, more mobile, more globally interconnected, and more collaborative. As he did, his projects helped perform to audiences that free jazz voice was alive and flourishing, communicating across scenes from around the world.

David Moss's Transnational, Transcultural, and Transgeneric Projects

There is no singer mentioned in this book that is purely a "free jazz vocalist." Most free jazz singers are bimusical or multi-musical, performing in more than one musical genre and working in more than one musical community or scene. Moss has shifted from working predominantly in jazz genres and spaces to developing a career split largely between jazz-identified and classical spaces. While the shift between the environment Tamia describes in the late 1960s and the very different environment she found herself in by the early 1980s was already in progress before the 1980s—transnational collaborations of vocal improvisers were already becoming frequent and voice-only free jazz was beginning to gain a significant presence in free jazz spaces—the 1980s and 1990s saw an acceleration of this process. And while many singers before Moss asserted that voice-only free jazz could be a space for transnational and/or transcultural collaboration and exchange, Moss has pursued this in a particularly ambitious and consistent manner.

In 1989 Moss organised a vocal quintet he called Direct Sound.[3] This would be the first of several voice-only (or nearly voice-only) quartets or quintets he organised that would stage the spectacle of the existence of a transnational free jazz vocal scene. Direct Sound brought together Dutch vocalist Greetje Bijma, West Coast American vocalist Anna Homler, East Coast American vocalist Shelley Hirsch, and Catalan vocalist/composer Carles Santos, thus combining five vocalists who all worked substantially with unconventional vocal sounds.

Shelley Hirsch

Moss and Hirsch were both active figures in the Downtown New York jazz scene in the 1980s. Hirsch's work is reflective of her movement between theatre and music contexts. At eighteen years old, in 1970, she moved from New York to San Francisco and joined Cecile Pineda's experimental theatre company, the Theatre of Man. She has often described being influenced by the company's method of collecting environmental sounds to use in rehearsals. Additionally, she describes leading the other actors in re-creating these environmental sounds using only their voices. Similar methodologies factored into her early work after she left San Francisco and returned to New York City. In 1973, she became involved with Kirk Nurock's Natural Sound Workshop, a group devoted to exploring the musical possibilities of "the myriad sounds of untrained voices."[4] Natural Sound Workshop performances were often inclusive, partially improvisatory voice-and-body-sound–only performances built around the philosophy that: "We are all musicians naturally . . . Music belongs to everyone. Each of us can develop an amazing variety of personal sounds which can be organised and performed as contemporary music."[5] These performances usually involved a large choir of 20 to 25 performers exploring sounds that included hissing, humming, breathing, and gurgling. Nurock encouraged audience members to join portions of the performances, which would subsequently transform them into large free jazz choirs with both ensemble and audience members vocally improvising.

Hirsch also joined smaller ensembles organised by Nurock. In one of these groups, Hirsch was one of three vocalists alongside the versatile singers John DeRobertis and Jay Clayton. Clayton is a central figure in a thread of free jazz vocal history that runs parallel to and sometimes intersects with the free jazz soundsinging thread I am most concerned with here. Her thread is rooted in traditional jazz vocal training and an aesthetic somewhat less invested in non–pitch-centred singing, although Clayton has certainly done some soundsinging, especially in her free jazz collaborations with Nurock. In this thread the term "extended vocal technique" seems appropriate, given its firmer rootedness in a more recognised, pitch-centred vocal pedagogy. Clayton's extensions of her technique in her free jazz work in the 1960s and beyond are notable and have played a role in inspiring some vocalists to move in the direction of free jazz soundsinging. Hirsch's work with Clayton in Nurock's ensemble led to her singing on some of Clayton's own projects. The personal style Hirsch developed often combines abstract singing with improvised storytelling or fragmented speech. She has been active in free jazz contexts consistently from the 1980s to the present.

Anna Homler

Anna Homler describes her entry into free jazz voice by pointing out her "background is in visual and performance art" and she "never thought of" herself "as a singer."[6] Singing entered the work she was doing as a performance artist in the early 1980s in Los Angeles. She felt that "performance art seemed to [her] like a big container—it was like a permission slip to be all of [herself], to live all of [her] aspects," and singing was one of those aspects.[7] In an early performance piece called "On the Egyptian Sleep of Unopened Books," she recorded her voice and played the recording in the performance space while she went to sleep among the books in Hunter's Books, a bookstore she worked at in the Westwood area of Los Angeles. This early work preceded a foundational performance art project built around a character she called Breadwoman. Breadwoman was a character "so very ancient, so old that her face had turned to bread. She lived in the centre of the earth and spoke in the root sound of all languages."[8] Part of the Breadwoman project involved Homler recording a cassette of five songs sung in the "mysterious and familiar" ur-language of Breadwoman.[9]

Homler's early recordings factored into her movement from performance art into music-centred contexts. She was introduced to Moss by the interdisciplinary artist Jacki Apple, who, Homler recalls, led her to a radio program Moss hosted called *U.S. Ear: The New Music Review. U.S. Ear* and the other radio programs Moss produced in the 1980s stand as one piece of Moss's extraordinary legacy of connecting and promoting musicians within and across the mixed-avant-garde and also within and across the emerging sphere of free jazz voice. Alongside the fifty-two thirty-minute episodes of *U.S. Ear* that Moss produced, he also created one hundred and twenty episodes of a three-minute new music program called *Soundspot*; a program called *Sound Sculptors*, where he "interviewed people who worked with objects, like Harry Bertoia and Richard Lerman;" and a program called *Vox Box* where he interviewed singers like Minton, Maggie Nicols, and Diamanda Galas.[10] After Apple introduced Homler to Moss's work, she had the opportunity to see him perform at Los Angeles Contemporary Exhibition. Later, while she was out on the East Coast for an artists' residency in Pennsylvania at the arts village Yellow Springs, she connected with Moss, and they spent an afternoon singing together. She describes meeting Moss as "a turning point." Vocalising with Moss led Homler to broader work as a singer in free jazz contexts, with the Direct Sound project serving as an important step towards free jazz involvement that remains active to the present.

Greetje Bijma

Greetje Bijma often sings melodic jazz standards in a manner that convinces audiences of her virtuosity and her command of dominant traditional jazz vocal technique. However, her practice emerged in a manner she says was "entirely autodidactical," and she commonly takes detours into "extensions" of her pitch-centred singing.[11] Her work explores a wide range of less conventional sounds in sustained manners that signal a strong commitment to and affinity with varieties of less conventional vocal sound. In other performances these sounds are not extensions of jazz vocal technique but are the base from which she works. She describes her approach, explaining: "The technical possibilities of my voice present a constant challenge but have been never a goal in itself. I find it beautiful to spontaneously discover new facets of my voice, and this is something that is still happening . . . I consider myself to be 'in development' where, from my first moments as a vocalist, I have worked with complete freedom" (Bijma 2006, 550).

Bijma's musical career began in the late 1970s in the northern Netherlands. She began as a kind of singer-songwriter "singing improvised songs, which she underlined with a few basic guitar chords."[12] Meeting Alan Laurillard in 1980, a Canadian saxophonist who was living and organising improvised music events in the northern Netherlands, led to her involvement in the broader Dutch and European free jazz music scenes, initially through her involvement with Laurillard's project Noodband.

Carles Santos

Most of Carles Santos's most recognised vocal work fits into a neighbouring category to free jazz soundsinging: pre-structured soundsinging. In this, his work resembles that of Demetrio Stratos, discussed in the previous chapter. Both Santos and Stratos could certainly be called soundsingers rather than specialists in "extended vocal techniques," as their work is less an "extension" beyond pitch-centred singing and more a product of a vocal field where pitch-based singing does not constitute a central position from which the singer extends. Both pre-structured much of their most recognised vocal work. Santos came to this work starting in 1977 from a background as a concert pianist and composer, influenced, in part, by encounters he had with the worlds of sound poetry and experimental theatre.[13]

Direct Sound's unmistakable transnational composition announced that interest in this unconventional vocal work was geographically widespread, and the connections across these distances were established and flowing. Significantly, the quintet staged concerts in 1989 on either side of the Atlantic.[14] One of these concerts occurred as part of an event that is notable in the context of this chapter for the way it both staged a concert of the ensemble and broke the ensemble down into smaller units to support a six-day vocal festival called *Urbane Aboriginale Vokal*.

Urbane Aboriginale Vokal began on October 11, 1989, with two days of vocal workshops led by Hirsch. The second day of the festival also featured a concert with Moss in a voice and percussion duo with Peter Hollinger; Sussan Deyhim performing a piece for voice and tape; and Gambian singer Buba Jammeh. The third night featured Jammeh again, as well as a piano performance by Santos, and a duo set by Hirsch and David Weinstein. On the fourth night, Direct Sound performed, adding Phil Minton and Deyhim to the group in place of Homler. Finally, the final two days of the festival involved a two-day workshop led by Moss. The blend of free jazz, new music, and Gambian traditional singing stands as an early example of Moss's desire to create spaces where singing could be explored from a trans- or multicultural perspective.

After Direct Sound, Moss continued to organise transnational voice-only or nearly voice-only ensembles. In the late 1990s, he organised what he called the Vocal Village Project, a quartet of vocalists—Catherine Jauniaux, Koichi Makigami, Phil Minton, and Moss—two of whom doubled on percussion, accompanied by one instrumentalist, Frank Shulte, on electronics and keyboards. In this project, Moss assembled four vocalists, each from a different country, and he highlighted the transnational nature of the ensemble prominently with his name for the group, a play on Marshall McLuhan's notion of the "global village."

Catherine Jauniaux and Koichi Makigami

Although Catherine Jauniaux and Koichi Makigami come from different corners of the globe, Jauniaux being Belgian and Makigami Japanese, both came to free jazz through their experiences in avant-garde rock bands and as actors in theatrical contexts. Makigami was aspiring to be a stage actor, and his entry into a musical career emerged as a by-product of this aspiration. He formed a band in 1978 called Hikashu to provide the soundtrack to an underground theatre performance called "Yochu No Kiki" (The Crisis of Larvae).[15] This led to an experimental, often improvisational band project that continues to the present day and is nothing short of legendary in Japanese avant-pop music circles. Hikashu's first appearance as a band, apart from the theatre production, occurred just over a month after the production "at Raoya, a free jazz joint in Kichijoji" Tokyo.[16]

His interest in improvisation was fostered by early experiences with improvised theatre. He describes one formative experience by explaining: "In 1974 at age 18, I went to London to participate in the Fringe Theater . . . It was a time when improvisation and theater were becoming intertwined. I appeared in a performance in which the entire dialog was gibberish. It was a big influence" (Makigami quoted in Grunebaum).[17] This carried into Hikashu; Makigami describes how "when [Hikashu] started out our gigs were half improvisation. Even further back, the band only played improvised material. After we signed to a major label, we ended up just doing songs, and we gradually accumulated a lot of them. We've been slowly getting closer to the original idea since then" (Makigami quoted in

Hadfield). The ensemble work in free jazz spaces led to Makigami performing as an improviser apart from the ensemble in solo performances and in combination with other improvisers in Tokyo and then globally. His connection to John Zorn, who he met in 1987 while in a chamber opera by Yuji Takahashi that Zorn was also a part of, eventually led to the recording of a solo vocal album, *Kuchinoha*, on Zorn's Tzadik label. This also connected Makigami to the New York free jazz scene that Moss was a part of. In 1990, he performed with Moss for the first time in New York.[18]

Like Makigami, Jauniaux worked early on in her career with avant-rock groups on the margins between popular music and free jazz. Aksak Maboul was a Belgian band Jauniaux sang with in the late 1970s. Like Hikashu, Aksak Maboul incorporated free jazz and fostered connections with free jazz communities. Their second album featured well-known English improvisers Chris Cutler and Fred Frith. Frith recorded with Aksak Maboul around the same time his label Rift was getting ready to release Phil Minton's *A Doughnut in Both Hands: Solo Singing*. Jauniaux recorded her first solo album, *Fluvial*, three years later (1983); it featured a number of other English free jazz players, like Lindsay Cooper, who had worked extensively with Minton and with Maggie Nicols. It also featured Tom Cora, who Jauniaux married and who released a duo record with Moss in 1983 on Frith's Rift label.

Moss first encountered Minton's singing via *A Doughnut in Both Hands*. He describes the encounter, explaining:

> Phil was a big, big influence; a very important person for me, and in some unspoken way almost a mentor for me. Fred Frith turned me on to Phil. We were all playing in New York in the abstract sound world and at the same time Fred had this new record label he started and I think he released one of Phil's records, I don't remember. One day I was at his apartment and he played me something I had never heard: it was Phil singing solo! …And I thought "Jesus Christ, this guy can do things I've just barely been scratching at and didn't know how deep and far you could go. I just knew there was something more, and Phil was actually doing it!" It was shocking. Almost too shocking. Not shocking intellectually, it was emotionally shocking because I thought I was by myself and now I found there was someone who was quite a bit ahead of me, or more vocally developed than I was in the improvisation scene.[19]

It was not that much longer until they performed together. One of Moss's regular collaborators in the trio Meltable Snaps It, saxophonist George Cartwright, describes an early performance of Minton with Meltable Snaps It, which took place at the New York City venue The Kitchen on January 23, 1982, as follows:

> Fred Frith asked us a favor. Would we would let his friend, Phil Minton, who was visiting from England perform with us? Of course, we all

did whatever Fred asked in those days even though we weren't familiar with Phil at the time, and didn't know how amazing a vocalist he was. Maybe David did. About half way through the second set they do a series of several duets that are quite something, personally I think rather historical.

(Cartwright)

It seems that Moss did, in fact, know Minton prior to this as he remembers a trio tour with Frith and Minton as their first encounter, one that took place shortly after Frith introduced him to Minton's solo recording:

> . . . a little bit later Fred said: "You know, Phil's coming. How about if we do a trio tour?" And I went: "Wow, okay." And this was 1980 something and we did our first gig in Boston, I think, and I had a drum set and Phil played trumpet still and Fred was playing guitar and I was totally learning what was possible listening to Phil. I was *really* influenced by him.[20]

Not only was Minton an inspiration for Moss, the transatlantic connection between the two singers would prove significant for the performative assertion of the transnational voice-only free jazz scene in the following decades.

Sussan Deyhim and Sainkho Namtchylak

Just prior to the Vocal Village project, Moss enlisted Minton for another project, an opera called *Survival Songs* that he composed with Bert Noglik. Like the other projects mentioned here, the opera staged transnational connections of free jazz vocalists. Minton was not the only first-generation free jazz vocalist involved in *Survival Songs*, Moss also recruited Jeanne Lee for the project.[21] Alongside Minton, Lee, and Moss were two other vocalists: Sussan Deyhim and Sainkho Namtchylak. Both entered free jazz vocal contexts after being trained in national fine and folk art contexts in their home countries, Iran and Tuva, respectively.[22] Deyhim studied folk music and dance in different regions of Iran while she was part of the Iranian national ballet company from 1971 to 1975. After moving to New York in 1980, she started to identify primarily as a musician and vocalist, drawing on her intensive study of regional folk music and performance methods she acquired during her time in Europe between 1975 and 1980, studying and performing with Maurice Béjart's Ballet of the Twentieth Century. She comments on her early years in New York, explaining: "I had been trained to do unusual vocals and I started doing choreography and composing music myself, using my voice as an instrument. Gradually I started getting very excited about music. My apartment was in the Village and I got into the downtown music and arts scene. I wanted to do something cool and an interesting hybrid relevant to our times" (Deyhim quoted in Iran Chamber Society). She sang for a period in the New York downtown free jazz scene, which overlapped with Moss's involvement there, and she worked in a number of projects and performances with both Moss and Hirsch.

Like Deyhim, the early stage of Namtchylak's performance career took place in the context of a state folkloric performance group. In the mid-1980s, before the fall of the Soviet Union, she was part of an ensemble called Sayani that toured the world performing what she called "a mixed pickle show: horse riders and drummers from the Caucasus, artists from Chukotka, from Krasnoyarsk ensemble of song and dance, from Piatnickiy's choir, Bashkir kurai players, and me" (Namtchylak quoted in Antufieva 2011). She explains that in the show she "sang Russian, and Northern, and Tuvan songs. A two-minute Tuvan song, Nanai song, a Saami song" (Ibid.). Prior to her time in this ensemble, she studied music extensively at the Kyzyl Art School, the Ippolitov-Ivanoc music school in Moscow, and the Gnessin State Music and Pedagogy School in Moscow. She described her training to *Musicworks* magazine in 1997, explaining she studied "the Western system, with tempered scale . . . I learned music theory first, and different instruments, as well as musicology. I studied the traditional music of all Russian minorities, and Russian folk music. I collected ethnographic recordings from different times and songs from different parts of the world. So it was more analytical than practical for me, because I was just starting to train my voice" (Namtchylak quoted in Dutton and Raine-Reusch 1997, 6). It was from these ethnographic recordings that she learned the harmonic singing techniques she sometimes employs in her work. She describes: "I learned by myself in Moscow. I had no teacher. I had to listen to old tapes and try to figure it out on my own, because there is no school for women to learn it; it's considered a man's art. In order not to destroy my normal voice I had to find a new technique" (Ibid., 5–6).

In 1988, Namtchylak moved to Moscow and began working in free jazz contexts. She credits an encounter with a recording by Vladimir Tarasov, "percussionist with the U.S.S.R.'s best known free jazz group, the Ganelin Trio," with inspiring her to quit the folk ensemble and move in the direction of free jazz (Corbett 1994, 161). Soon after Namtchylak began working as a free jazz vocalist, where she discovered that she was not the only singer working with the kinds of sounds she was exploring at that time. The experience was somewhat traumatic. She explains that while touring with her first free jazz group, a trio project, in 1988: "In one night I heard tapes by Diamanda Galas, Laurie Anderson, Cathy Berberian. I was shocked. I was sure that I was the first to do these things. I said, 'It's mine, I found it!' I stopped singing and lay in bed saying, 'Should I suicide?'" (Ibid., 162). Soon after this and after the dissolution of the Soviet Union in 1991, Namtchylak moved to Austria and quickly became known as one of the most celebrated vocalists in transnational free jazz.

Through Direct Sound, Vocal Village, and *Survival Songs* alone, we have encountered a broad array of the most active and accomplished free jazz vocalists on the soundsinging side of that spectrum. Each of these projects announces that the present is unlike the past; that an era in which a singer like Tamia could look for and fail to find others exploring free jazz soundsinging is a bygone era. All four of these projects also perform to audiences that free jazz voice is a practice that has taken hold in cities all over the globe and/or that free jazz is a space in which vocal practices from all over the globe can come into and are coming into contact and collaboration. These, of course, are two very different perceptions that may be afforded by the same performance. Which of these might manifest will depend on the prior knowledge and cultural assumptions of each individual listener as well as the ways they perceive and position both the sounds and the bodies of the performers. Despite the fact that Namtchylak learned khöömei from tapes in much the same manner a non-Tuvan singer might, despite the fact that her "mixed pickle" folkloric training involved learning a broad range of vocal styles from places she has never lived, and despite the fact that her free jazz style, like that of all free jazz soundsingers, emerges from an idiosyncratic hybrid sonic vocabulary inspired from a broad range of self-developed and borrowed approaches to vocal and non-vocal oral sound creation, she points out that: "People ask if I really sing traditionally and I have to say honestly, 'No' . . . Western audiences can't tell" (Namtchylak quoted in Dutton and Raine-Reusch 1997, 6). Listeners knowledgeable enough to recognise Namtchylak's free jazz performances are no more "traditional" than other free jazz vocalists who also developed personal sounds informed by mimetic encounters with recordings of various styles of global folk music are likely to recognise the performances she gave with Moss as transnational but not necessarily intercultural, given the fact each of the singers is emerging, most substantially, from the "tradition" and culture of free jazz. However, as Namtchylak points out, this type of recognition is frequently not how audiences receive her free jazz performances.

This is not to say that free jazz has not afforded a space for intercultural encounters between practitioners of varying vocal traditions. Moss's Institute for Living Voice (hereafter ILV) sought to create an intercultural space for vocal sharing and collaboration. The institute took the form of a travelling series of sixteen multiday sessions involving workshops, panel discussions, and concerts in different cities around the world from 2001 to 2012.[23] Rather than primarily performing the transnational connectedness of free jazz vocalists, the ILV positioned the free jazz vocal tradition as an important part of the broader shared global transcultural practice referred to by the term "singing."

The first edition of the ILV advertised its "intention . . . to break down the boundaries between entertainment, classics, experimental, artistic, traditional and world vocal techniques . . . From postmodern pop and electronic hip-hop to opera and belcanto, from the 20th-century 'extended voice' to traditional ethnic and folk songs, from cabaret and chanson to extreme vocal experiments, and much, much more."[24] Every one of the institute sessions consisted of workshops led by singers that emerged from distinct singing traditions (though, as discussed above, many emerged from multiple traditions). Though it was an impossible goal, the aspiration of the institute was to specialise in "workshops and concerts in all vocal genres."[25] The hope was that such an approach had "genre-erasing potential"[26] and participants could develop their voices in "an 'Exploratory' not a conservatory," thus "giving participants the chance to mix and measure the lively variety of contemporary vocal music for themselves."[27] As I've discussed, this kind of mixing of styles and traditions in the creation of an idiosyncratic vocabulary was already what the space of free jazz afforded many singers. While free jazz singing is a tradition in itself, it is a tradition that empowers singers to combine inspirations from various traditions and to enable a wide range of dynamic sonic sources to inform the ways one utilises their own body and voice.

Two vocal traditions clearly dominated the diverse offerings of the ILV: Western art music and free jazz singing. A number of the workshop leaders, including Moss himself, occupied middle spaces between these two traditions, having carved for themselves the kinds of mixed vocal practices and pedagogies the institute aimed to give students increased access to.[28] By weighting these two traditions roughly equally in the structure of the institute's offerings and by featuring vocal instructors who were already carving a space between these two traditions, Moss was suggesting that the vocal arts could benefit from these two traditions, in particular, being placed in conversation with one another and treated equally in terms of the potential value they could bring to individuals negotiating their own personal vocal practice. This was, like the transnational voice-only free jazz groups Moss put together, a bold means of claiming space for free jazz voice, of performing the established, transnational presence of the practice and the value it holds for the broader field of vocal arts.

Alongside the steady and roughly equal presence of Western art music and free jazz at the ILV, the ILV also invited practitioners of popular music vocal styles and a broad variety of global vocal styles, as well as a few experts from the field of theatre voice. A rough breakdown of these general categories as they appeared over the sixteen sessions of the Institute can be found in Figure 4.1.

The musical interculturalism that the ILV fostered happened largely through the experiences of ILV students who attended multiple workshops with instructors from distinct traditions. The ILV as a whole suggested to participants that transcultural encounter and improvisation exist as a method and principle for the shaping of vocal practice, one that stands as an alternative to devoting oneself to a singular vocal tradition. The exploratory concept was firm at the ILV. Moss insisted:

> If you wanted to come to the ILV as a participant, as a workshop member, the rule was you had to go to at least two workshops. So suppose you were a Meredith Monk freak and you only wanted to learn Meredith's techniques, you only wanted to be next to Meredith and you wrote "I want to be in Meredith Monk's workshop," we would write back and say: "That's very nice but what other workshop do you want?" "No we don't want another workshop I want to be with Meredith." We'd say: "Sorry you can't come here." That was the rule we had.[29]

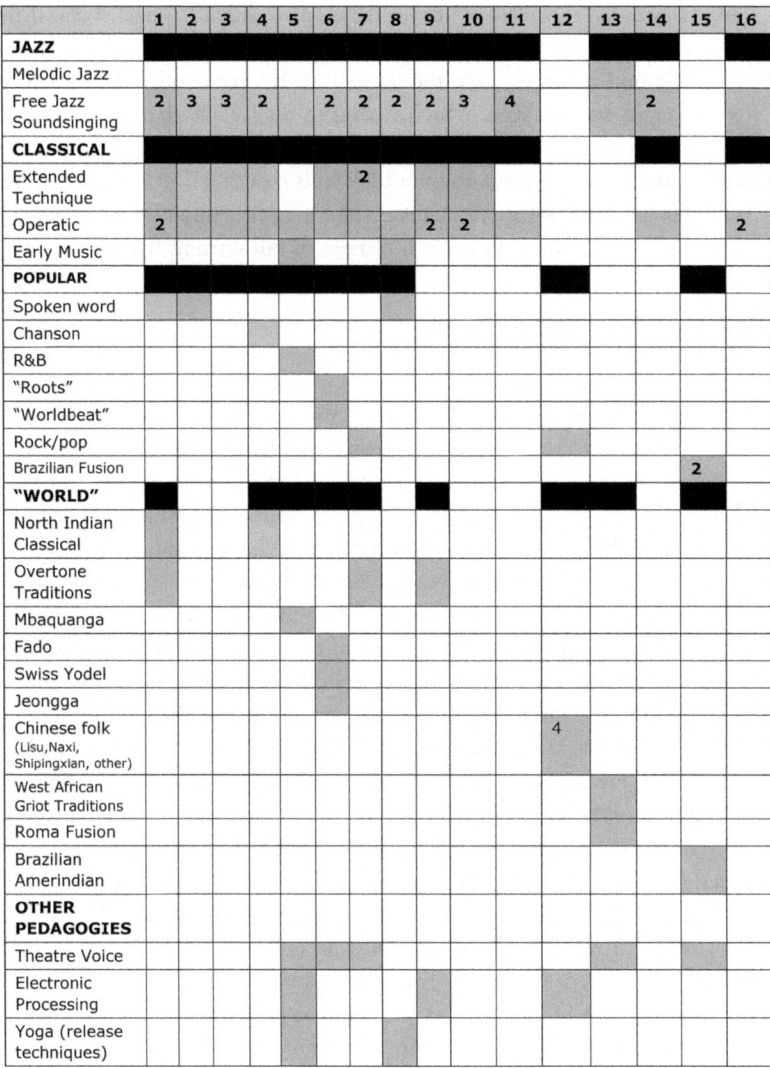

FIGURE 4.1   Overview-Institute for Living Voice Workshops 2001–2012, Sessions 1–16[30]

While interculturalism was the core principle of the ILV and free jazz does provide a musical space in which various traditions can sound together and try to find a musical middle ground, Moss acknowledges that even in that dedicatedly intercultural space the constraints of capitalism got in the way. He reflects:

> It took time . . . When a performer from another tradition came to us, say in Antwerp, and they only came for one night, if that happened, the

improvisational aspect could never develop . . . What happened was if they sang together with someone else they did their shit and someone else did their shit and it happened at the same time. If, on the other hand, some of them stayed for five days, which I tried to do—we'll give you a hotel for five days, we'll feed you for five days, why don't you stay with us for five days and we can sing together and try stuff together and see what, if anything, is possible? What we neglect is the idea that this stuff needs time . . . the time factor is unfortunately not there in our current lives.[31]

Conclusion: Next Generations

Most of the singers discussed in this chapter began their practices in the late 1970s or the 1980s and are part of the second generation of free jazz singers. The transnational projects they contributed to asserted that free jazz soundsinging was a widespread established musical practice, a musical option for singers seeking a path. Substantial third and fourth generations of free jazz singers have established practices amongst a rich array of mentors, often with intergenerational support.[32] The final set of interview excerpts ahead conveys some of the experiences of members of the third generation. However, there are, of course, so many more members of the third and fourth generations I have not had the chance to interview, including Sarah Albu, Fabrizia Barresi, Gelsey Bell, Loren Benedict, Claire Bergerault, Mossa Bildner, Theo Bleckmann, Julian Bonequi, Lynn Book, Audrey Chen, Arrington de Dionyso, Helga Davis, Isabelle Duthoit, Alessandra Eramo, Jodi Gilbert, Maki Hachiya, Carole Hemmard, Christiane Hommelsheim, Susanna Hood, Viviane Houle, Maja Jantar, Sofia Jernberg, Amirtha Kidambi, Kyoko Kitamura, Antoine Läng, Elizabeth Lima, Moo Löhken, Leïla Martial, Antoine Mermet, Elaine Mitchener, Cassondra Murray, Dylan Nyoukis, Wanda Obertova, Neal D. Retke, Carol Sawyer, Dorothea Schürch, Kazehito Seki, Amanda Stewart, Tanya Tagaq, Sophie Tassignon, Ijeoma Thomas, Liz Tonne, Josephine Truman, Ken Ueno, and Ami Yoshida, and many others I have yet to discover.

By tracing a few of Moss's projects, we begin to get a glimpse at the expansion of free jazz voice in the 1980s and 1990s. These projects, of course, represent only a small part of the relevant activity that could be examined. Many other free jazz singers developed similar collaborations in this era; festivals focused on the intersection of voice, experimental music, and/or improvisation were formed; and hundreds of singers carried on the everyday work that gives life to this practice. The next set of interview excerpts helps to fill out some further details of this era. The contributions of many other important figures from this generation—including: Beñat Achiary, Bonnie Barnett, Iva Bittova, Mari Boine, Stepanida Borissova, Uschi Brüning, Han Buhrs, Ellen Christi, Iqua Colson, Viv Corringham, Diamanda Galas, Iris Ederer, Géraldine Eguiluz, Sidsel Endresen, Yamantaka Eye, Zusaan Kali Fasteau, Annette Giesriegl, Sylvia Hallett, Ron Heglin, Charlotte Hug, Dalila Katir, Kathy Kennedy, Dagmar Krause, Joëlle Léandre, Cathy Fern Lewis, Bernard

Lubat, Vanessa Mackness, Janice Misurell-Mitchell, Lauren Newton, Mike Patton, Jean-François Pauvros, Maja Ratkje, Lisa Sokolov, W. Mark Sutherland, Tenko, Tina Pearson, Karolyn Van Putten, Jean-Michel Van Schouwburg, Saadet Türköz, Ute Wassermann, Linda Lee Welch, Pamela Z, and Christian Zehnder, as well as figures I was unable to cover in more detail from the first generation, including: Irene Aebi, Thomas Buckner, Jay Clayton, Urszula Dudziak, Floyd LeFlore, Christine Jones, Sheila Jordan, Karin Krog, Nobuo Kubota, Joan LaBarbara, Daniel Laloux, Meredith Monk, Charlie Morrow, Rita Omolokun, Ingrid Sertso, Tamia, Penelope Taylor, Ghédalia Tazartès, Julie Tippetts, Patty Waters, and Norma Winstone—will, I hope, be discussed in detail in many more future studies.

Notes

1. The other three singers were Karen Irving, and Ros Plotkin and Marg McDaid, two British singers of note both of whom worked with Nicols, Tony Wren, David Roberts, and Georgie Born in a project in 1980 called Voicings.
2. David Moss, interview with the author 6 and 7 July 2013. Moss's emphasis.
3. I discuss the expansion of the group to a sextet later in the chapter.
4. This description comes from Nurock's official website: kirknurock.com/bio. Accessed 10 September 2018.
5. Kirk Nurock quoted in a 27 May 1976 press release promoting the New York Museum of Modern Art's Summergarden concert series. The Natural Sound Workshop was featured on 4 and 5 June 1976 in the series. Available online at www.moma.org/momaorg/shared/pdfs/docs/press_archives/5395/releases/MOMA_1976_0055_44.pdf.
6. Anna Homler, interview with the author, 23 July 2013.
7. Ibid.
8. Ibid.
9. This characterisation was included on the packaging of the cassette, released in 1985.
10. David Moss, interview with the author, 6 and 7 July 2013.
11. The biography on her website refers to her as "geheel autodidactisch" (entirely autodidactical). See www.greejebijma.com/biografie. Accessed 28 December 2018.
12. See www.enjarecords.com/GREETJE_BIJMA.htm. Accessed 12 June 2013.
13. Jackson Mac Low's liner notes for Santos's 1981 solo voice album *Voice Tracks* explain that Santos was deeply influenced by the Catalan experimental poet Joan Brossa and that he worked in the 1960s with Albert Vidal Paz's theatre company.
14. David Moss, interview with the author, 6 and 7 July 2013.
15. See www.makigami.com/bio.html. See also hikashu-as.blogspot.com/2010/04/ for a detailed account of the production.
16. See hikashu-as.blogspot.com/2010/08/. The performance reportedly took place 29 August 1978.
17. Makigami's website, makigami.com, indicates the company was Lumiere & Son.
18. See makigami.com/bio.
19. David Moss, interview with the author, 6 and 7 July 2013.
20. Ibid.
21. Minton and Lee are discussed in Chapter 1.
22. Tuva has officially been part of the Soviet Union and then Russia since 1944 but was sovereign from 1921 to 1944.
23. It is possible Moss will revive the ILV in the future, however it was discontinued by the series producer Musiktheatre Transparant in 2012. A listing of host cities and guest instructors from 2001 to 2012 is available online at www.instituteforlivingvoice.be.

24. See www.instituteforlivingvoice.be/events.php?sess=1.
25. www.instituteforlivingvoice.be/articles.php?id=1. Accessed 22 September 2018.
26. Ibid.
27. See www.davidmossmusic.com/institute-for-living-voice.html. Accessed 22 September 2018.
28. By 2001 Moss had begun devoting much of his time to performing in operas and orchestral works. He also developed and performed several evening-length solo theatrical/musical performances like his *Einstein for Aliens*.
29. David Moss, interview with the author, 16 January 2019.
30. Moss notes "more than 75 world-renowned singers, performers, teachers, composers from 15 different countries 15 vocal 'genres' have been guests at the ILV" (See www.davidmossmusic.com/institute-for-living-voice.html). My rough slotting of workshops leaders into genre categories here employs 25 different traditions/emphases/genres and thus adopts a taxonomy distinct from his. My intention is to provide a loose proportional sense of the traditions represented, despite my understanding that the vocal practices of instructors in nearly every case span multiple genres.
31. Ibid.
32. Phil Minton, for instance, has worked extensively with younger singers like Audrey Chen and Dylan Nyoukis. As another example, Paul Dutton has performed with both Maja Jantar and myself.

In Their Own Words II

IN HIS OWN WORDS—DAVID MOSS[1]

CT: I thought it might be smart to start just by getting a sense of your preferred nomenclature for your vocal practice. Do you have a name for it? Do you call your vocalisation anything other than vocalisation?

DM: What to call what I do has been an issue for a long time. Now I simply say I sing, as a kind of a social-political statement, which is to say that what I do is as much singing as any other form of singing, using the apparatus and brain power to activate the voice. In certain circles, people refer to my work as extreme singing. The word "extreme," initially, years ago, was an interesting word for us. It indicated the extremes, the edges. Now it has been kind of subverted by pop culture to indicate danger and risk. You see all these extreme sports and other events that have the possibility of injury and bodily harm involved—and therefore I now shy away from this word extreme. I call myself a performer. I'm a performer who sings and manipulates time and rhythm with the voice. That's how I work.

CT: For the sake of the interview today, is there any preferred term that we could use to indicate a type of vocality that goes beyond standard speech or sequences of pitches? Is there a term that you like for this?

DM: I always used, for a long time in my own music, this simple word: texture ... Truthfully, people who work in my area or the area that I'm connected to are all so individual. There is no easy way to find a name that fits us all, aside from this old phrase improvisational singing—yes we use improvisation as one of our tools, but that's not the main focus of our work, that's one thing *inside* of our work. There is no easy word for this kind of singing. When I go into the opera world they all ask me what kind of singer am I. It's the first thing they ask me when I'm singing a new opera (I get a call from the opera house before I sign the contract), because in the contract in Europe they have to put what kind of singer I am: So, am I a bass, baritone, tenor? They have to. It's almost a rule. And I always say I'm none of those because I actually have made a stance against this categorisation of the voice. For me, it's very uninteresting. But then the opera-house says: "well, ok, *we* know you're not any one of those, but let's just put baritone in the contract."

CT: Why a stance against categorisation of the voice?

DM: There are two things to categorisation. Categorisation of the human voice is, first of all, dismissal of anything outside of the category. When you categorise something, you close it off from the outside world and you say: "aha, this is what it is, I understand it now." That's the first thing about categorisation. And the second thing about categorisation is once you categorise you have rules and hierarchies to obey and to live up to and people have expectations, their expectations are generated by these names. You can dash the expectations of people or you can fulfil their expectations or you can play a game with their expectations—oftentimes people think I'm a baritone and I come out and sing and they say: "that's no baritone, what the hell was that?" For me, part of my history has been to say: "Look, I'm doing personal music. I love this stuff. That's what I do. It's been my whole life. It uses this, this, this, this. I think about it a lot. I bring these things together and here it is. You need more than this? Why?" . . .

CT: When you did your first solo show that incorporated the voice in 1974 or 1975, at that point what other textural vocalists or unconventional vocalists or inspiring vocalists were you aware of? Were there other people working on that kind of vocalisation that you were conscious of?

DM: I was mostly conscious of people from pop music. I actually thought of James Brown, Sly Stone, and Aretha Franklin as "extended vocalists." Which, in fact, I still think they are. I was not aware, until a little bit later, of Joan LaBarbara, of Cathy Berberian. I had only very limited access to the contemporary music scene, I had to find it myself later on. Then, as fate would have it, I found an LP of Gyuto Tibetan monks chanting, playing gongs and horns. This deeply affected me, influenced me then, and does even today . . . I was extremely attracted to that kind of extended voice, not knowing anything about multiphonics, or overtone/undertone singing at the time, attracted to its intensity and the fact that it was a historical music, a historical sound that was not avant-garde but that sounded completely experimental, contemporary, timeless and most importantly, necessary! So, happily singing between the Tibetan monks and the pop world. I would drive to gigs in my Datsun pick-up truck, sometimes 800 miles in a day and I would sing along with James Brown, Aretha Franklin, Sly Stone, the monks . . . I would sing an octave higher or lower, working on the extremes of my voice, getting it bigger and wider and looser and more in control—not thinking of it as experimentation, just thinking of it as practice, or a kind of "body-building." "Experimental" singers I knew almost nothing about . . . It was a few years later that I heard the Demetrio Stratos records and Diamanda Galas. Actually, I shared a bill together a couple of times with Diamanda. In some way we're contemporaries. And Meredith Monk, there was an interesting first meeting with Meredith. Well, in 1974 Steve Paxton, Lisa Nelson, and I shared a farmhouse for six months, and I was invited by a professor at Goddard College to curate a concert performance there and so I asked Steve: "would you be interested in doing a concert together with Meredith Monk?," because I thought Meredith was an interesting mover and I could imagine the two of them on the same floor. Steve said "sure," so I called up Meredith and she said "sure." This was 1974 or 1975. So I got them both to go up to Goddard and it was a really weird, unexpected event because when I asked Meredith she was singing more than moving. She sang at a microphone, sang at the piano, sang acoustically at one crouched position, worked with a few gestures. So they gave this incredible performance in which, as I remember, Meredith was there squatting on the floor singing for 30 minutes and Steve was dancing around the whole giant barn, sometimes seemingly trying to get Meredith to dance with him. But she wasn't going to dance, she was just going to sing and I thought: "wow, this is a weird moment, they're not actually going to dance together or move together." And they didn't. So, Meredith was an influence. I heard of Meredith in the early 1970s. I thought it was magnetic. But I had my own approach/avoidance problems with Meredith then because she triggered something that I was having difficulties with at that time: storytelling. I was trying to develop an abstract vocal arsenal, a warehouse of sounds that were non-connotative enough to fit in with my percussion, that could do instrumental things and do sound things and not separate themselves so much from the percussion world. Meredith was telling stories, singing songs, and using narrative. Gorgeous, and I was attracted to it, but I didn't know what I could do with it. It was so different from my world, her tonal command, her sound range, her timbre qualities, her seduction of the audience was beautiful, but in a different way from mine . . .

In the mid to late 1970s, I heard players coming from new music and coming from jazz who were dissatisfied with the limitations of the genres. Around 1979, the experimental impulses began to spark out of jazz, from contemporary music and from what you would have to call alternative rock or punk or non-mainstream rock came singers who were unsatisfied, even frustrated, with what they could do, *or were allowed to do*, in their area and who were searching for another ground, another "sound space." And many of us met in the developing improvisation scene, which only happened after this particular improvisation scene I was part of as a drummer finally tacitly accepted the possibility that "the emotional, live human voice" could be part of it. It took a while. People like Phil Minton and Shelley Hirsch and me. Phil was a trumpet player first, so he had to break out of that world and people had to accept that from him. Jaap Blonk is another wonderful voice, who initially came out of a totally "other" scene that formed in the Netherlands and northern Europe. This "emotional live voice" finally became an acceptable and interesting spring of information for the improvised music world, and the theatre world, to incorporate. Several of us vocalisers who had jettisoned our genre affiliation quickly became very attractive to theatre people because we were new, energetic, and malleable material for them. We were usable, un-categorised stuff for their work. We were not formed and finished. We could be placed in a live situation and we would change and fit in and do something interesting and it would work. It wasn't as if we were a screw going into a hole, a director would find an entry point for us—and we were flexible enough to use it. By not being affiliated with one genre we could be seen as an actor or a singer or a performer, not just a jazz or classical or world-music singer playing a role or being a weird sound maker. We could be part of this very different work and world and that was a great change of direction for those of us who were able to "mentally" move there. And it all began to take shape not so much in the good old U.S.A., but in Europe—which is a later part of the story for me, and for many of us—that we could begin to be theatrical in our outward performance . . .

I've always been looking around for the people, the singers, the bodies, the personalities, the voices, that I can physically resonate with, or the ones that stretch and challenge me beyond all hope or reason. What's interesting to me about a live singer is: that person is making a *living* sound. What would it feel like for me to make that sound? I hear it. Can I get to it? How do I have to organise my body to get to that sound that that person is making or that kind of movement that that person is making? That is information that singers, all singers, give me. Of course, I can't sing like every singer, I can't sing high like some singers, or low or whatever, there are lots of things I can't do. But what I can do is try to touch on the way they go about their work. Breathing, placement of their muscles, of their vocal cords, projection of the sound, of their energy and focus and a glimpse into how their mind organises time, that's incredibly precious information for me that I get from people . . .

The reason I do certain things is, I think, that for a long time the music that I cared about and was developing starting in 1972 or 1973 was not central to many people. I had to make some choices: should I get angry, should I get bitter, should I get negative, should I get mad, should I get aggressive, should I get smarter? How do I deal with this fact that they laugh at it, call it noise, or animal sounds. And my answer to this was to contrast it with what existed, to present both things next to each other . . . The concept or framework of *contrast*—that was my ultimate material: contrasting the daily, normal, mainstream real world with the wider sonic realm I was developing. I wanted these things to rub up against one another, to create usable friction. Unless I brought them together my world would always be untouched, unseen, unfelt, or when rarely heard, almost always rejected. I had to find my own ways to do this—through special projects or unique groups . . . This is the way I've found to bring my work back into focus as a counter-weight to the mainstream, to what is considered important in our society.

Words/opinions of David Moss appear in this volume excerpted and condensed from a longer interview conducted by the author. More information on Moss can be found at www.davidmossmusic.com.

IN HER OWN WORDS—ANNA HOMLER[2]

CT: Let's start at the beginning. Can you tell me about the beginnings of your performance practice?

AH: My early performances were rituals then I started singing as the character *Breadwoman*. I imagined *Breadwoman* was so very ancient that her face had turned into bread. She lived in the centre of the earth and spoke in the root sounds of all languages. My background is in visual and performance art and I never thought of myself as a singer. The songs came to me in a very organic way and were so much a part of me that I didn't think of them as something I did; it was more like something I was. I started to do performance art at the end of 1981. I took classes at Otis [College of Art and Design] with Rachel Rosenthal. She was the person who taught performance in L.A. at that time. I loved performance art because you could use everything happening in your life, images, and dreams. It was a form big enough to contain all that. Because we don't usually have places to house the more mythic parts of ourselves, there's really nowhere for them to go. So, performance art seemed to me like a big container—it was like a permission slip to be all of myself, to live all of my aspects. At the time of one of my pieces, I was leaving the book-store where I worked. My job had been to arrange books on the gift tables. I would get so tired at work—my shift was 6 to 10 p.m., and all that I wanted to do was lie down and go to sleep, but I had to pyramid the books. So, one of my earliest performances was called "On the Egyptian Sleep of Unopened Books." This was before *Breadwoman*. I never spoke in my early performances, but rather, played a recording of my voice while I performed actions. I had asked everyone to bring objects to the performance to place on me.

In ancient times people would go to temples of healing. They were temples of incubation where you would go if you had a problem, or an illness. You were given something special to drink then the gods would visit you and answer your question in a dream. I was duplicating this sleep, by performing at Hunter's Books in Westwood. While a tape described my life in the book-store, I wrapped myself in a sheet like a mummy and went to sleep. The audi-ence then placed the objects they had brought on me. The background tape played included the sound of books being opened and my voice reciting page numbers and book titles. So, at that time, there was an element of English.

In the early 1990s, I went to Europe. David Moss and I had performed in Europe in Direct Sound[3] in 1989 and then I went back the next year on my own.

CT: *Direct Sound* is what brought you to Europe for the first time?

AH: Yes. At that time I was a new vocalist and wasn't known. I was coming from the art world, not from jazz or new music. I worked with objects and told stories. David was the first person I sang with. Meeting him when I did was a turning point.

CT: So he helped you identify as a singer somehow?

AH: Yes. I was just getting started and already I was on tour with these great sing-ers. I was onstage in the dark with a light on my head, making improvised high-pitched sounds. It took me to Europe the first time, then I went back to find my niche. I am entirely an improviser, but I improvise melodies, and melodies are anathema to many improvisers. On my albums, some of the tracks really are songs. I make choices, with noise and sound, but I always try to bring in the melody; it's like a lost continent that comes up and then goes down. I think you can only absorb so much excitement with the nervous system, so much noise. The ears and the nervous system have to rest, and a melody and silence let you do that.

CT: Has there ever been a time where your focus on melody prevented you from working with people?

AH: Oh yes! But, I've been really lucky in finding people to work with. I went back to Amsterdam the year after Direct Sound and went around with my *Bread-woman* cassette and got it into record stores. I eventually met radio people. One person with a radio show had seen me play with David at Apollohaus. This was the late Anton Vergiever. He connected me to an arts organisation where I ended up doing a *Pharmacia* exhibition, the Melkfabriek. Later, on another radio show, I met people from England who were putting on an evening in Amsterdam's Melkweg, but nobody came—we had no Dutch audience but we all watched each other perform. One of the acts was the Voices of Kwahn, which reminded me of performance art. We admired each other's work and arranged to meet in London and do some recording. I was trying to work outside the system. However, I didn't realise that you can't. You have to be part of some system. So what I did find was the Dutch underground, but the way I found it was by accident. From 1991 on I went to Europe every year, two or three times a year. It was through Butch Morris that I got back to Germany the third time to play at the cloister that A.R. Penck owned in Heimbach. The TTT organisation brought improvisers from New York so Penck could play drums with them. Penck had the resources to bring Jeanne Lee, J.A. Deane, and Paul Lovens, improvisers from New York and Europe. Penck's place was also a rest stop for people on tour. It was because I was in Germany that I met Frank [Schulte] and Axel [Otto] who had also played with David Moss. I played with them for years in a project called *Sugarconnection*.

CT: Let's step back a bit. You discovered your singing style in 1982. When did it first appear on a stage?

AH: In 1984. *Breadwoman* appeared in the Mask Festival, which was part of the Olympic Arts Festival at the time, in Los Angeles.

CT: And at that stage were you thinking of it as music, theatre, performance art?

AH: I thought of it as performance art. Then Jacki Apple introduced me to David. David had a radio project called *U.S. Ear*. Jacki sent him some of my early songs. Eventually, I saw him play music at LACE in L.A. I wanted to run up on the stage and sing with him. I was doing a Residency at Yellow Springs in Pennsylvania, so I met with David when I was on the East Coast. We spent an afternoon singing together. I didn't have the sonic vocabulary that David had, but I had characters, stories, and objects. What I was doing was related to the puppetry of objects. My performance practice then had elements of music and theater in it.

CT: Before meeting David Moss were there other singers that you were compelled by?

AH: Yes—Irene Pappas, female Fado singers from the '30s, Idjah Hadidjah, and women singers from Burundi. Also, there was Tsai Hsiao-Yüeh, she's a Nan-Kouan singer. This is vocal music from Western China, a bit obscure. This music, this woman's voice, and her life story moved me. There's something in the purity of her voice that I like. Lisa Fischer inspires me and I also love how Shelley Hirsch has so much fun when she performs.

CT: Do you ever imitate the technique from recordings? Do you learn from recording in that way?

AH: Not really, I would simply sing in my car and play with my voice. I studied the Roy Hart technique. That was life changing.

CT: How?

AH: I saw what was possible. My range expanded. I loved the exercises . . .

CT: The speechlike elements you use that you call your Bread Language, they're language-like without semantic content. Audiences must sometimes assume it's a semantic language they don't understand. Is that effect interesting to you?

AH: Yes. Because I'm dark complected, people sometimes think it's Spanish.

CT: We talked before about emotion and humour. Do you find more acceptance of that from women improvisers? I don't want to generalise, but do you find yourself working with more women because they're more open to these elements?

AH: Oh, no. It isn't about gender. It's about openness. When my album *Do Ya Sa Di Do* first came out, I was playing in a women's solo music festival in Switzerland. And I remember some of the other performers were really friendly before the concert, then afterwards, they wouldn't talk to me. I wasn't edgy enough. I want to nourish my cells with sounds. I used to want to sing lullabies or create sonic landscapes. Now I'm playing in projects that are conversations between improvisers. I prefer *quirky* to edgy.

Words/opinions of Anna Homler appear in this volume excerpted and condensed from a longer interview conducted by the author. More information on Homler can be found at www.annahomler.com.

IN HIS OWN WORDS—JAAP BLONK[4]

CT: I thought it might be nice to start by talking about very recent history and then go back and talk about the very beginnings of your practice. You performed last night with a variety of other improvisers in the *Snugs* concert series in New York City. What moments from last night's performance stood out to you?

JB: I remember, starting with the very last collective performance we did, we were supposed to, well, improvise with the whole group and at some point I noticed that the dancer wasn't participating so I went out to her and started sort of talking to her in gibberish and trying to get her involved as well, and it worked, so it was a nice moment . . .

CT: That moment with the dancer stood out with me as well. It seemed like there was a politics to the fact that at the end everyone was performing together and you noticed the one performer that wasn't participating and you made an effort to get them involved. I'd like to talk about the politics of your practice, but first I'd like to sort out what terminology I should use for your vocal practice. I often use Paul Dutton's term "soundsinging." Do you like that term?

JB: He's coined a few, I think, useful terms. His one CD is called *Mouth Pieces*; actually I was quite envious of that title.

CT: Ah, why is that?

JB: Quite a few sounds don't have to do with the voice in the sense that the vocal cords are not involved, just air pressure. But it does happen in the mouth, so that's a more general title.

CT: How about soundsinging as a term?

JB: Yeah, that to me is less useful because you could also just call it singing and someone like David Moss says, "everything I do is singing." We should widen the definition of music by telling that music is organised sound and singing is just anything produced by the voice, well not ordinary speech, but anything that is meant to be art or music.

CT: Okay, I'll use the term vocal improvisation then. So that moment last night— you weren't specifically inviting her to vocalise but there was politics of inclusivity at work. Could you talk a bit about that aspect of your practice? You seem to be willing and interested in performing with any other improviser. There seems to be a politics of inclusivity to what you do.

JB: Yeah that actually goes back a long way. I benefited greatly through the politics of inclusivity of other people when I started out as a vocal improviser in the early 1980s. I was in Amsterdam and there was a really open and vibrant community of improvisers then, involving many dancers as well, and many small improvised performances still stand out for me involving also some musicians who had recently come to stay in Holland from North America like Michael Vatcher, Tristan Honsinger, Michael Moore, and also dancers. So there were quite a few small venues where people would gather and improvise, and for me it was a very fruitful environment to develop my vocal vocabulary and flexibility. So it has always been for me, right from the beginning, very inclusive . . .

CT: Could you tell me about some of the vocal workshops that you've done, how you structure them, and how people have responded?

JB: I usually start with some simple games and improvisational things. Sometimes people are really shy and you have to sort of gently push them and get them to lose their shyness. Sometimes people are already advanced and very spontaneous and I try to introduce somewhat more structured improvisation because when the spontaneity and the intuitive improvisation is already there I try to go towards more formal stuff. But it's not so much about vocal technique in this area. There's no standard technique, like for instance bel canto, or specific jazz styles. People can do different things and it all depends on the motivation of people and what for them is fun to do. I try to give them ideas and open up new alleys and new vistas for them, rather than focusing on specific techniques. I give a few useful exercises usually.

CT: Is that something that you think attracts you to this as a performance medium? The fact that there is no sort of hierarchical way of learning it?

JB: Yeah for me actually that was very liberating when I discovered this area. Also for creating new pieces, you can set your own rules for every new piece and no sound is excluded. This I'm very happy about. And sounds that many people would consider ugly or even inappropriate can be used here.

CT: That's something I am thinking about a lot, why it is that many vocal sounds are considered ugly or inappropriate. You tell stories about having beer thrown at you while performing the *Ursonate*. I read another story in one of your interviews, where you performed the *Ursonate* in a formal concert hall and the audience reacted strongly.

JB: It was a formal concert hall in Amsterdam, the Concertgebouw, in the chamber music hall. It was actually a nice move of a program for them. They had this subscription series where you have four or five concerts through a season, so you get a reduced price and you go to all those concerts, and usually they have a theme. The theme was the sonata, in general. At every concert some chamber sonatas were played, or piano sonatas. So the *Ursonate* was sandwiched between a Bach sonata and another classical piece, I don't remember which. So people were the typical audience for a subscription series, like elderly well-to-do people, the bourgeois, more women than men. So the atmosphere was sort of formal, like a chamber music concert, and so they didn't dare to laugh: they started taking their handkerchieves and covering their mouths with them . . . More generally, these sounds are not to be considered art or music in any way. Yeah, I've encountered that prejudice or attitude a lot.

CT: Do you have a theory of why these sounds can be threatening? Why people make efforts to not include them?

JB: Partly because they're disquieting, or the idea that "well educated" people don't do that anymore. I remember doing a project about sound poetry and vocal improvisation in elementary schools in Holland and, so, well, after these lessons we had the kids talking to each other in gibberish and making a lot of fun with sounds, but then some mothers came to pick them up from the school, immigrants like Turkish and Moroccan people, and they said, "Our children are in this school to learn proper Dutch, not for this nonsense." . . .

CT: I wanted to ask you what the important performance spaces for you were in your early period, in Amsterdam or Utrecht.

JB: Well what was very important for me was the work with a group of students of Dutch literature at Utrecht University where we made programs of poetry and music. Not our own poetry but poetry by, usually, well-known Dutch poets. I was not reciting poetry. They thought I didn't do it very well, or I did it in a strange way, or I don't know. I was playing saxophone and composing all the music for those programs. We did quite a few performances, usually in student societies or at a theatre as part of university programs. This was very important for me to develop my music and also one important thing was that I could compose any kind of music that I was considering appropriate for that, so it didn't have to be in a certain style. Like, if you have a band you're supposed to play a certain type of music, otherwise you wouldn't get any gigs. But in this context I could use any kind of music. I started to experiment with other styles of music like atonal music, using random things, aleatoric music, more towards modern classical, and some jazz of course as well. And I also put some poems to music. There was a woman in the group who sang with them, and there was a pianist, we had a cello, and later on a violin also, so there were some instrumental possibilities. And, this was only when the personnel of that group had partly changed and moved to Amsterdam, then at some point we made this program of Dada and Surrealist poetry, and there were a few texts that none of the others found a way to do, so that was when I made a breakthrough as a vocal performer of poetry on stage and I did some Schwitters, not sound poetry but the "An Anna Blume" poem, for instance, and some Artaud, also not sound poetry but translations of French texts, which were pretty extreme texts. This was a seminal experience for me.

CT: And then, as you tell the story often in your interviews, there's this moment where you put on an Archie Shepp and Roswell Rudd record and sang along to it.[5]

JB: Yeah . . . It's true, that happened. Actually it happened when I got home in the afternoon after doing a vocal workshop with some actors from Poland who were students of Grotowski. So it was a very physical voice workshop I had been to, and then that happened after . . .

CT: And what were the next stages then if that was the kind of genesis moment for you as a kind of vocal improviser, adding vocal improvisation to the sound poetry practice that you had already established? What were the next steps? How did it creep further into your practice?

JB: As I mentioned before, I had many chances to improvise with instrumentalists and dancers in Amsterdam. So I noticed that instrumentalists of different kinds found it interesting and stimulating to improvise with me and dancers also, so I had many chances to develop it, and I began to incorporate it. I had a band at that time with two horns, I was playing saxophone, and this trumpeter I mentioned, with guitar and double bass and I started to incorporate vocal improv in that also, and a little later to write some vocal parts in the music, gradually.

CT: So you would incorporate it a bit into your band. Were there other ways, other spaces you'd explore this beyond your band?

JB: I didn't do really much solo improvisation yet. But I began, from the mid 1980s, to make little pieces of sound poetry. Some of them were partly or just improvised. Some had some texts which grew into a sort of sound poetry cycle called *Songs from Heaven* (*Liederen uit de Hemel*). And from about 1985 I started to do performances of that. I had at that time performed the Schwitters *Ursonate* in many places already and I got invitations to do performance of my own work, so I had opportunities to do that.

CT: And you started incorporating solo vocal improvisation into those?

JB: Yeah, mostly it was pieces, but some pieces were partly improvised. Some pieces were pretty harsh vocal sounds . . .

CT: Do you remember the first time you publicly did a free vocal improvisation?

JB: Yeah. The first time was with my band when there were no vocals yet in the band, and this was not very long after this breakthrough in my room with the free jazz record. At some point I was to announce the next piece we were going to play and instead of doing that I got into a vocal improv. Even my own band members were sort of worried. I remember the trumpet player coming to me and saying "Are you okay?" [*laughs*] . . .

CT: At the time of the Archie Shepp moment you've said that you weren't really aware of other people doing vocal improvisation. Could you tell me about discovering others? Who were the first and what were your reactions?

JB: I don't remember the first time I heard another vocal improviser. I do remember hearing The Four Horsemen in 1985 and I think they did this European tour. I had heard some other sound poets like Bernard Heidsieck in Amsterdam. I remember a poetry night in Amsterdam, I think it was even earlier, in 1981 or so, where they had John Cage not on stage but reading on the telephone from New York. He read some of *Empty Words*. But I think the first vocal improvisation I heard must have been David Moss. He came to Amsterdam rather frequently in those days. I didn't hear Phil Minton until much later . . .

CT: I've read in your interviews that part of your practice at some point was imitating the sounds in your environment of animals and machines and cities. How does imitation play a role in your performances?

JB: Not so much in the performances. Imitation has played a role in finding new sounds, mostly. And for me the use of imitation is to not to realise a perfect imitation, but to find new sounds to add to my vocabulary . . .

CT: When you happen into those sounds when you're improvising, are you reminded of those moments, those sources, or do they feel like your sounds?

JB: No not anymore. They're sort of a natural part of my vocabulary.

Words/opinions of Jaap Blonk appear in this volume excerpted and condensed from a longer interview conducted by the author. More information on Blonk can be found at www.jaapblonk.com.

IN HIS OWN WORDS—PAUL DUTTON[6]

PD: The biggest influence on me and my writing, the real soul-opener—I was going to say eye-opener, but it was really a soul-opening for me, and an art-opening: it opened up the whole field of poetry to me—was my association with bpNichol . . . When I met Nichol I had just entered psychotherapy. I had previously been psychiatrized . . . my psychotherapist saw that I didn't have a context, and I wanted to be a poet; and he was personal friends with bp and he asked me if he could show some of my poetry to bp. And he did. bp agreed to meet with me and he accepted a couple of poems for his magazine that he was publishing, *Ganglia*, and he talked with me about my work . . . He was a few months younger than me, but he was so much more developed, both as a person and as an artist . . . He was involved in visual and sound poetry, which I had no knowledge of whatsoever. I learned of it through him and that opened up all that territory for me and I tried my hand (and mouth) at those kinds of poetic expression . . .

CT: You've written about the first time that you saw a reading by bp and David UU . . .

PD: It was in a studio shared by [visual artist][7] Aiko Suzuki and [free-improv musician] Bill Smith . . . there was a poet named George Swede . . . operating a reading series there. It was called "Poetry and Things." I went to hear bp and David UU [he was David W. Harris then; the UU came later and was supposed to be pronounced "double u" but everyone who saw it read it and spoke it as "you-you"] give a reading there. And it was a room about thirty by forty feet. They both had microphones and a PA and they were both shouting and carrying on. It was overkill. There was no need for such amplification in that room. It was just riveting. It scared the shit out of me and thrilled me, excited me tremendously.

CT: I'm interested in that contrast, excited and frightened at the same time.

PD: This was very visceral, quite apart from the amplification. It was very, very visceral and emotional and some of the pieces had real anger in them. He wasn't up there throwing a temper tantrum, but it was a good healthy expression of outrage. There were all these intense emotions happening. Anger and also fun. So, it was liberating at the same time as it was frightening . . . I believe that somewhere in me I sensed that this was an area where I could apply both my literary and my musical talents. When Hugo Ball started doing his sound poetry in Zurich at the Cabaret Voltaire, in 1916 or 1917 or whatever year it was, he called what he was doing "Verse ohne Worte," poetry without words . . . a play on Mendelssohn's "Lieder ohne Worte," songs without words . . . Sound poetry, at least in its twentieth-century manifestation . . . when the Dadaists and the Futurists came up with it, there was a conscious application and a conscious recognition of it being a vehicle for the integration of both the literary and the musical impulses and I think somewhere bp and David's performance awakened me to the prospects of that . . .

CT: Did they do two-voice pieces?

PD: Yes, they did duos. Barrie [that's bp] at that time . . . I didn't realise it but—and this is why The Four Horsemen happened—he was tiring of solo sound poetry . . . So what was happening in this reading: some of it was chant-based, it was mostly verbal, it was rhythmic and it was intense and, as I said, it was loud and it was very visceral. It was intelligent without being intellectual. It wasn't like they were doing sophisticated vocal effects or sonic effects. They weren't making a point of inhaled sounds or multiphonics or any of those kinds of things. It was mostly rhythmically driven and phonetically and verbally based . . .

CT: And the year of the duo performance?

PD: Well, I think it would have been in 1969. I first met Barrie in '68. The Four Horsemen formed in 1970 . . . I started trying my hand, or mouth, at sound poetry, and I would take it to Barrie and I was getting encouragement from him . . . he started doing readings with Steve McCaffery as well . . . Rafael [Barreto-Rivera] was in the audience at one of their readings and . . . he was tremendously excited by what he heard Steve and bp doing and he knew bp well enough to send him a message and he suggested that he'd like to get together with bp and Steve and jam sometime. bp took that ball and ran with it, immediately got excited about the prospect of bringing me into it. I still remember getting the phone call at the publishing company where I was working as a copyeditor, a call one day from Barrie, very, very excited about the prospect of a four-man poetry group . . . He came up with the name

The Four Horsemen of the Apocalypse which we used for that first reading May 21st, 1970 at Poetry and Things on Yonge Street; after that, just The Four Horsemen . . .

CT: You had published "Jazz Musician," years prior, right? 1966?

PD: I had written it around then, '66, '67 . . . the way "Jazz Musician" happened was that I had read a lot of poems about jazz and what struck me was how unjazzlike they were. I wanted to write a poem that was informed by jazz: jazz rhythms, jazz sensibilities . . . I continued to listen to jazz and love it and grow in my knowledge of it, although I considered free jazz too much for me. But that changed with The Four Horsemen. Barrie adored Ornette Coleman, and the way The Four Horsemen worked, very much, was that we built up repertoire. After that first performance, we decided to get together and, as Barrie put it, woodshed. Another musical term. Borrowed very much from jazz, of course. So we woodshedded some repertoire and one of the techniques we used for building a piece was to do free-improv vocal work. And some of the early pieces you can hear on *Canadada* [or *Nada Canadada*, to give the LP its full and proper name] were very clearly structured improv . . .

In around 1977, 1978, I started working more with instrumentalists . . . I say instrumentalists as opposed to musicians because singers are musicians, although we don't get called that very often . . .

CT: I think it was 1982 you discovered the Extended Vocal Techniques Ensemble and 1984 was your first time hearing Phil Minton. Did you feel just as connected to the Extended Vocal Techniques Ensemble as you did to Phil's work?

PD: Nowhere near. The Ensemble was, well, technical; Phil, on the contrary, so impassioned . . . I've always been impressed by how uncompromising Phil is. He won't make any concession to it being anything other than just singing. When anybody asks him what he does he says he sings. I've come up with this term soundsinging. Of course, I come from sound poetry and that's why a lot of people still call me a sound poet. Fuck 'em. I hate it. It's like I never wrote a novel or something, not to mention all the other books that I've written, the collections of poetry that I've published . . . When I heard Phil in England in 1984, that was at the 14th International Sound Poetry Festival, which was produced by Bob Cobbing and Clive Fencott . . . At the end of the festival, Clive had arranged an evening . . . with some of the London Musicians Collective improvising musicians, and some sound poets from the festival . . . Phil was on this program. He just floored me. I had never seen anybody doing something so similar to what I was doing . . . I could tell that what Phil and I were doing was very close and also the way he held himself and contorted, wrenching the sounds out of himself. I felt a great affinity . . .

I thought of myself more and more as a musician as I moved more and more into free improvisation. As The Four Horsemen, as the group started to lose wind I continued my own solo sound compositions and also collaborations with any number of different instrumentalists . . . When the group performed [during its last five years or so] we were performing, really, as a free improvising vocal quartet. We would still use text, but none of it was planned. None of what we did was structured, preordained. It was totally free improvisation. We'd pull in text from our own individual writings at will, as it occurred to us, or we'd start spontaneously improvising verbal material on the spot. But that was it . . . Then in 1987, bp approached me and said, "You're the only one of the Horsemen that's really doing sound" [i.e., in individual practice], and he said that he wanted to keep his chops up, so he proposed to me that he approach CCMC, who had, I think, at that time, four members, and get their individual consent to have him and me sit in with them once or twice a month. He made the proposal and they all agreed to it. I was there faithfully every second week. His schedule didn't allow him to do that. So that was '87–'88, and then the CCMC season and the Music Gallery shut down for the summer and then Barrie did a very stupid thing in the fall of 1988: he died. So I continued on playing with the band and they eventually invited me to become a member of it. So I did.

When I wrote the essay "Beyond Doo Wop or How I Came to Realize That Hank Williams Is Avant-Garde" I talked to a lot of people who were in varying degrees undertaking these kinds of what I was then calling free-voice singing. They were using extreme utterance effects, not necessarily vocal—most of them were. And every one of them—man, woman, singers, instrumentalists, musicians, writers, every one of them—I'd ask about how they arrived at it and basically it was from just fucking around. So this takes us back to that whole question of training, which sounds so totally foreign to me in the context of this kind of creativity. It's not trained, no. Develop, discover, emerge. Don't train . . . I've known some singers who wouldn't go near [radical vocal effects] because it's going to wreck them for their bel canto singing. Well, there's Cathy Lewis [Canadian soprano Catherine Fern Lewis, performer and teacher]. She did Schafer stuff and various other things. That's her profession. She was all for doing sound improvisation. When I'd say, "Most singers like you don't want to touch it," she'd say, "They're just ignorant. It's not doing any harm to the voice" . . . I have come to consider training as violation.

CT: Where does that come from?

PD: It comes from being violated . . . Sonny Boy Williamson, the original Sonny Boy Williamson, John Lee, or whatever his name was, he had a cleft palate. He didn't let that stop him from singing and he didn't try to sing with perfect enunciation. He sang the way he sang and he was so fucking good that other singers imitated his cleft palate. True story. To me, art is working with what you've got and creating with what you've got. And it doesn't mean that you're lazy . . . you're working on developing your other skills that you *can* develop. And I think I've hit some new territory in some of the things that I do. And I know that I'm still constantly surprising myself with some of the sounds that come out of me. That's why I don't do electronics: because I still haven't exhausted the acoustic capacities of utterance . . .

Have you ever heard of horse whispering? I hadn't. I thought it was a contemporary phenomenon. It apparently actually goes back centuries. There was a guy on this talk program who was a horse whisperer. He didn't train horses. He worked with them to get them to cooperate. And he himself had been brought up by an abusive—he talked quite openly about this—he'd been beaten the shit out of by an abusive father. And he wasn't going to pass it on, unlike his older brother who decided that was the way it should be done and continued passing it on. But the horse whisperer, he was working with horses, getting them to cooperate . . . and it was a way of treating the horses kindly and working to get their cooperation instead of forcing them into doing what you wanted them to do. And to me, this is a model. One of the reasons why I'm convinced to this day that I cannot stand bel canto singing—this might sound funny to some people who've heard what I do—is because it sounds so fucking unnatural. Am I wrong in this, that it's all built around projecting the voice more, that all these techniques are in order to be heard over the orchestra? We don't need that anymore. We can use a more natural voice. We've got technology to handle that . . . But as far as I'm concerned, it's a violation. That kind of training is violation . . . Training is moulding somebody. There's a foregone conclusion. You're going to wind up doing *this* . . . I'm not utterly against it . . . It's fine if people have been violated and cooperate with it and manage to do stuff with it . . . All I'm trying to do in a workshop is lead stuff out of people. Lead them, let them find their own strengths and abilities and get them to open up their ears and lose their inhibitions a bit and start exploring the sounds that they can make . . .

CT: Is there a politics to unconventional vocal sound?

PD: Yeah. I think, again, implicitly, subtextually. And it's those same kinds of elements that I suggested earlier: lack of conformity, an anarchic element, a life lived on the basis of the intuitive, sensing your way rather than reasoning your way. If that can be considered political then I would say yeah, that's implicit in it. Making those kinds of sounds you are certainly expressing a willingness to go beyond the conventionally accepted.

Paul Dutton interview excerpts appear with the permission of Paul Dutton condensed from a longer interview conducted by the author. More information on Dutton can be found at www.pdutton.ca.

Notes

1. This interview was completed over two days on 6 and 7 July 2013 in St John's, Newfoundland. Moss subsequently reviewed and edited the transcript.
2. This interview was conducted in Los Angeles on 23 July 2013. Homler subsequently reviewed and edited the transcript.
3. Direct Sound was a vocal quintet organised by David Moss that included Moss, Homler, Greetje Bijma, Shelley Hirsch, and Carles Santos. For more on this group see Chapter 4.
4. This interview took place 8 November 2013 in New York City. Blonk subsequently reviewed and edited the transcript.
5. See Chapter 3 for another description of this breakthrough moment.
6. This interview took place 11 and 12 August 2014 in Toronto. Dutton subsequently reviewed and edited the transcript.
7. Square-bracketed comments, with the exception of italicised comments, in this excerpt are clarifications added to the transcript by Dutton.

5

POLICING THE NON-HUMAN VOICE

Liberation movements can quickly turn into their opposite.
—*Maggie Nicols quoted in McKay 2005, 255*

In this chapter, I depart from broad histories and focus instead on two fleeting moments in the reception history of free jazz singing. By telescoping in on these, I examine how some free jazz singing has affected certain listeners, and caused socio-political effects in particular contexts. The particular effects I discuss represent only a fraction of what free jazz singing has afforded. However, I feel they are significant enough to become the focus of this chapter. They help us understand important lessons not just about free jazz singing, but about the social functions of vocal sound more generally.

In the introduction I discussed Paul Dutton's term soundsinging, its use as a genre term describing employment of less conventional vocal and non-vocal oral sounds, and its potential as a theoretical term describing musical uses of the human voice that listeners categorise as non-Singing or as non-Human human sound (more on these capitalisations below). This chapter extends this discussion. Free jazz soundsingers commonly experience attempts by others to contain and correct the sounds they sing. Sit down with a soundsinger and most will have more than one story to tell about a time an audience member or fellow performer made efforts to discourage them from exploring less conventional forms of singing. The two instances of reception I will discuss fall into this category—they were both corrective responses to instances of soundsinging. I will use language borrowed from the philosopher Jacques Rancière and focus on ways soundsinging is "policed." I will insist that the very fact certain human vocal sounds are contained and corrected, "policed" by various forces in our everyday lives, is one particularly important factor motivating soundsingers to dedicate themselves to giving voice to those sounds.

The first moment I will discuss has something to teach us also about the value of practice-based research, as it emerged as a result of my own performance practices. It is the incident that first made me curious about why certain listeners go beyond merely ignoring vocal sounds that may not appeal to them and actively act to discourage singers from making them. The details of this incident motivated the theoretical framework that this chapter offers. This particular occurrence was a listener's response to a duo performance I gave with Dutton in Toronto in 2004. I will describe this response and how it suggests vocal sound is an important material component feeding into processes that Humanise certain bodies at the expense of others. The second moment emerges from Yoko Ono's reception history. I will suggest we can productively understand both the correction I experienced in the personal incident and containment or correction Ono has endured as defence of a social category I will refer to, with a capital H, as the category of the Human. This capitalisation of Human will distinguish a category of the "human" that is strictly material, rather than ideological, and includes *all human bodies*, from an ideological category, signified by the capital H, that posits that *some human bodies* are more fully-Human than others. Such a category reinforces a hierarchy that denies full-Humanness to subsets of the materially human population. I will argue that while there is a level on which the specifics of each case need to be attended to—the meanings Yoko Ono's sounds, body, and persona affords are distinct in many ways from those of Dutton and me—on another level it is productive to recognise the common elements of these deHumanising efforts, as this can teach us both about the tactics of deHumanisation and the role vocal sound plays in both undergirding such tactics and undermining them.

The processes through which sounds afford and are articulated with meaning are always contextual; the work sounds do in one context won't be the same in another. Soundsingers, by definition, have made audible categories of vocal sound that aren't sounded often and that are often disparaged as ugly, as noise, and as "non-musical" or "not singing." In certain contexts these negative valuations do not emerge, nor do listeners imply these human sounds are non-Human. In this chapter, I focus on contexts in which, I believe, these negative valuations manifested. In such contexts we can witness soundsinging doing important work—disrupting symbolic structures that undergird deHumanisation. However, these contexts and these disruptions do not fully define what free jazz voice is or has done or what it will or can do in the future. They can only show us what certain sounds have done in certain past contexts, and, only possibly, what they may have the future potential to do.

Indeed, the dimensions of the incident I will describe convinced me that what the sounds Dutton and I were making were doing, in that specific context, in the mind of at least one specific listener, was threatening the listener's access to a self-perception as a fully-Human individual amidst other not-fully-Human humans.

However, I have come to realise that this perception aligns with the discourse in fields like disability studies, ethnic studies, and gender and sexuality studies, that deal with how social hierarchies are created via perceptions of bodily materiality. I follow scholars like Alexander Weheliye who observe "a set of sociopolitical processes that discipline humanity into full humans, not-quite-humans, and nonhumans" (2014, 4). In addition to employing this discourse, I follow the lead of cultural theorist Lindon Barrett in also identifying the term "modernity" with these processes of self-privileging. "Modernity" invokes a range of diverse and often contradictory meanings. However, my usage refers to Barrett's sense that the concept of modernity is tied to the ubiquitous, systemic, and pervasive nature of Humanising and deHumanising processes. By linking the content of this chapter to the concept of modernity I point to how the micropolitics of the encounters I describe are part of a broader systemic cultural logic that we need to resist and reject to diminish suffering and inequity.

I believe that the microscoping of this chapter synthesises themes hinted at in this book's other chapters to bring us closer to understanding what motivates soundsingers to embrace less conventional vocal sounds. If soundsingers witnessed their sounds disrupting a self-privileging and deHumanising symbolic order, it follows that that potential would become part of their reason for working with those sounds. However, the incidents I discuss will also help us understand other motivating factors, including the physical pleasures of vocal exploration and the symbolic pleasures of placing one's body and self into the intersubjective or subjectivity-muting flux of freeform vocal improvisation. Within the chapter, these sounds are theorised not merely in relation to performers but also listeners. I will discuss how in the act of policing, listeners sometimes avail themselves of soundsinging's pleasures, becoming soundsingers while discouraging others from soundsinging. One of the questions that occurs to some listeners when they first encounter free jazz soundsinging is: why would anyone want to make these sounds?[1] This chapter will suggest that both the pleasures of vocalising and the social-political potential of sounding the sounds of soundsinging answer that question.

Furthermore, I seek to underscore the importance of diverse and inclusive approaches to human vocality. I attempt to show that when we construct and validate spaces that display only "perfect voices" while correcting and containing voices possessing other abilities and qualities, we, on some level, contribute to symbolic structures grounded in exclusion and deHumanisation. This argument, I contend, is not purely my own. Rather, it is an argument implicit in certain manifestations of free jazz soundsinging; it is an imperative that has kept many free jazz soundsingers engaged in their practice when other forms of reward were negligible or discouragement ensued. Listeners who struggle to place soundsinging within the field of musical and artistic values most familiar to them may think differently once they gain exposure to the ways these sounds challenge processes of Humanisation and deHumanisation. Hopefully, this chapter makes this audible, conveying what soundsingers already know to be the potential socio-political force of these sounds, in certain contexts.

Example One: Policing the Voice at the Gladstone Hotel

The Gladstone Hotel is the oldest continuously operating hotel in Toronto. Built in 1889, it served for decades as an upscale establishment catering to wealthy business people and tourists (Graham and Roemer 2007). Gradually, it became a flophouse, home to daily and weekly renters. In 2000, ownership changed and a process of gentrification began. The new owners devised a business plan that initially, seemingly, sought profit without removing the long-time flophouse residents (Ibid.). They arranged for the downstairs "Melody Bar" and a new "Art Bar" space they developed to frequently feature art events which would attract business. By 2005, this plan fell apart. Flophouse residents were removed and a full renovation was undertaken (Ibid.). Room prices skyrocketed, and the gentrification that had begun five years prior fully materialised.

In 2004—while the space was still shared between residents, artists, hotel customers, audiences, and regulars of the Melody Bar—on a Sunday afternoon Dutton and I performed improvised soundsinging duets for an audience of both listeners that had come for the *Glad TOES* series our performance was a part of and patrons who abided the music but were there to socialise and drink.[2] After our performance, the microphones were still live and one member of the latter group decided to take the stage and respond to our performance. He proceeded to perform four short improvised pieces. He introduced himself and then vocalised a buzzing sound into the microphone while tracing an arced path through the air with one finger in imitation of a fly. The path eventually led to his cheek, and, when it did, he slapped himself loudly in the cheek, then thanked the audience and took a bow. Following this, he dedicated the next song to his dog and proceeded to play the roles of mutt and master, calling "here boy" and then barking in response. He alternated between these roles several times and then took his second bow. For his third piece, he mimed the action and imitated the sound of drinking from a cup and followed by imitating violent vomiting. He took another bow and then announced that for his last piece he'd be "performing a song that is always a hit . . . silence."

Unlike Dutton and I, this guerrilla performer provided an imitative visual supplement to the vocal sounds he produced, to help the audience imaginatively insert the image of an animal or context alongside the vocal sound he was producing: during the fly piece his finger was the fly; during the dog piece, he bent over and called to his dog as if he could see him in the room; during the "purge piece," he made efforts to look inebriated and queasy before he acted out his purge. His performance felt to me like a form of symbolic policing. It felt as if he was reinstating a sonic-visual order Dutton and I had disturbed by using our voices in ways that did not map "properly" to the sight of our bodies. He intervened and, in my estimation, policed what visual bodies were appropriate signifiers for the kinds of sounds we were making.

Rancière writes, "[p]olicing is not so much the 'disciplining' of bodies as a rule governing their appearing, a configuration of *occupations* and the properties of the spaces where these occupations are distributed" (1999, 29). In effect, this guerrilla performer was reminding us of certain unspoken rules of where the sounds we made should and should not appear. He may have been justified in reminding us that these sounds should not have appeared at the Gladstone; in retrospect, it is clear that the artists that appeared there between 2000 and 2005 certainly aided the gentrification processes transforming the space. However, he did not seem to imply merely that our sounds shouldn't have appeared at the Gladstone—his performance suggested that our sounds should not have emerged from our bodies; it pointed to the fact that these were the sounds of flies, dogs, and humans who have lost control of their bodies. He may have been acting, on one level, consciously or unconsciously, in response to our role in the gentrification of the space, but on another level, his reaction clearly dealt with the content of our performance and not merely its location.

The theatrical images he used invoked two of the core symbolic binaries that fuel structures of privilege: the Human/animal binary and the able/impaired binary. Though I will later consider other interpretations, one possible reading of his response to our performance was that he was restoring a divide between Human and animal and between bodies considered able and others perceived as lacking certain abilities (here the ability to control one's stomach). Concurrently, he was articulating the animal and insect with the not-in-control human by placing them in proximity as the proper sources of the sounds Dutton and I were employing. Donna Haraway, in her *The Companion Species Manifesto*, makes reference to "the pure of heart who long for better protected species boundaries and sterilization of category deviants" (2003, 4). In my interpretation of the guerrilla performer's actions, I feel justified in identifying him with this figure described by Haraway. And, by doing this, I am identifying the space of soundsinging as one where these boundaries and categories are sometimes challenged.

Understanding what is at stake in these spaces is made easier when we consider the extent to which the idea of "the modern" helps us make sense of the world. Modernity can be understood as a structure of beliefs founded on the notion not just that the present is different than (and a progression from) the past but on the paradoxical notion that the past is manifest in the present. Or, in other words, that we can identify some things in the present as modern and others as not-modern or primitive—as belonging to the past.

Lindon Barrett's work helps us understand these processes, linking modernity to histories of suffering, identifying it as a mechanism of deHumanisation. Barrett argues the epistemic disjuncture of modernity first emerged with the rise of mercantilism and its dependence on enslaved labour and global colonisation. For

Barrett, "the partitioning and reorganisation of the hemisphere of the Americas constitutes the fundamental, ongoing event of Western modernity," an event that "begins earnestly in the sixteenth century and remains the extended geopolitical episode that . . . revises the materiality of the body and the relations of the body to the discursive mechanisms by which it is socially apprehended and managed in the modern exclusive paradigms of personhood" (2014, 1). Crucial here are "ongoing" and "exclusive paradigms of personhood." When we view modernity as a cultural logic that emerged from a need to justify slavery we link economic imperatives with processes of deHumanisation. When we view modernity as a logic that helps justify overlooking deHumanisation, we begin to understand how certain nations could be founded on notions of universal freedom while propagating slavery or other forms of systematic deHumanisation. The imperative to see oneself and one's nation as modern, which spread globally from the sixteenth century onward to the present, betrays the vast scale of this disjuncture. Further, if we can acknowledge that modernity acts as an ongoing force behind continual social reorganisation, one that cannot function except through exclusion of certain humans from full personhood, we make visible an invisible mechanism always within our reach, offering us a sense of self based on a notion of our own superiority, our own connection to "the greater good," absolving us of responsibility for suffering due to our contribution to the progress of that "greater good," our role as "more modern, " as "more fully-Human."

The logic of modernity is, naturally, fundamentally ideological and flawed to its core. The notion that people can exist at the same moment in time yet some can belong to the present and others to the past is a self-privileging myth. However, it is a myth we all experience to some degree as truth because of the system of interrelated binaries that exist alongside and support the primitive/modern binary. These binaries come to shape one another through their co-presence; when we invoke these binaries, we appeal to other categorical distinctions we have made to make sense of and shape the terms we invoke. As a result, the Human/animal binary problematically comes to be shaped by the past/present and primitive/modern binary, and we justify our systematic privileging of Human over animal life through convincing ourselves animals are primitive and primitive life is less valuable. The *ongoing* history of slavery contains ample horrific evidence that this hierarchy of Human and animal is utilised to aid the dividing of Human from human; the Human/animal binary comes to shape conceptions of racial divides, fuelling the deHumanising practice of slavery and its legacy of tolerance of both deHumanisation and the suffering of the Other. Disability studies theorists have demonstrated how this system of binaries fuels the deHumanisation of those perceived as or who identify as disabled, and we see the same system invoked by listeners in their responses to soundsinging.[3]

My reading of the guerrilla performer's actions implies that they reveal that soundsinging disturbed this system of binaries, and he acted to repair it in light of this disturbance, to put the sounds of soundsinging back in the bodies in which he felt they belong (even as he put the sounds more tangibly, and possibly pleasurably, into his own sounding body). This reveals that the voice can play a clear role in the maintenance of these binaries. It also reveals that sounds can play some small role in their dismantling. Dutton and I, by embracing sounds this listener felt to be not fully Human or nonHuman, unsettled him to the degree he felt the need to counter our articulation of our human bodies—white male bodies the listener may have experienced as his categorical equivalent—with these sounds. It is this argument I will expand in the rest of this chapter. However, before pursuing this further, I want to consider the possibility I'm wrong.

Policing or Participating?

The guerrilla performance felt *to me* like policing. It felt *to me* like the performer was invoking a rule governing the appearance of my sounds, a rule that dictates that my sounds were not in fact mine. It felt *to me* that his performance was his way of saying what so many others have said to free jazz soundsingers in more direct ways, that we should self-police and abandon the parts of our voices they feel aren't proper for the categories to which we belong. However, I can't read his mind. Any theorisations here about his intentions are guesses, albeit informed by patterns I have witnessed over nearly two decades as a vocalist. I can speak authoritatively about the effects of his actions on me but not about his intentions. So what are the implications if I'm wrong? What if his performance came from a conscious or semi-conscious impulse to encourage rather than discourage us? What if the imperative to take the stage uninvited was, on some level, in favour of soundsinging?

I believe both readings are necessary to fully understand these encounters. One simple likelihood at the heart of this incident is that the performer made sounds he likely didn't often make in public. The theatrical and referential framing he improvised, to some extent, functioned to divorce his body and identity sym-bolically from those sounds, but they emerged from his body nevertheless. After witnessing two soundsingers perform, he took an opportunity to use his voice in public in ways that he is likely prevented from in most other social settings he occupies. Theorising his embrace of this opportunity is as important as theorising the effects he had or may have attempted to have on others in the room.

Freya Jarman-Ivens's work on what she refers to as "queer voices" underscores the importance of understanding this embrace. Her use of "queer" in her book *Queer Voices: Technologies, Vocalities, and the Musical Flaw* is, like in many other queer theory texts, entangled with histories of homosexuality but cannot be understood solely in relation to those histories. Instead, "queer" refers to a more general pro-cess of "upsetting, making strange, unsettling" (2011, 15).[4] For her, "the voice is always potentially queer" (Ibid., 162). It exists "in between bodies and at the bor-ders of the body and language . . . it is genderless, and it is performative" (Ibid., 18). The in-betweenness of the voice causes it to frequently invoke intersubjective and intercorporeal fluidity: we hear the voice of another and we often semi-consciously try on that voice, we imagine what our bodies and identities would be like if the body producing that voice was ours. We can see intersubjectivity is a factor in our reception of voices by simply observing how often we impersonate the voices of others and recognising the ways our embodiment is altered in the course of these impersonations. The power of the voice to launch us into these imaginations is substantial, and the experience can be sudden, unwanted, and feel like a violation of our body. For Jarman-Ivens, the queering power of the voice lies in its potential to lead us into moments where intersubjective experience blurs our sense of self and other and, sometimes, illustrates to us the constructed and arbitrary nature of our identity by showing us other ways we could think, act, and feel.

Jarman-Ivens discusses identification, pointing to "the role of the voice—as the active carrier of both language and music in song—in drawing the listener in to identification, or . . . push[ing] the listener away and clos[ing] down the possibility of identification" (Ibid., 26). However, what I find most fascinating and instructive in her work is her acknowledgement that this is not a simple dichotomy. The guerrilla vocalist seemed to be performing his counter-identification with soundsinging, illustrating that this is not the way Humans with control over their bodies should comport themselves in public. Yet at the same time, he was embracing the opportunity to feel what it is like to configure his body with sounds similar to the ones Dutton and I were making; as such, to some extent he was extending the imagined intersubjective experience many of us have when listening silently to the vocal performances of others into an actual public performance that embraced soundsinging while also performing a rejection of it. To focus merely on the rejection and not also the embrace would be reductive.

If I am correct, the guerrilla performer was trying to police our voices. Equally, it follows that he was also trying to police his own partial identification or intersubjective entwinement with our voices and the symbolic chaos he perceived such an identification to entail. Jarman-Ivens writes that "vocal identification . . . serves both to assert the subject's being and to threaten it simultaneously, negotiating precisely the precariousness of subjectivity" (Ibid., 28). It is possible our guerrilla performer was attracted momentarily to the kind of fluidity our embodiment allows us, a kind of fluidity that does not have to restrict the voice to the kinds of utterances deemed coherent with the constructed categories of body we are placed into. Plausibly, he momentarily identified with a state that is non-identificatory, that doesn't conform to a reductive sense of who or what we are, a state arguably more "natural" than the kinds of identification our liberal humanist culture demands we adopt, which restricts us to identifying with bodies in the culturally constructed categories we are placed in rather than with all worldly dynamisms. We could call this an *assertion of his non-identificatory being*, a being with the potential for constant fluidity and identification across all categories rather than containment as a liberal humanist subject that is unified, coherent, and categorically the same over time. We may also theorise this fluid moment as giving simultaneous experience of a threat to the unified identity he, like all of us, has always been cultivating. His performance can be understood both as a prolongation of the feelings of fluidity and a return towards his unified identity through reinstatement of the symbolic order through which the categorical distinctions that afford that Human identity become felt as real.

This is naturally conjecture. I only know what I felt and can't claim authoritatively he was "a listening subject brought into a moment of crisis" by the queering power of the voice.[5] However, my experiences as a soundsinger have convinced me that Jarman-Ivens is right to posit both the commonality and complexity of such moments. It is not likely, in my estimation, the case that the guerrilla performer was simply counter-identifying with soundsinging through his performance. He was both having a policing effect and participating in the very thing he appeared to be policing. Yet the reinstatement of the symbolic order was, seemingly, the most immediate surface-level message and function of his performance, a more easily noticeable meaning than prolongation of identificatory fluidity. Despite the complexity that may have been present, it seems plausible the dominant message of his performance was that our human vocal sounds do not belong in the category of the Human.

Example Two: Policing Yoko Ono

To illustrate the coherence that may exist between various attempts to police soundsinging, I shift now to response to the world's best-known soundsinger. With the significant exception of human, many social categories in which Ono's body can be located differ from those of Dutton, myself, and the guerrilla performer. Comparing the reception of any two soundsinging performances or body of performances requires sensitivity to the ways the racial imagination, gender, class, ability, age, and other factors figure into how the body is received. Differences between the reception of mediatised and live performances must also be taken into account. Undoubtedly, the threat Ono has posed in many instances has been that of a woman claiming space in a male-dominated sphere, an Asian claiming space in "white" and "black" musical traditions, a practitioner of high art claiming the relevance of practices from that tradition outside of its institutions, and a celebrity asserting herself through the power of the media into the lives of others without the access she enjoys. When proceeding into consideration of reception of her work, all of these intertwined transgressions must be considered. Equally, however, comparing Ono's reception history to the Gladstone incident reveals significant similarities that once again point us to modernity and the problem of the Human.

My goal is not to give an overview of the complicated history of reception of Ono's soundsinging. Rather I focus on one particular but rather typical moment. On October 29, 2014, radio talk show host Howard Stern broadcast a segment reacting to Ono's June 29, 2014, appearance at the Glastonbury Festival. The segment expressed incredulity over her incorporation of what Stern referred to as "screaming" and "moaning" (Stern 2014). He suggested what she was doing was "weird," that "she might be mentally ill," and that this was strange "behaviour" for an 81-year-old (Ibid.). He also insisted the performance lacked "musicality" (Ibid.). Like the Gladstone intervention, Stern alternated between expressing that he didn't understand why she would make these sounds and vocalising similar sounds himself. In fact, in a period of less than twelve minutes he experimented with the kinds of sounds he heard in Ono's Glastonbury appearance at least seven separate times. He also alternated between expressing that the sounds she used are difficult to produce—saying after trying out one technique "and by the way, that's not easy to do"—and suggesting that anyone could make this music—stating, "We should make a Yoko cover band . . . everyone just do their thing" and then suggesting to his co-host Robin Quivers, "you could play in this band," to which she responded: "Absolutely, I don't have any musical talent whatsoever and I can play" (Ibid.).

Essential to an author-centred understanding of Ono's output in and beyond her soundsinging is the recognition that she has long been highly interested in work that breaks down the division of labour that makes art the exclusive domain of specialists. Many of her performance works, visual works, and concept pieces are simple to realise, both in terms of economic cost and the skills required to produce them. Many of her works invite active participation and encourage audiences to understand they too can break down the barrier between art and life. Stern's reaction, his realisation that he too can participate in this musical practice, reveals quite clearly that this is also one of the concrete effects of Ono's soundsinging and, perhaps, of soundsinging in general, despite the virtuosity often involved in the practice. Though Stern did not acknowledge this inclusive impulse as part of her intention or a meaningful effect of her work, he, like the guerrilla performer, became transformed quickly into someone who feels invited to create this kind of work. Despite his mockery of her practice, he must reasonably have enjoyed making the sounds—why else would he have engaged in his own soundsinging *seven* times in twelve minutes?

As previously mentioned, it is important to acknowledge how pleasurable it can be to explore unexplored avenues of one's voice. The pleasure can be purely physical or can be ideological pleasure derived from breaking free of arbitrary proscriptions or hegemonic value systems. Both this pleasure and the message of inclusion so much of soundsinging is interested in forwarding (see Chapter 6 for more on this) are palpable when those compelled to police soundsinging engage in soundsinging as a means of policing. However, as in Stern's reaction, it is common that neither that pleasure nor those inclusive politics are enough to make these listeners feel they understand and accept the practice. We can lament the fact that the fun Stern has making unconventional sounds doesn't legitimise the practice for him, just as we can lament that so many people who encounter Ono's work fail to perceive the ability of the work to invite the participation of others as itself an important artistic achievement (dare we say as socially beneficial as the display of special talent?). Ono's sounds at once require a virtuosity to achieve and suggest to listeners that they too can participate in this practice, that this virtuosity is present but is not a requirement for participation. Stern's comments and the fact the guerrilla performer felt invited to take the stage uninvited both stand as evidence that the listener often perceives that free jazz soundsingers are operating in a musical space that lacks strong aesthetic criteria regarding correctness.[6] The sounds and contexts they appear in each play a role in generating an invitation to participate. Jarman-Ivens may be right when she insists listening to voices often involves intersubjective imagination. However, we should also acknowledge that, like the guerrilla performer and like many who encounter soundsinging, Stern followed this temporary fluidity with a withdrawal back into ideological normativity and identity hierarchy. Listeners like Stern and the guerrilla performer seem, after allowing themselves some license to explore vocally, to remind themselves of the prohibitions for exceeding vocal norms, and they return to the policing and self-policing behaviours those ideologies generate.

Stern and the guerrilla performer are also similar in their invocation of several of modernity's binaries while restoring their symbolic order. Like the guerrilla performer, Stern invoked human bodies that lack self-control, saying, "I think she's mentally ill or something." Moments later he invoked a second out-of-control body, the body involuntarily vocalising during sexual encounter. In the same breath he also invoked the Human/animal binary in a manner similar to the guerrilla performer, remarking, "this sounds like Benji being fingered." The suggestion of this comment is both that Ono's sounds are proper to the category of animal, not Human, and that the sounds belong to the category of bodies that have lost self-control.

The suggestion that Ono's sounds are sexual was not mirrored by the guerrilla performer, suggesting distinct gendered and sexual-identity related components at play here. These are not as simple as Stern-as-publicly-heterosexual sexualising Ono's female voice. The full statement Stern made was "this sounds like Benji being fingered by Perez Hilton"; Stern's invocation of a gay male celebrity and his repugnant association of homosexuality and bestiality reflect the ways straight/gay or normal/queer binaries are also viciously invoked in Stern's reception of Ono's persona, her sounds, or both (Ibid.).

In both incidents, the human sounds of soundsinging were positioned as non-Human. One can recognise the clear presence of racism, misogyny, and homophobia factoring heavily into much of the kinds of discourse listeners inject into the public sphere in reaction to Ono's soundsinging performances. Though a close reading separating misogynist attempts to contain Ono's challenges to male privilege from racist attempts to contain her Japaneseness, Asianness, or "foreignness," from attempts to contain her use of unconventional vocal sound would be a significant contribution to our understanding of Ono's complex history, this difficult disentanglement is, unfortunately, both beyond the means of the present study and, arguably, not entirely possible. However, related to this, it is productive to remind ourselves that while we do need to understand the specificity of distinct manifestations of the racial imagination and of particular sexisms, homophobias, ageisms, and ableisms, it is also productive to consider the ways in which racism, sexism, ableism, and policing of unconventional vocality are all part of the same broader imperative to counteract threats to a symbolic logic that creates intertwined binaries and hierarchies that co-create one another. Barrett invokes this broader imperative by labelling it modernity; Weheliye reminds us it only manifests through fleshy specifics. Modernity's symbolic order attempts to give license to the positing of divides that deHumanise subcategories of the human in service of other subcategories. When we identify this broader superstructure as the source of all of these self-privileging impulses we may be seeing the forest rather than the trees, but this may be a valuable heuristic—provided that Weheliye's caveat is also remembered—as it can help us recognise that to invoke and naturalise any one of modernity's interconnected divides is to strengthen the entire apparatus of deHumanisation. Stern's invocation of a rational/irrational binary in connection to Ono's performance is not disconnected from his invocation of a Musical/unmusical binary, and neither is it disconnected from the Modern/primitive, Civilised/uncivilised, Able/disabled, and Human/animal divides we have discussed, nor to the Male/female binary, the Singing/non-singing binary, and Unmarked/marked notions of the core of any racial imaginary.[7] Treating any one of these imaginary binaries as real strengthens modernity's entire system. As such, the impulse to police unconventional vocalisation represents one form of a broader imperative to reinstate a symbolic superstructure after moments in which the validity of any one of its binaries have been demonstrated to be false. By blurring the borders of self and Other and creating the intersubjective confusion Jarman-Ivens calls queer, and by disrupting the sonic-visual articulations of modernity's symbolic order, soundsinging performances can demonstrate the fragility and falseness of that order. If this is correct, and this threat is manifested in the imaginations of certain listeners of soundsinging, it might also explain the lengths listeners go to to contain, correct, and silence soundsingers.

Conclusion: Things Become Their Opposites

When we theorise deHumanisation as a singular imperative to grant only certain human bodies and voices the status of fully Human, we must also consider the distinct consequences of deHumanisation for different bodies. Though the slight of an audience member repeating the widespread proscription against human bodies making sounds some categorise as non-Human is mild compared to the extreme abuse Yoko Ono has endured, and even that abuse cannot compare to most of the physical forms of injury, abuse, and death wrought by the logic of modernity upon bodies today and throughout history, it is my hope that it is not an insult to speak of these all in one breath. My goal is not to reduce the specificity of any particular instantiation of deHumanising logic. Rather, my goal is to remind us of the far reach of this logic and ask us to listen for the ways this logic extends into domains like singing, as seemingly innocuous as those domains often seem. My goal is to pay tribute to the devotion of free jazz soundsingers to a practice that is often misunderstood and devalued by a significant portion of the listening public, a practice whose small contribution to resisting the logic of deHumanisation is evidenced by the existence of the forms of policing I describe here. The fact that listeners act to correct and contain soundsinging is evidence that soundsinging has at times disrupted the logic that sustains it as a category in the philosophical sense I introduce in this book, however minor or temporary that disruption proves to be.

This chapter's epigraph is an observation Maggie Nicols made after her decades of political activism in organisations like the Workers Revolutionary Party. This observation is, for her, a justification of why an improvisational attitude is always necessary in all domains of life; if things become their opposites when contexts change, a constant re-evaluation is what is required for continual progress. Similarly, sounds that are policed also have the potential to turn into the sounds on whose behalf a form of policing unfolds. Essentially, the lesson offered in this chapter is not that certain vocal sounds or vocal practices are innately subversive towards deHumanisation. The lesson is that vocal sounds get caught up in symbolic processes that are dynamic and unstable, processes in which the symbolic functions of sounds and bodies are constantly being negotiated. While the encounters I have detailed here seem reflective of patterns that repeat in many of the contexts in which "extra-normal" vocal sounds appear, Nicols reminds us that we "need to maintain our improvisatory approach" as we attempt to determine how certain vocal sounds are functioning (quoted in McKay 2002). Disruptive potential is not imminent in the sounds themselves but is an effect of the co-presence of the particular sounds and bodies that encounter one another in particular contexts of reception. However, free jazz soundsingers largely seem consciously or semi-consciously aware that the methods and sounds they have gravitated towards have the potential to do this kind of work. In the following chapter, I will discuss other experiential and socio-political benefits free jazz singers associate with their soundings and with the methodologies of the solitary and collaborative dimensions of their practices.

Notes

1. See www.youtube.com/watch?v=TwjUcyoRkW4 for one manifestation of this impulse. At present, the sole comment beneath this document of a duet between myself and Laurel MacDonald is "porque hacen esos sonidos?" (Why do they make those sounds?). While the question might be sincere, it might also imply there is no good reason.

2. Alan Glicksman was the organiser of the *Glad TOES* series. *TOES* stood for Toronto Original Experimental Sessions. The "O" in TOES stood, at first, for the venue, the Oasis restaurant. The "Glad" in "Glad TOES" indicated that the Gladstone became the new venue for the series.
3. For an examination that draws more substantially on disability studies and invokes other anecdotes from soundsingers about audiences "policing" their work, see Tonelli 2016.
4. Of course, Jarman-Ivens acknowledges that "[t]his is not, however, to say that there is no link between queer and sexuality . . . we can understand queer as a system (albeit a peculiarly unsystematic one) of interrogating structures of sexuality as one expression of power and identity relations" (2011, 16).
5. Jarman-Ivens 2011, 28.
6. I do not mean to imply that these rules never arise in contexts of soundsinging. They do. I discuss this in Tonelli 2017. However, the emphasis here should be on "strong." While some spaces of soundsinging manifest these types of "rules," others foster a radical openness, an implicit or sometimes explicit acknowledgement that any sound is acceptable (also discussed in Tonelli 2017 and in Chapter 6). Relative to many other musical traditions, assertions of correctness and incorrectness seem to be more sporadic and less pervasive.
7. For more on the Singing/non-singing binary, see Tonelli 2017.

6

RADICAL INCLUSIVITY AND THE PARTICIPATORY POLITICS OF IMPROVISING CHOIRS

"Professionals don't have a monopoly on doing exciting stuff."
—*Maggie Nicols, interview with the author, 25 June 2014*

We can hear the echo of a gaping social divide when Maggie Nicols recounts a period in her career when male musicians began to validate her in ways that counteracted a lack of self-worth she had developed through previous interactions in the London jazz scene. She describes how she "went from feeling like this low-status, no-status nuisance scrubber to then starting to get gigs as a jazz singer and then people going: you're different from other singers, you're not like other chick singers."[1] She had longed for this validation. But, as this quote implies, it was validation that came at the expense of an Other—the "chick singers" that had to be marked as lesser to prop her up.

For Nicols, this validation arrived at the right time. While she began to receive this recognition, she was engaged in a quid pro quo arrangement with Peter Oliver, the warden in charge of the Oval House Theatre in South London. A band Nicols was part of at the time needed rehearsal space and approached Oliver about using the Oval House.[2] Oliver agreed on the condition that the musicians offer workshops in return. As a result, Nicols found herself, for the first time, in charge of ushering rooms full of people into vocal and instrumental improvisation, and this, she feels, inoculated her against the seduction of the special status being offered to her in the jazz scene. She recalls:

> I'd gone from no status to feeling like I was special because I wasn't like these other chick singers, buying into that because it felt so good to be accepted after feeling like nothing, to suddenly being in a room full of

people where I've got these things going and was thinking "wow, everybody sounds so amazing," to just realising how magical all these voices together were. So that just saved me from really, maybe, getting into that competitive thing. I could've. I was heading in that direction, from feeling so insecure to suddenly being accepted and lauded.[3]

Her appreciation for the sounds that emerge when a mix of professional and non-professional singers improvise together led her away from a vocal practice dedicated exclusively to specialised vocalists sounding above the silenced crowd. The "everybody" that sounded "so amazing" included experienced vocalists and amateurs, trained and untrained voices. The magic that emerged came from the surprising sound events that occur when these voices explore together. This was, as Nicols refers to it, a "mixed-ability" environment.

Though not every free jazz singer has devoted themselves to creating inclusive spaces for vocal improvisation, a substantial number have devoted a sizable portion of their practice to doing this. Inclusivity in free jazz choral practices is not merely the openness these groups often have to anyone that wishes to participate but also openness to any kind of vocal sound these participants choose to employ in these choirs. In the previous chapter, I discussed the ethico-aesthetic motivations of some free jazz singers, the desire some have to embrace human vocal sound others categorise as non-Human and chastise soundsingers for making. Through improvising choirs, that desire can be sated to an even greater degree given that more voices come to violate those proscriptions. In this chapter, I will consider how these choirs have not only reconfigured the public voicescape along these lines but also how they counteract prevailing ideas of whose voices deserve to be made publicly audible. I will argue that these kinds of improvising choirs, while often still retaining a degree of hierarchy, frequently work against the positioning of music as a space where exceptionality is acquired, conferred, desired, and necessary. The ethical rewards of contributing to these inclusive practices exist alongside the aesthetic or "musical" rewards of these ensembles. While some leaders of improvising choirs describe them as ensembles where aesthetic ideals are sacrificed for the sake of ethics, some describe them as forms of music making that yield uniquely valuable aesthetic rewards. Nicols insists that "professionals don't have a monopoly on doing exciting stuff,"[4] and in mixed-ability settings she's "experienced some of the most beautiful music of [her] life" (Nicols quoted in Cowley 2008, 16).

Though traditional aesthetic theory might imagine aesthetic quality as a universal characteristic detached from ethics, recent thinking has argued ethics and aesthetics are highly intertwined. Following the latter impulse, it is difficult to separate the aesthetic pleasure improvising choirs offer from the distinct ethical affordances that listeners feel are at work in a given context. As this chapter proceeds, I trace some of the histories and methods of improvising choirs and examine the ways participants have benefitted from the access these choirs offer to community, intercultural and intersubjective experiences, and public presentation of one's voice. As in the previous chapter where I argued that exposure to or awareness of specific contexts of performance and reception was necessary for understanding certain meanings and potential functions of the sounds of free jazz soundsinging, in this chapter too I will argue that an understanding of what improvising choirs have afforded in particular contexts can yield an understanding of the value and potential of the practice that may not be immediately available from isolated experiences of the practice.

The Rise of Free Jazz Choir

Following her initial workshops in 1969, Nicols sustained a lifelong dedication to creating spaces for inclusive, mixed-ability improvisation. She often uses her non-hierarchical, leaderless notion of "gatherings" in place of the concept of the workshop. From a series of regular sessions she led in collaboration with the Jazz Centre Society and John Stevens in the early 1970s to workshops she led in roughly the same period in "a mental hospital in Friern Barne," (Hyder 1973) to Contradictions, an interdisciplinary improvisation environment and ensemble for women which she began hosting in the early 1980s to "The Gathering," an inclusive space for improvisation she began hosting regularly in London in 1991 and continues to host in Carmarthenshire, Wales, Nicols has devoted a massive portion of her time and energy to the creation of inclusive spaces for improvisation. Some of these have been voice only, but many have been open to any form of musical or non-musical participation. Important to this chapter is the fact that the voice-only workshops she led at the Oval House may represent the beginning of a free jazz choral movement that has since touched the lives of many.

In Chapter 1 I outlined aspects of the long working relationship Nicols has had with Phil Minton. The vocal quartet, Voice, that Minton formed with Nicols, Julie Tippetts, and Brian Eley in 1975 stands as one of the most important projects in the history I am tracing here, as it represents an early development in multi-voice a cappella free jazz, though this work did blend free improvisation and pre-composed structures. Chapter 4 traced how this small, voice-only ensemble format became common for the second generation of free jazz singers. Of course, this type of ensemble is, in some sense, the free jazz variation of a small ensemble vocal format that exists in many varieties of art, folk, and popular music, from Renaissance SATB quartets to barbershop ensembles to doo-wop groups. However, Voice was also an early professionalisation of the free jazz vocal ensemble work Nicols was doing in her workshops, one that, unlike those workshop groups, left behind a recorded document; while, unfortunately, little documentation of Nicols's workshop groups and their performances exists, Voice, despite being a relatively short-lived project, recorded a live album on October 13, 1976, and released it in 1977 on Ogun records.

Interestingly, another Voice recording was made in 1977 with a slightly different line-up, singing with Ken Hyder's Celtic jazz project Talisker on their album *Land of Stone*. The line-up change is notable with Frankie Armstrong appearing in place of Julie Tippetts. Armstrong has since gone on to found an organisation called the Natural Voice Network that espouses many of the same ideologies that circulate in free jazz choral communities and that Nicols herself espouses—ideologies like "singing is everybody's birthright" or the importance of creating spaces "where everyone's voice is accepted without judgement."[5] The role or type of improvisation, however, seems to be one difference between what occurs in most Natural Voice Network workshops and performances and what occurs in the improvising choirs I am focused on here. Despite the presence of some improvisation-based methods, Natural Voice Network practices seem to often focus on the performance of pre-composed songs and, as such, may not offer an equivalent amount of space for inclusion of any and all vocal *sounds*, even if they do indeed create "a community where singing together is . . . open and accessible to all."[6]

Curiously, Voice, Nicols's work, and the entire history of British free jazz/improvisation makes no appearance in ethnomusicologist Caroline Bithell's book-length study of the Natural Voice movement, *A Different Voice, A Different Song*, despite the presence of a substantial section on Armstrong's history and despite the fact Armstrong worked not only with Voice, but was, for a period, part of the Feminist Improvising Group with Nicols and a regular contributor to performances that included other members of the British free jazz community. These absences might be explained by the fact Armstrong's own recent promotional materials also omit these activities from her biography.[7] These segments of Armstrong's work do not factor into how she is currently choosing to represent her past work, so Bithell may have opted to convey Armstrong's past in the manner of her consultant's preference. Jazz vocal traditions are only fleetingly mentioned in Bithell's study, and the choral practices I will discuss here are not represented in her chapter on "The World of Community Choirs." The great divide between dominant notions of what constitutes "proper" singing and an imperative within Natural Voice Network practices to challenge those norms is palpable in Bithell's book and the NVN's own promotional material, but, unlike the current study, French Ultralettrism, New York Fluxus, Toronto sound poetry communities, Cathy Berberian, or Western free jazz vocalists are not invoked as voices that have challenged these norms. When discussing "other voices less often heard" Bithell mentions "keening voices, chanting voices, clamouring voices, ululating voices; the voices of Mediterranean fishwives, Swiss cowherds, West African praise singers, Argentinian shamans, Bahrainian pearl divers, Taiwanese farmers, Korean *p'ansori* opera singers, Tibetan monks" (Bithell 2014, 46). These are positioned as the voices that do not "all sound "musical" or "nice" to the modern Western ear and as the "other voices" that "often seem to draw inspiration from the natural world" (Ibid.). Though Bithell does allude to the Roy Hart School and Alfred Wolfsohn being "among the first people in the West to recognise the profound value of 'unacceptable' human sound" (Kalo, Whiteside, and Midderigh quoted in Bithell 2014, 58), no aspects of the free jazz voice tradition that Armstrong clearly brushed up against in her career are mentioned, creating a problematic impression that the Natural Voice Network is relatively solitary in its bucking of the dominant Western vocal norms and sustaining an unfortunate erasure of a seemingly important connection between Armstrong's philosophy and the core beliefs of improvisers she formerly worked with.

Clearly, the imperative toward inclusivity present in the Natural Voice philosophy deserves to be placed in conversation and comparison with the related mandate as it manifests in the history of improvised music in the UK and the history of improvising choir communities that grew out of it. After all, regardless of which might have come first or may have influenced the other, both emerged from the same political context. Armstrong, Nicols, and Minton were not just performing in some of the same musical spaces; these spaces were often also activist political spaces. For example, Armstrong collaborated with members of Henry Cow and Mike Westbrook's Brass Band, including Minton, in a performance at the Moving Left Revue on March 13, 1977, a Communist Party benefit concert held at London's Chalk Farm Roundhouse.[8]

The communitarian ideals of the political movements Nicols, Minton, and Armstrong were active supporters of in the 1970s align with their devotion to musical practices that prize community above virtuosity and inclusion over exclusivity. Certain core ideals expressed in the Natural Voice movement seem well stated by a passage from a 1972 article on Nicols's Oval House workshops that reads: "Maggie feels very strongly that everyone has the latent ability to create, which needs only a little encouragement and channelling to bring it out into the open. She practices what she preaches at the workshop, coaching all kinds of people in her vocal lessons" (Williams 1972). This passage was followed by a quote from Nicols that reads: "I get people who've never sang before, and who reckon that they can't sing at all. But eventually they find they can do really marvellous things. They just need to be given the chance. If everybody realised that, it could be beautiful, rather than having select performers, performing for people who think they're not capable of anything creative" (Ibid.).

Though, again, recordings of Nicols's early choral improvisation performances do not seem to have been made or have survived, she has shared memories of them that convey both the inclusive spirit they fostered and the deeply spontaneous nature of their working methods. Describing a performance at one of the festivals she organised at the Oval House, she recalls:

> Harry [Vince], my ex-husband, it was Harry's idea to run a jazz festival at the Oval House. This would be 1970 or 1971. We had Derek Bailey. We had everything from mainstream jazz to free improvisation. This was one of the most exciting experiences of my life: Derek was taking a while to set up. There were problems with amps and Harry was getting anxious and he said to me:

"Do something, do something." I gathered the current workshop group and we went onstage . . . we did one of the pieces I used to do a lot, which was wait in silence for ages and not have imitative responses, in other words if a car went by you'd avoid going "vroooom," to wait until we had an emotional or musical feeling, until the sound affected us to respond to them, rather than just imitating. Well, there we were, just sitting, getting into a deep trance and somebody came in late and stumbled over the rostra. We all jumped out of our skin and we all [*she gasps ingressively*] and the audience all started joining in. The whole room did a vocal improvisation and Derek came up and he said: "Keep going." And, he started playing with us and we slowly, slowly just dissolved and Derek did a solo. And the audience got Derek. I don't think they would have got what he was doing if they hadn't participated in what we did. And it was so obvious it was because that person stumbling was so clumsy, bless them, I think the audience saw that our reaction was so genuine because there we were in a deep trance waiting for little sounds and some-body went "clang, clang, clang" and we went [*she vocalises in a manner that rhythmically parallels "clang, clang, clang"*]. It was amazing. So that was [impor-tant] for me and then we started doing more. And Peter would ask us to do [things]. So, right from the off I did performances with the workshop group. We did it at the Oval House first, because that was our room.[9]

While Nicols's workshop ensemble performances clearly set a precedent that informed the work she did with Voice and the later free jazz choir movement as a whole, she does not appear to have ever sustained and given name to a large vocal group in the manner she did with Voice. This is likely, in part, because the inclusive mixed-ability communities she formed, like Contradictions and The Gathering, were too radically open and interdisciplinary to be focused only on the voice or imagined as a stable ensemble. However, this type of "narrowing" proved valuable when Minton began devoting himself to free jazz choral work in the mid-1990s. His concept of The Feral Choir helped substantially in sparking a broader free jazz choir movement.

Minton's Feral Choirs have emerged from temporary workshops he has been leading since 1994. He identifies the beginning of this work with an invitation he received to lead a group of singers at the Muiskcentrum in Sweden. This led to subsequent invitations and a realisation that this was an important way he could contribute to the well-being of others. His description of how this took shape speaks to the power dynamics of improvisational choral practices; it displays that they are not entirely about the conductor (when they are conducted) shaping the ensemble to reflect their artistic vision or, of course, the vision of a composer, but instead involve the conductor accepting and adapting to the vocal contributions of the choristers:

I was invited first in a music college in Sweden, to do [an improvising choir]. It was with trained singers, mostly. And, I wasn't really that happy with it in the early days. But, then I got invited to do some in housing projects in France . . . The actual choral results weren't that impressive; the actual sound of the singers, it wasn't exactly what I wanted, how I was hearing it in my head. But, afterwards the people were so enthusiastic and loved it so much. They said: "Oh, we had such a great time. It was the first time we'd ever been onstage and sung and used our voices." And, it really literally brought me to tears and I thought I really want to do this more in lots and lots of different situations. Now, the aesthetic idea of trying to get a group of singers to sound like some preconceived idea I had in my head, that's gone.

(Minton quoted in Tonelli 2015)

Minton developed his own idiosyncratic gestural vocabulary for conducting his Feral Choirs, but, as is the case with most vocabularies used to conduct improvisation, within the parameters of each conducted instruction he gives there is substantial room for improvisation. Conduction is the most common term for these gestural instructions, and "parameter" here refers to the fact that each gesture indicates a zone to improvise within, like a "sing a pitch" sign that allows each singer to choose their own pitch or a "whistle" sign that asks for whistling but does not determine how the singers will choose to whistle. The Feral Choirs tend towards dense voicescapes in which individual choristers follow their own improvisational ideas or work with what Minton refers to as the "seeds" he plants, singing variations on the vocal ideas he sings as he leads the choir (Minton quoted in Howard). Minton, as he conducts, tends to sing, and there tend to be long sections where he stops conducting and the choir explores a particular undulating collective texture with energies building and dissipating on their own, as individual members vary their contributions to the voicescape. At other times Minton conducts sudden or gradual shifts in texture, volume, or pitch range; he prompts rhythmic patterns to begin or cease; or he feeds the choir or sections of the choir with new seeds that they approximate with their voices or that prompt them in new improvisational directions.

The term "Feral Choir" comes from a reappropriation of a description of Minton's singing as feral. Chapter 5 discusses the desire of certain listeners to associate the human sounds of free jazz soundsinging with animal sounds, and there I theorise that this functions to protect certain notions of humans as superior to animals and, relatedly, of certain groups of humans as superior to other groups of humans. Minton describes that his use of the term comes from a friend of his, the multi-instrumentalist, improviser, composer, actor, and co-founder of the IOU Theatre company, Lou Glandfield (Minton quoted in Broomer 2012). Glandfield's reference to Minton as "a feral singer" seems to fit into the general pattern discussed in Chapter 5 since the term feral is usually used in conjunction with non-human animals. However, given the fact Glandfield was a friend of Minton's, the term may well have been entirely or partially honorific; rather than invoking the animalic as a form of policing, in the manner discussed in Chapter 5, Glandfield may have intended it as a form of praise. Minton contemplated the designation and decided he liked the association of his vocal practice with "release" or "escape" from "domestication" (Ibid.). He began using the term widely in the 1980s in the name for his ensemble with Hugh Davies, Roger Turner, and Alan Tomlinson, The Ferals, and as a description of his music, especially when promoting his duo with Roger Turner as "feral music." The use of the term in the choir settings derives from these earlier employments of the term.

Glandfield's comment may or may not have come from and fed back into a kind of primitivism. The notion that Minton's soundsinging emerges from a less "domesticated" or "civilised" state than other forms of musicking, that it is somehow "wilder," might function in some contexts as the honorific flip side of the disparagement of these sounds as "less than human." Romanticisation of certain humans as "closer to nature" than others can feed the same symbolic logic as disparagement of certain humans as "too close to nature." Such romanticisation, a conceptualisation of soundsinging as a return to some pre-civilised state, is meaningfully distinct from thinking of it as a vocal practice that disregards certain arbitrary vocal proscriptions embedded in our cultural norms. When Minton invokes the term "feral" he does conceptualise a kind of escape from "domestication"; however, arguably, he does not seem to indulge in primitivist imaginations that his improvisation allows him to access some state of nature that other humans lack access to. Rather, his focus is on the ways cultural permissions and proscriptions have shaped the voice. When he explains that he's "interested in discovering the voice beneath the shrouds of culture that have suppressed voices in the West and East for thousands of years" it is desire for a space where the vocal "possibilities are infinite" that he focuses on, not some claim his improvisation accesses some romantic "primal" state (Minton quoted in Tresham 2012).

His desire to create a space where all vocal sound is acceptable and celebrated goes hand in hand with his desire to foster spaces that are radically inclusive in terms of who can participate. Minton insists: "I always say it's open to absolutely anybody."[10] He has led Feral Choirs catering to people suffering from homelessness in Tokyo and São Paulo; to residents of economically depressed neighbourhoods in Vancouver and London; to prisoners in England and the United States; and to postgraduate scientists in England whose work environments reward vocal monotony.[11] He estimated in 2009 that he had by then led between fifty and sixty Feral Choirs, and the number is now likely between seventy-five and one hundred.

Minton's Feral Choirs were one of the important influences on a free jazz choir movement that has grown and spread across Canada thanks largely to the efforts of two choral improvisation conductors—Christine Duncan and DB Boyko. In 2007, Duncan and her partner percussionist Jean Martin received a Canada Council grant to support research that would lead to the development of an improvising choir. This led to the formation of The Element Choir, an improvising choir based in Toronto. To develop the conduction vocabulary she uses to lead the choir, she drew on past experiences with conduction she acquired when singing in the Hugh Fraser Orchestra and Dave Clark's Woodchopper's Association; she studied Butch Morris's conduction system, John's Zorn's game work Cobra, the conduction system Jean Derome developed for his game piece *Canot-Camping*; she took a soundpainting workshop with Sara Weaver; she enlisted composers Peter Hannan and Juliet Palmer to advise her on the development of her system; and she hosted one of Minton's Feral Choir workshops in Toronto.[12] Taking elements from all these sources, she developed a conduction language and approach to improvisational choir conducting that helped to spark improvising choirs in several other Canadian cities.

The idea to form an improvising choir was partly inspired by work Duncan was doing with Martin and Boyko prior to 2007. Boyko was the music curator at a prominent and historic artist-run centre in Vancouver called Western Front, and she began collaborating with Duncan, who was also Vancouver based until 2000, in the late 1990s. They began to dually conduct impromptu improvising choirs together for community events at the Western Front, which Duncan described as "just like us improvising with each other, but using the choirs as our instrument."[13] They revived the idea for a pair of CD release concerts in 2006 for Duncan, Boyko, and Martin's trio Idiolalla. Duncan referred to these concerts as "the experience where the switch gets flipped," and she recognised the potential to deepen her approach to this type of work.[14]

Boyko relocated to Toronto for a period in 2008 while Duncan was completing her research and starting The Element Choir. Duncan shared the research with her, and she became a custodian of the method Duncan developed. She later brought it back with her to Vancouver and adapted it, using it as a main method in two choirs she organised in Vancouver, the Voice Over Mind Choir, which she started in 2010 in conjunction with the Voice Over Mind Vocal Festival at Western Front, and the Express Your Voice choir, a choir she also began in 2010 for seniors and people dealing with chronic health issues.

The Element Choir has always been entirely open at no cost to anyone interested in participating. There is no obligation to attend choir events, as the choir can function with any constellation of its members present. When an event is coming up, Duncan sends an email to the list of hundreds of individuals who have attended one or more of the workshops she has given teaching her conduction vocabulary, and those interested and available gather and form one version of the ever-shifting choir. This flexibility is an important element of the radical inclusivity I am claiming these choirs often offer; members are not prevented from participating if their schedules prevent them from regular attendance, and this feature enables many who would not otherwise be able to commit to membership to be part of a choir that welcomes them whenever they can make it.[15] Even the basic requirement of learning the hand signals that make up her conduction system is not an absolute prerequisite for participation; Duncan describes how "sometimes, once in a while, someone who hasn't done [one of her conduction workshops] ends up performing. [Her system] is organic enough, the communication is clear enough that people can follow if it's just one or two people buried in a group who knows what they're doing."[16]

The Voice Over Mind Choir has existed largely in connection to the Voice Over Mind festivals that ran from 2010 to 2015 and several other special projects in the Vancouver area. It "is dedicated to the practice of improvisation and spontaneous choral composition" and has been composed of an almost even mix of participants who identified as singers prior to participating in the choir and those that wouldn't have.[17] Duncan's work has also served as inspiration for Montreal based vocalist/saxophonist Joane Hétu, who described wanting for many years to develop some kind of radical choir and finally taking the initiative to do so when she saw The Element Choir. This led to the formation of Joker (a playful combination of her first name and the French word for choir, *chœur*). Joker is a small invitation-only "chorale bruitiste" founded in 2012 that is predominantly improvisational. Joker, in turn, helped influence another similar group, Phth, that includes several members of Joker (Gabriel Dharmoo, Elizabeth Lima, Kathy Kennedy, and David Cronkite) to form in Montreal in 2018. Duncan's work also served as the basis of a series of improvising "Vocal Exploration" choirs that I founded in Guelph, Ontario in 2013, St John's, Newfoundland in 2014 and in Groningen, the Netherlands, in 2017.

Other musicians have also independently developed improvisational choir practices and/or conduction systems. One is Austrian vocalist Annette Giesriegl, who has been leading improvising choirs and orchestras in the Styrian region of Austria in recent years. Giesriegl lived in London for a period, and her interest in community music was informed by her involvement in Nicols's The Gathering; Giesriegl founded her own free and inclusive Gathering series in Kumberg, just outside of Graz. Another example is Thomas Johannsen, an improviser with a background in theatre who has formed a choral improvisation community in Amsterdam called The Genetic Choir. A third example is Marten Archer's Juxtavoices, an improvising choir formed in Sheffield that works nearly exclusively via improvisation. A fourth example, of the various improvising choirs David Moss has organised, included his Berlin based New Babel Choir. Each of these groups has formed choral improvisation communities in distinct ways using distinct methods.

Experiences and Affordances of Choral Improvisation

To close this chapter I approach the question of the social value of these choirs via research I conducted with participants in Duncan's Element Choir and one of my Vocal Exploration choirs. My choice to foster these choirs emerged out of a sense of obligation I felt to the legacy of Minton, Nicols, Dutton, Boyko, and Duncan. I felt privileged that the postdoctoral support I was receiving from the International Institute for Critical Studies in Improvisation was allowing me to meet and understand the work of these vocalists, and when I came to realise the positive transformative effects their creation of an inclusive space for voice has had on many of the participants in their choirs, I felt an obligation to help expand access to these practices. It gradually became clear to me that it might help expand the practice even further if I treated the choirs I was building as a form of practice-based, applied ethnographic research. Documenting and analysing the experiences participants were having might help others decide whether or not they too might be motivated to create these spaces for their communities. It is my hope that you, by reading this, might realise you can also go out and start an improvising choir.

I am laying my bias towards these choirs bare here. I must begin by stating that I remain frustrated by the ways much of the research on choral practices and communities has celebrated the benefits of community singing while remaining relatively blind to the limitations of these practices and the potential harm they may cause. I can understand the desire not to dwell on those who are alienated or triggered by the music you are making, especially when you see the positive effects it is having on others. And I am certain there are blind spots and negative consequences that we simply cannot access when we are leading these projects. However, I feel we have a responsibility to try and understand not just the benefits of our practices but all of the processes our music making contributes to. As such, I argue here that free jazz choral music has qualities unique to free jazz—like its ability to include not only all people but also all sounds, its ability to freely and fluidly foster connections across musico-cultural divides, and its ability to foster a form of music making in which individual participants feel their contributions and the contributions of others were singular and irreplaceable in the production of the music—while also admitting and documenting that not everyone who experiences this form of music making has a positive experience.

I mentioned above that Minton's Feral Choirs are short-term choirs that emerge through one or more workshops and commonly disband when Minton leaves town. Of course, some of these workshop choirs take the initiative to continue after Minton has left. The experiences afforded by the short-term workshop versus the stable, long-term localised improvising choir can be quite different. In the sustained local choirs, there is the opportunity to build deep relationships over long durations between regular participants. Both types of improvising choirs are collaborative, and much of the experience they afford depends on the particular people participating and the experiences and values they bring to the choir. Nearly all of the diverse manifestations of these choirs create a space where participants come into contact and collaboration with others who have quite distinct musical and cultural backgrounds and distinct understandings of what kinds of vocal sounds are valuable and deserving of public presentation. To illustrate the various kinds of encounters and affordances these distinct varieties of free jazz choir offer, I will describe and compare my fieldwork experiences with one workshop choir and one sustained local choir.

The workshop choir I will discuss was a touring version of The Element Choir. While The Element Choir most often refers to the sustained Toronto-based collective, Duncan also offers Element Choir workshops in other cities and performs with these workshop groups under the same name. One such group was a part of the 2013 Ottawa Chamberfest. Duncan and Martin, who often performs improvised percussion with the choir, were invited to present a concert they titled "The Element Choir Project."[18] Ottawa is more than a four-hour drive from Toronto and due to the distance, only a few of the members of the Toronto-based choir participated in this event. Most of the participants were drawn from the Ottawa area via recruitment emails and web postings. These specified that Duncan was "looking for singers—whether professional or enthusiastically amateur, and in any style" and that "singers of any skill level and experience are invited" (Duncan's call for singers quoted in McGregor 2013). Interested singers were asked to commit to attending two three-hour-long evening workshops and to participate in two distinct Chamberfest performances. Participants were enticed by compensation in the form of a Chamberfest Artist Pass "good for admission to all events during the Festival except Gala shows" and a Chamberfest T-shirt (Ibid.). The invitation also announced that the choir would work in improvisational collaboration with the "exceptional instrumentalists" Jean Martin on drums, trumpeter Jim Lewis, and Veryan Weston, who would be coming from England to improvise with the choir using the organ installed in the performance venue, the Dominion-Chalmers United Church (Ibid.).

The invitation attracted approximately fifty choristers, some of whom had worked with Duncan before, but also many singers who had no prior experience with Duncan or with choral improvisation. As a component of my research, I distributed a qualitative survey to participants. Most of those surveyed who had no previous experience with Duncan listed their primary reason for participating as the opportunity to "expand" or "broaden" their "musical horizons." However, for some, "receiving a free artists pass to the complete Chamberfest was also a lure." These various motivating factors, the diverse classical, jazz, and gospel music communities through which the invitation circulated, and the invitation's welcome to singers of any skill level and style yielded a choir composed of individuals from a diverse range of ages and musical backgrounds, many of whom would have been unlikely to have collaborated with each other in any other musical context. Though this particular context seemed to involve few, if any, participants who had no prior experience singing in public it certainly brought together musical professionals, semi-professionals, and "enthusiastic amateurs."

The second Vocal Exploration choir I founded was called the St John's Vocal Exploration Choir, or VocalX for short. The choir employed the conduction method I learned singing with The Element Choir as well as strategies for free and structured choral improvisation I learned in workshops or rehearsals with Minton, Nicols, Dutton, Hétu, Tina Pearson, and W. Mark Sutherland. VocalX was founded in December 2014 with the intention that the choir would be self-sustaining and not dependent on any one particular leader. I acted as the primary conductor for the first year and then began sharing conducting duties with choir members who expressed interest in conducting. At present, my career has taken me out of Canada, and the choir is continuing in my absence under the primary direction of two of the choir members, Alison Carter and Mack Furlong, that gained the most experience conducting prior to my departure.

Between December 2014 and August 2016, ninety-nine individuals participated in one or more of the free sessions that I offered twice monthly, fifty-three of whom participated in one or more of the fourteen public concerts the choir performed in that period. The twice-monthly sessions were never obligatory, and they ranged in size from three singers to thirty singers with an average of ten singers per session. Participants were recruited through posters, flyers, and social media posts. The language on these invitations differed from the Chamberfest emails; rather than inviting "singers of any skill level" these invitations read "Free Vocal Workshop Series. Everyone is Welcome. Appropriate for all ages and levels of experience." While the Chamberfest project attracted singers from a range of genres and levels of professionalism, VocalX participants attracted fewer individuals who identified as professional or semi-professional singers and a far greater number of individuals who had never performed publicly as vocalists prior to their involvement with the choir or who had but whose participation in public vocal performance had lapsed for a significant period of time for various reasons. VocalX and the Chamberfest choir were similar, however, in that both groups brought together individuals of a wide age range and individuals whose diverse professions, interests, and musical backgrounds would have made it unlikely that certain of them would have met and collaborated in any other context. The diversity of age was wider in VocalX, as children frequently participated, while the youngest members of the Chamberfest choir were young adults.

The Chamberfest choir led to singers becoming temporarily part of a choir that can be considered radically inclusive when compared to most other choirs these singers have experienced. While some of the less professional choirs that served as the home choirs of participants may welcome any interested participant, they would not be inclusive in the sense of allowing participants to introduce any sound of their choosing into sections of the choral performances. Of course, many of these choirs would also have been much less inclusive in terms of membership; singers would need to be proficient in the particular vocal style of the choir and would have to pass an audition process to be admitted to many of the classical and jazz choirs familiar to participants in the Chamberfest group, and many of the jazz specialists would not likely be qualified for the classical choirs and vice versa. VocalX could be considered even more inclusive given the absence of a suggestion that potential participants should identify as singers.

Surveys I conducted with participants in these two choirs made it clear that these varieties of inclusivity yielded distinct challenges and benefits to different kinds of participants. Unlike the events connected to VocalX, which were all voluntary, involving no prior promise of compensation, and requiring no promise of commitment, members of the Chamberfest choirs entered the group knowing that signing up to participate meant committing to both workshops and both performances. This meant that unlike certain Chamberfest audience members (about "a dozen or so" by the estimation of one of the choir members I spoke with) who left Dominion-Chalmers during the first portion of the concert, choristers were obliged to stay for the duration of both concerts and listen to and improvise with voices they found "difficult to bear," "discordant," "embarrassing," and/or "not warranted."[19] Due to the presence and employment of an "imitate" sign in Duncan's conduction system, participants were ushered into moments where they were encouraged to imitate sounds they found "weird," "not particularly musical—sort of like colouring outside of the lines," or sounds they felt "reluctant" to attempt.[20] Reflecting, some participants indicated that this experience had little bearing on their future: "I cannot see me ever using this again," or "[t]he positive encouragement to experiment . . . likely had less effect on me than on others."[21] Others, however, found it transformative, stating, "I may continue to explore to expand my courage and challenge my aversion to risking being wrong"; or "I was reluctant to do this, but once I started and gave into it, it felt cathartic and enjoyable"; or "There were some very moving moments of wonderful collaboration with the other singers. I dared make sounds, for the sheer joy of it. I noticed that I became much more attentive to the sounds around me. I think that increased 'sound mindfulness' has persisted till now. What a wonderful discovery."[22]

Alongside ushering singers into vocalisation of sounds they previously heard as sonic Others, one singer in the Chamberfest choir commented that the choir afforded them the opportunity to experience "a sense of true empowerment" through the way Duncan's system of conducted improvisation allows for improvisatory ideas generated by individual singers to expand out into the choir and serve as structural elements in the broader improvised compositional whole.[23] While improvised choral performances can involve the experience of being ushered into embodying sounds perceived as Other, conversely, they also involve the experience of your sounds entering the voices of the other bodies around you. One Chamberfest singer commented on this, describing how the experience involved "the feeling of conversing with the whole choir."[24] Others in the choir made similar comments, acknowledging that they felt as if "the outcome all depended on us, and would have changed if any chorister wasn't there, or if they were replaced by someone else."[25] Through comments like this, we see that the kinds of inclusivity these choirs can foster involve not only making singers feel welcome but making them feel like a necessary part of the whole that the group co-composed. While this may also be true of choirs that perform composed music, it would be true only to a distinct degree, of course, as choral compositions are nearly always composed with the intention that a variety of distinct choirs will realise the piece. Conversely, in free jazz, the improvised contributions of each participant create an event that is not only irreducible in its singularity, as all events are, but perceived and felt to be irreducible by most of the individuals attending to the sounds, including, crucially, the individual producing the sounds.

Conclusion: The Stigma of Inclusivity

The practice of creating inclusive improvisatory choirs is, of course, not entirely altruistic. Nicols's Oval House workshops were offered in exchange for rehearsal space, and different forms of cultural and economic capital accrue to singers who choose to cultivate these spaces. However, these sometimes hidden rewards exist alongside costs that might also be inaudible in considerations of these practices. Nicols discusses "how painful it had been not being understood in terms of wanting to work within community."[26] Many of the same musicians that began to welcome her into a privileged inner circle in the late 1960s withdrew that welcome, replacing it with "that feeling of not being seen as a 'proper' musician because you're doing stuff in community."[27] Nicols realises that when she works with inclusive groups "there's that thing of 'oh God, she's working with all these amateurs.'"[28] Many improvising vocalists have cultivated inclusive, mixed-ability improvisational choirs despite the possibility of stigma that Nicols describes. Service to a politics of inclusivity and the sincere enjoyment of the aesthetic and social results of mixed-ability vocal improvisation have been central motivations driving singers like Nicols through the stigma.

The extremes and the potential healing power of this kind of inclusivity are perhaps encapsulated best in a story that Veryan Weston shared about Nicols's approach to The Gathering. He explained:

> Of course, Maggie's thing is The Gathering. She was the founding member of The Gathering. Which is a very important group of people that still meet, actually. The only bit of leadership there is the person who has the key that opens the door of the places that they choose to meet and play together. And, what's quite interesting about The Gathering is that when there is conflict, say for example if someone in The Gathering might feel that someone else is being too dominant, or not listening enough to what's going on around them, Maggie would say the way to alleviate the conflict is through the person who is making the complaint. So, for instance, if somebody comes in to The Gathering completely unfamiliar with what is going on and so seems to be being almost musically disruptive as a result, a way of resolving such a conflict is to not actually tell the disruptive person to stop what they are doing, but try and resolve any of your own inner conflicts by taking time out, or to give the situation more silence in order to allow the music to start from nothing again. It feels to me, and this is where the discussion comes into it, you kind of think "okay, if somebody's being like this, how do you deal with this in a group situation?" And, perhaps certain people in The Gathering might want to sort of say "well, can't we just tell

the person to stop?" and Maggie would say "No. In actual fact you just let them do it." Maggie's always been very resolute in allowing the music to flow and do the healing.[29]

Nicols has come to an understanding that the impulse to police the sounds of others is an opportunity for self-reflection. Rather than following the impulse and silencing others, we can reflect on why that person might need to take up that space and how we likely have the strength within ourselves to let them work through whatever they need to be working through while supporting them with our presence and growing personally through the process of accepting the sounds we have the impulse to silence. Further, that acceptance can sometimes have transformative effects on the individuals needing to take up the space. Often they come back to listening and leaving space for others once they've worked through what they need to work through or felt heard.

These kinds of encounters in improvised music provide us with a space for personal growth that can extend into and inform our approach to all our encounters with others in daily life. Voice is the least expensive and most widely accessible of the musical instruments, and free jazz singers like Nicols, Minton, Dutton, Duncan, Boyko, Hétu, Giesriegl, and others have developed effective methods we can all use to open spaces for every voice and to all vocal sound.

Notes

1. Maggie Nicols, interview with the author, 25 June 2014.
2. The band in question here was called Voice but is not to be confused with Nicols's vocal quartet called Voice. This Voice was a larger group of singers and instrumentalists formed by Nicols and her former partner Harry Vince.
3. Maggie Nicols, interview with the author, 25 June 2014.
4. Ibid.
5. Both quotes are taken here from Armstrong's Natural Voice Network webpage. See naturalvoice.net/about and naturalvoice.net/about/more, respectively. Accessed 2 January 2019. Nicols has said "singing is a birthright" (quoted in Cowley 2008, 15), and she describes The Gathering as "open to clumsiness, open to anything; anyone can just walk in off the street" (Ibid., 16).
6. See naturalvoice.net/about. Accessed 2 January 2019. Armstrong alludes to improvisation's role in her workshops, writing "doing movement . . . helped open the potential for vocal improvisation, as well playing with melody and harmonies, rhythm, imagination, vocal range and quality, mood and expression." (See naturalvoice.net/about/nvn-president-frankie-armstrong. Accessed 2 January 2019).
7. See naturalvoice.net/about/nvn-president-frankie-armstrong and frankiearmstrong. net, respectively. Accessed 2 January 2019.
8. *A Melody Maker* review of the concert in the 19 March 1977 issue documents that the group performed that night as the Occasional Orchestra and Big Band. On other occasions, like a 26 June 1977 concert at Regent's Park or a 15 October 1977 concert at the Jazz Pulsations festival in Nancy, they performed as The Orckestra.
9. Maggie Nicols, interview with the author, 25 June 2014. Despite Nicols's reference to 1970 or 1971, it is more likely this took place during the second festival she organised with Vince at the Oval House, 21–23 April 1972, with this particular moment occurring on Sunday

the 23rd. I base this on the fact that Bailey's solo appearance was discussed in Williams's 1972 *Melody Maker* article on Nicols's work at the Oval House. The previous festival she organised ran from Friday 20 June to Sunday 22 June 1971. It was advertised to feature Nicols (1) performing a piece "for singers" by John Stevens alongside Julie Driscoll (known later as Julie Tippetts), Norma Winstone, Pepi Lemer, and Carolann Nichols; (2) performing duets with Driscoll; and (3) performing with her group Okuren, which, curiously, was referred to in a *Melody Maker* announcement as "Miss Nichols's vocal group," despite the fact that Nicols doesn't recall applying this name, which was the name she used for a piano/vibes/voice trio she had with Derek Foster and Georg Jensen, to a "vocal group" (email to the author, 19 May 2018). See *Melody Maker*, 19 June 1971, p. 5.

10. Phil Minton, interview with the author, 24 June 2014.
11. Ibid. Minton explains that the scientists explained that if they don't speak in a consistent timbre and at a consistent rate "they won't be taken seriously."
12. Duncan, interview with the author, 11 August 2014.
13. Ibid.
14. Ibid.
15. Though she did during the early stages of the choir, since The Element Choir currently performs frequently, Duncan no longer holds regular "rehearsal" sessions for the group. The performances serve to keep the members connected to the practice of working with her conduction.
16. Duncan quoted in a dialogue between her and Tomomi Adachi arranged and recorded by the author, 29 September 2013.
17. The quote here was taken from https://front.bc.ca/events/voice-over-mind-festival-3. Accessed 7 January 2019. The estimate is from DB Boyko, interview with the author, 18–22 March 2015.
18. The Element Choir regularly works with instrumental improvisers. I give other examples below.
19. Comments from anonymised participants in the 2013 Element Choir at Ottawa Chamberfest. Each of these comments was used to describe sounds the singer heard other choir members make during one of the two concerts they participated it.
20. Ibid. Each of these comments was used to describe sounds the singer made themselves during the concert. I say "encouraged" because singers have the agency to ignore the conductor's instructions and are often encouraged to exercise that option when they see fit.
21. Ibid.
22. Ibid.
23. Ibid.
24. Ibid.
25. Ibid.
26. Personal Interview with Maggie Nicols, 25 June 2014, Guelph, Canada.
27. Ibid.
28. Ibid.
29. Veryan Weston, email to the author, 30 January 2019.

In Their Own Words III

IN HER OWN WORDS—CHRISTINE DUNCAN[1]

CT: So let's start today by talking about when you first began performing free improvised music. When was it? . . .

CD: I moved to Toronto in September of 2000 and it was not long after that . . . I had been doing some kind of improvised singing in Vancouver, which is where I lived before Toronto, with DB Boyko, a friend of mine . . . But the reason why it's a difficult question is I believe I've been improvising vocally for my whole life . . . My father is a Pentecostal minister and I was raised in fundamentalist Pentecostal churches and one of the coolest things about that environment is the environment of musical improvisation, group musical improvisation that happens all the time. And often it's in conjunction with praise and worship. And so there's talking in tongues, which is kind of like a sound poetry or improv kind of non-idiomatic vocalising . . . the idea of free improv music absolutely resonated with me as an extension of that kind of channelling of energy . . .

CT: It sounds like Toronto was a kind of accelerator.

CD: I think so . . . I just did a bunch of research when I first moved here and checked out the different scenes and kind of made a clear decision that the improvised music scene and new music scene and the experimental music scene was what captured my interest most at that point . . . Another really seminal experience that that is based around is Barnyard Drama with Jean Martin, my partner. My first experience of an entirely improvised gig was with him . . . The first completely improvised show I did with DB was at a festival in Québec . . . Somehow she got us a gig there with a group that she called Off the Cuff, which consisted of her, Jean, and me . . . two voices and drums, which became Idiolalla. Since then we've recorded an album and released it on the label D.A.M.E. . . .

CT: For you is there a preferred term you have for singing with unconventional techniques?

CD: I don't know. I just ripped off Paul Dutton's soundsinging term. I quite like it.

CT: Do you know why you like it?

CD: Because it's sounding and singing. It's super basic, for me. I don't really worry that much about the labels . . . even in my full-on improv gigs, I'll sing songs if it feels like the right thing to do. That's pretty unusual. For a lot of people who are "sounding" people, that's kind of taboo. They're not into it. But, I really, really firmly believe that if you're actually in that space and it's actually happening, whatever the resource material is should be at your disposal to use.

CT: Have you gotten pushback from other musicians for employing something melodic?

CD: Not people that I've played with, ever. But I remember a musician once after a gig gave me the feedback that they didn't think this song thing worked as well as the other stuff. And I just kind of took the info and went "okay, whatever." I said for me it's really very much a part of what I'm all about, that it's all available and should happen . . .

CT: When did extended techniques find their way into your vocal vocabulary?

CD: Again, I've been aware of improvisatory sound making. I was always a mimic. I was parroting things and pushing the voice. I discovered whistle tones when I was young and used to walk around squealing like the kettle is done and my dad would just say: "Christine, would you stop that squeaking?" . . . But I do recall there were two things that happened that were interesting little focal points for me. One was not long before I moved to Toronto I was at the Vancouver Jazz Festival . . . and I heard an ensemble that Kate Hammett-Vaughan was singing with, doing free improv stuff, and I remember being very taken with that performance . . . It stuck with me . . . Then, newly in Toronto, I was asked by Glen Hall to perform with his group the redShift orchestra, subbing for their singer, Sook Yin Lee. She was doing some vocal improvising too. Glen gave me some live recordings, and I learned the material by listening to her live performances and mimicking. This was right at the same time that I was starting to heavily get into Diamanda Galas. And the way that I do that when I'm starting to get into a new artist, I obsessively listen to them for hours and hours and hours and I mimic them. The combination of these experiences opened something up for me . . .

CT: People put a hierarchy on specific sounds and a lot of the unconventional sounds we're talking about gain negative associations.

CD: Yes, of course.

CT: As a pedagogue you must have encountered students who have those associations. So you must have some insight as to where those associations come from, how you can break through them, or how they're sustained. One question I wanted to ask you is what has sustained your interest in unconventional vocality and I guess one opposite question is what maintains other people's interests in maintaining those hierarchies?

CD: Fear. I believe people maintain their structure in terms of their perspective of the world largely based on fear. And I understand that. That makes perfect sense to me. But, for me, the way that I operate with people who are concerned about that or worried or nervous about sounding—because there are times when I am teaching in such a way that it actually goes directly to these kinds of sound making in conjunction with breath, in conjunction with body and it is making sounds that freak people out—is that I will always just address it. I say, you know, because of movies, the scores and the soundscapes we see in movies, we often have negative associations with certain kinds of sounds, like those that sound ghostly, or that sound like a death rattle. All these things, right? And because we don't understand it we're going to just pitch it into the basket of negativity, right? But the way I couch it is, yeah, that is true, it can be that but it's also just the sound of breath leaving the body. It's also body sounds . . . And, when you think about these kinds of sounds, we associate them with pain, we associate them with grief. It's because the body is making those sounds to comfort itself. We associate it with those things, but actually they're not. They're the sounds of the body comforting itself and healing, in a way. So if you can contextualise it so people think of the glass as half full rather than the glass as half empty it can start them down the path of being okay with making less normal kinds of sounds . . . It's just part of the natural thing and it's part of the sound palette of the body. Why wouldn't I want to get in there and get into the attic and get through all the dusty cracks and see what's in there? Go into the basement, go into the cellar and check it all around? Why wouldn't I want to find out what the whole instrument has to offer? The only thing that can do is make whatever I choose to use that much deeper, that much more informed, that much more authentic. So, even for people who only want to sing songs—which is great, I work with a lot of people who only want to sing songs—I still have this approach with them. If it's unknown or if it's hidden or you're hiding from certain parts of your instrument or voice that translates into how you express and your ability to communicate . . .

CT: If I'm remembering correctly, the genesis of the Element Choir was when Idiolalla . . .

CD: Did a CD release concert.

CT: Yes. Could you tell me about that?

CD: It was in November 2006 that Idiolalla was doing two CD release concerts. One in Toronto and one in Montreal. It's a pretty hard gig, just two voices and drums for a whole concert. It's pretty intense. So, Jean, my partner, who has usually come up with some of my best ideas, I must say, he suggested that perhaps we get a group of singers together to conduct. Now this was something that DB and I had kind of been playing with a little bit here and there and I think she was doing it before I was doing it, this very gestural kind of improv conducting of choral groups. In fact, we had done a little bit of two-conductor play at the Western Front block parties for a couple of years where they just have a bunch of people show up, a bunch of people from the community, and she would put them into an impromptu choir. It's just like us improvising with each other, but using the choirs as our instrument, in a sense. And so we'd done it recreationally a few times and it was super fun. So Jean suggested that and we went: "oh, what a great idea." So we got on it and put together these little vocal groups. Very small. There weren't that many people. In Montreal, Kathy Kennedy put together a little group for us from the people she works with. That was very kind of her. So we had about ten singers there to work with. And in Toronto I tried to put it together from a student base. Five or six people showed up to rehearsal and three showed up to the gig . . . Anyway, so, we did that for the gigs. Again, for me, it's like you have the experience where the switch gets flipped: "Oh, this has actually got incredible potential here." And then after that was over, Jean and I went: "you know what? We're going to apply for a Canada Council grant to develop an Improvising Choir." So it was really a decision that we made together based around an idea of his . . .

CT: For you, what are the most important outcomes of the Element Choir project so far? . . .

CD: Being in the Element Choir and participating in this community has changed a lot of people's lives, actually, in the art community in the city. I think that's a very important thing. People are different. People are acting differently. People are living more artfully. People are making connections with each other and going on to do spinoff stuff all the time in different kinds of projects. It's amazing. So that's a really important thing for me because it keeps people interested in coming back. I mean, being able to have a "band" (the biggest band in the world!) that can play anything from new music events, to free improv events, to poetry and word-based/text-based events, to indie guerrilla interventionist kind of performance, to alternative indie rock hipster kind of events, it's completely insane. I've never had a group or musical collaboration that has spanned so diversely through all different scenes and age groups. It's kind of crazy where this group can turn up and fit in. So that's kind of cool. The other thing that's really amazing to me is you can have everybody from retired people to teenagers in the same group and they're all totally engaged together doing the most cool things. Different languages are cool; it all doesn't have to be in English. People from different disciplines and different backgrounds. People with art backgrounds, people with no art backgrounds. They can completely come together in this environment and do something that feels kind of important and useful and musical and connected and good . . .

Christine Duncan interview excerpts appear with the permission of Christine Duncan condensed from a longer interview conducted by the author. More information on Duncan can be found at www.barnyardrecords.com.

IN HER OWN WORDS—MANKWE NDOSI[2]

CT: Can you tell me how you came to your vocal practice?
MN: Maybe. If we have a two-minute sing first.

CT: Oh, sure!

MN: We've got the music happening right now [here Ndosi was referring to the environmental sounds surrounding us as we sat outside the Siskel Film Center in Chicago]. What would you add to it? [*we sing together for about two minutes*] Okay now we can begin. When did I start improvising?

CT: I asked when did you come to your vocal practice, but if you'd rather answer when you started improvising that would also be interesting for me to hear about.

MN: What do you mean by vocal practice? The act of singing regularly?

CT: Yes.

MN: As opposed to being an improviser?

CT: Not necessarily. I'm interested in that question too, so you could answer either.

MN: I would just sing along with the radio and then I would sing, there was this cat across the street, my parents were both at the University of Minnesota, my father had abandoned biology and theatre for economics in graduate school, he had gone to undergrad in biology and theatre, he was British boarding school raised inside of the colonial country from mountain village people. He was the one sent off to learn the white people's education and to go across the sea and to make the money and to bring the money back home and save the family. We lived in a basement apartment and across the way was a cat in the window and I started to imitate the cat so well that it would react as though there was a cat around. You know, as a kid. And when I could do that it was very satisfying and I felt like I was speaking to the cat. I think that's probably when I got hooked. And because the music that I was hearing was classical and pop radio and I never assigned people's names or beings, I never knew who, I would just listen to the songs and the music and my father would play piano himself, Beethoven and Bach and Schubert and Schumann and others, Chopin, and he would play Miriam Makeba and Hugh Masekela. And then I would hear the music on the radio and then I would talk to the cats. I think I got hooked on music that way.

CT: So, your beginnings were vocalising in these private spaces. When did you start vocalising in performance spaces or more public spaces?

MN: I was singing for a long time in school choirs. I did have one vocal teacher when I was in high school who was an opera singer from the Ukraine. Her name was Oksana Bryn. In the Twin Cities, she was at MacPhail [Center for Performing Arts]. So I took voice lessons from her, and so she helped me think about breathing and helped me think about performing and I sang . . . I was a performer throughout high school in ways that were not happy-making for my father, who was looking for a profession for me. I did some theatre through college even though there wasn't a theatre program there. I got interested in theatre and dance and stumbled through, performed spoken word, and in spoken word I was starting to be with other live musicians and singing that way rather than just making up songs myself and being in more organised choirs. So that was when I started to "sing sing" more as a little bit of myself and started to improvise. We would make up little songs, make up little grooves, that kind of stuff and I got into the realm with Douglas [Ewart]. I actually had known him and Janis for several years and actually moved to live above them when I was married at the time and he heard me playing. I had begun to play with my voice after singing with this spoken-word and music group I would sing with sometimes. It was called Arkology. It was three theatre and music kind of people and three musicians and we would do our own poems with music and sound and then we would do Black Art Movement, 1960s and 1970s movement, poetry, more political and personal-political poetry with music, and we did that for several years. And then I was starting to also do my own performance artwork as well in the Twin Cities through a few different organisations. And then Douglas took me from doing the more out things to a stage where that was sort of expected and I got to try it out more with people. But I was singing for a long time. Like I'll just sing, like I sing. I recognise the tones and the music so part of the joy is similar to making the cat meow, it's like singing with the crickets and seeing if you can get a bird to recognise you, if you can talk back or if you can pay attention even and find a way to make that happen then that transfers with your own music to washing machines and the white noise from the computer and the hum of the refrigerator and, you know, the tires.

Douglas started bringing me to Chicago in 2000 and I got to be in Inventions with him and at that time Dee Alexander was also very active with Inventions. Her solo career hadn't quite skyrocketed as it has now, which I'm so excited about. So she was the first other female vocal improviser that I felt was like me that I have met and actually engaged with in that way. We had Dee, who was primarily a vocalist, we had Duriel Harris who was primarily a poet and then me who sort of weaves back and forth between them. So Chicago helped me go from doing 15-minute shows for cabarets (there are a lot of those in the Twin Cities) to thinking about and actualising longer scale shows and works. I started to produce work in the Twin Cities. So I've been producing as well as performing and then singing and improvising. During that time when I was in the spoken-word group Arkology I was also part of the whole small creative arts scene and focusing on communities of colour in the Twin Cities which I had not grown up around because my father was pretty tight with the leashes on his children. So I just started to improvise with people, with all different kinds of artists. I just would want to sing because I was in a mode of saying yes.

CT: You said that Douglas heard you experimenting at home?

MN: You'd have to ask him what he remembers because he might remember it differently. That's a story that I tell myself about that.

CT: You said that when he heard that and invited you to make music with him that more unconventional uses of the voice were almost expected of you?

MN: I mean, it was welcomed. I was already doing it.

CT: Do you think that was part of what attracted him?

MN: Yes, definitely . . .

CT: In Arkology did you use your voice in similar ways or was that something that came after?

MN: I don't honestly remember. Listening to Miriam Makeba and learning the rhythmic percussive breathing with her, trying desperately to imitate the click sound of the Xhosa, but doing it very lazily. And then I took Chinese when I was in high school because I went to a private high school. So I heard music from all over the place and was aware that in Beijing Opera they used their voices in this particular way and over here they use their voices in this particular way, so I didn't feel like I had a limit to what I could do.

CT: And so you were singing along with recordings and incorporating those sounds later into your performances?

MN: That was part of, I think, singing and singing and singing and singing. But then, also, because I was first trained in the theatre I hadn't been told: "don't have this emotion when you perform; don't do this; don't use your voice this way." I mean they will do some work in terms of breath but so much about it had to do with work with the audience, filling the space, being present in yourself while you're performing, being open to receive a story and able to receive it differently even if the context of language and story may, in block letters, be the same: to find the difference and the similar in the same thing that you do . . .

CT: How did Arkology come about?

MN: A couple of friends had been asked to do a performance for the opening of the Twin Cities Black Theatre Festival, to do something live. It was a piece about Nina Simone called "Blues for Nina." So they put together poems and they had one other singer and some musicians and I actually couldn't make that gig. But the reception was so healthy and happy. People wanted to hear more of it and they decided to do more, but the original singer who was there didn't want to do it for whatever reason. She couldn't do it or didn't want to do it, so they were looking for somebody else and I was like, "Okay, I'll sing, let's see what happens," and I fell in love with it and it was really beautiful. And I got to be way out. I would read and sing recipes. That's where I could exercise my performative situation too.

CT: Nina Simone is a singer that used vocal timbre in a way where in certain moments she can really change the timbre of her singing style in a way that can be so powerful. You seem to do this too.

MN: I call it texture. I haven't been to music school, though I've taken a bit of theory. So, my terminology is different. I call it: I like to change the *texture* of my voice.

CT: One of the things that I don't see often are singers who change their timbre substantially while singing a melody, where it's so dramatic it's almost multi-vocal. Most people establish a general timbre, in speech or song, and rarely stray from it. But rarely there are these speakers or singers . . . who change. You seem to change dramatically for good reasons, when there are particular texts that you want to highlight in a certain way. Have you always sung that way or is that something that developed at a specific point? . . .

MN: I recognise it in other singers. Miriam Makeba does it. She does it mostly with expanding and contracting in a similar line. I think I've been influenced by them and so I've known that was an option without ever thinking that that was not an option. And then my other vocal coach/vocal peer, a woman I check in with who has been through music school and has a lot of very concrete approaches, Libby Turner, I think as I started to meet with her every once in a while, and there were some periods of more concentrated study with her, I started to know more intimately my own voice and find ways to enjoy it as well . . . I do come from theatre. The stage is a space of ritual and so I use my voice as part of the message and the texture or that aspect of colouring of the voice is part of the message, it's part of being effective in that role and also part of how I keep it interesting . . . Mostly it's having fun because it's not intellectual, it's a split-second decision. It's allowing and following your curiosity because as scary as improvising can be—it's frightening sometimes because you're jumping off a cliff, kind of—it's amazing when it really works. It's like nothing else when it really works. I think the place where I started to get more comfortable is knowing that if you don't like what you're doing you can stop. Wow, it's really simple. If you're in a place and it's bugging you, you stop singing. You're not going to make the other person stop because you don't have this mind meld, but you can stop singing and make another choice. Go back to listening. It's as, if not, more important than sound production itself.

Words/opinions of Mankwe Ndosi appear in this volume excerpted and condensed from a longer interview conducted by the author. More information on Ndosi can be found at www.mankwendosi.blogspot.com.

IN HIS OWN WORDS—TOMOMI ADACHI[3]

CT: Could we begin by speaking about the beginnings of your vocal work?

TA: I started using my voice as my instrument, I think it was when I was eighteen years old. At that time, I was playing many instruments. I studied almost everything by self-education. I was playing piano, percussion, electric guitar, violin, flute, and saxophone. At that time I was interested to do many things at the same time. Still, I am interested in that. In performance, I was using drums and electric guitar at the same time. I figured out that still I had room to do another thing. It was voice . . . I thought the voice is the most interesting instrument for me. I quit the other traditional instruments. Also, I started using electronics, like a multitrack tape recorder and guitar effects and I processed recorded samples, including many voice samples, with the effects devices. Soon I started to connect my own voice and electronics . . . This was just after I moved to Tokyo to go to university.

CT: What year was that?

TA: 1990. Then I knew many improvising musicians. At that time, John Zorn was living in Tokyo and also TAKAHASHI Yūji's[4] activity was very important for me. They integrated the ideas of composition and improvisation . . . After that, I thought I got some clear idea about improvisation . . . Maybe it was in 1992, I found a flyer. It was an improvisation workshop by YOSHI-ZAWA Motoharu at P3 Art and Environment and I took part in it . . . I joined that workshop and I met several interesting people there. One of them was one of the curators at P3, MURAI Hironori, he's a musician also. At that time, P3 was working a John Cage exhibition. They were planning to make some concerts during that exhibition. He asked me to join a performance of Cage's work. It was really my first participation in a public performance . . .

CT: And it was in that context that you started working with Butch Morris?

TA: Yes, exactly. It was my first public concert in the context of improvisation. Actually, I remember someone cancelled his participation in Butch Morris' conduction at P3 and I was a substitute musician. I don't remember well. YOSHIZAWA Motoharu was working with Butch Morris and fortunately loved my performance, then he asked me directly. That was an amazing experience . . .

CT: Could you tell me about how you used your voice when you first started experimenting and how your vocal practices changed over time?

TA: When I began using my voice at eighteen years old I went to many gigs of hardcore punk. They were just shouting and also I just shouted. Also, definitely, David Moss and MAKIGAMI Koichi were important. I received many influences from them. I learned how I could use voice from them . . . I bought the David Moss Dense Band *Live in Europe* CD when I was 18 years old. I went to several gigs of Hikashu. Also at that time already I was very impressed. On that CD of David Moss, he used effects on his voice. It was amazing. It's not a big part, but particularly I was impressed with that part where he used effects on his voice. The personal voice changed to some different voice.

CT: Regarding this idea of being able to change vocally, of having multiple voices, yesterday you were speaking about having one body but many subjects. Do you think you're interested in doing the vocal work you do because it helps embody that sense of having multiple subjects within one body?

TA: I think so. When I was around 22 years old, I was convinced with the theories of Jacques Derrida. He was talking a lot about voice. He discussed the connections between voice and modern society and the idea of origin. He basically criticised the use of voice, he criticised the false relationship between voice and the origin in modern society. But, I thought there are many other uses of voice. For example, Daniel Charles discussed the voice of Demetrio Stratos and multiplicity of voice. We could make many interesting observations on voice after Jacques Derrida. Now, I don't think I need Jacques Derrida to explain my practice, because my practice became more complicated . . .

CT: In 1996 you had your first solo show.

TA: Yes. It was the first time one whole concert was played only by me . . .

CT: You had discovered sound poetry by then. Could you tell me about how that happened for you?

TA: I'm not sure when it was. Maybe when I was 21 years old. Already, I believe I had known the name of *Ursonate* but I had not heard any recording. I bought Eberhard Blum's recording in, maybe, 1995. And it was the first time I listened to the whole poem and I thought it was a really, really interesting piece. Also, I found it was published and I made a copy at the library at the Goethe Institute and I practiced it.

CT: Was that the first piece of sound poetry that you worked with?

TA: Yes, I think so.

CT: Your piece *Minna no Uta* (Song for Everyone), did you compose it and first perform it in 1995?

TA: I think so, yes. I composed that piece for a particular event. It was also at P3. I was organising several concerts from 1994. The name of the series was Oto Aruiwa Mimi ni Tsuite (音あるいは耳について; About Sound or Ears). It was the third one.

CT: It's a very powerful title, *Song for Everyone*.[5] And it's been reflected in so much that you've done since then, the idea that everyone can participate. Why were you thinking like that?

TA: "Song for Everyone" is just a translation of *Minna no Uta*, and *Minna no Uta* is the name of a TV program.

CT: Oh, like the radio program.

TA: Yes, it's a radio and TV program by NHK. It's an educational music program for children. They commission composers or singers for one song each week. They change the program every week. They broadcast those songs with animations.

CT: Your title was a reference to that?

TA: Yes.

CT: Why make reference to that? What was the purpose?

TA: The idea was connected deeply with Jacques Derrida, also I was thinking about Benedict Anderson's *Imagined Communities*. Benedict Anderson discussed about the role of publishing in modern nations; I extended the ideas to how singing together in a relationship with public broadcasting, how the idea of melody or harmony, could be connected to nationalism.

CT: Why were you interested in nationalism?

TA: Because I was thinking, really, we need to overcome it, it was really my enemy. I imitated the same structure with the origin of nationalism. Collective singing/choir works as a homology of the modern nation. Typically, with national anthems, all people can sing them and it shows their belonging to the nation. Also, the anthems are spread in the nation through modern technologies like TVs and radios. National anthems are unison/monophonic. This process has the same cultural structure with the origin of nationalism which Benedict Anderson discussed in terms of language. But, in my piece, the realisation process and the final sequence was very different. I gathered people and made a strict unison, also I imitated the broadcasting system in the headphone distribution system—these processes are imitations of the processes of national anthems—but the performance itself was very far from unison. I can probably call it a deconstruction of musical process in nationalism.

CT: So it was an ironic title?

TA: Yes, it was ironical, but also it's a really direct expression about what I was doing.

CT: Could you tell about why you wanted to do what you did, then in terms of the structure of the piece?

TA: There is no musical structure [*laughs*]. That's an important thing. There is only instruction. It's an instruction how to build a human P.A. system. The turntable player can improvise and then the signal goes to the performers and the performers imitate it as precise as possible and as loud as possible. It's human amplification.

CT: Why were you interested in that?

TA: This is an egoless and highly conceptual piece. I made just an instruction and the piece is not related with anyone's personal expression. But, also I wanted to realise a very energetic performance. It must have some intensity and also, at the same time, it should be humorous.

CT: When did your Royal Chorus start forming?

TA: 1997.

CT: For the Music Merge Festival, right? Can you tell me about that festival?

TA: It's a music festival organised by OTOMO Yoshihide and several people. I performed in the second edition of the festival. I remember in the first year I played as a member of P-blot, a group of melodicas. The next year I sent the proposal to realise that choir idea and they accepted.

CT: Why were you interested in the choir idea?

TA: I made one theatrical piece titled *Table Music*. I called it an opera, ironically. And several performers cooked during the performance and we sung my choir pieces. Then I thought I can develop those choir compositions . . . It was not really the first time I tried to make a choir without pitch. Already I did this for the theatre, for OOKA Jun's group. I used, I think, four or five people. It was a play about Walter Benjamin. I composed only rhythms for Benjamin's texts, without any pitches. Then performers can choose any pitches. I must confess, I cannot make precise pitch well by myself. It was a really simple composition . . .

CT: Why were you interested in working with vocalists that couldn't make pitches instead of hiring traditional singers?

TA: I'm interested in working with people who have many different kinds of backgrounds. I think it's really connected with the ideas of Cornelius Cardew. It was political in some meanings. That's the reason it has this ironic name, Royal Chorus. I can say it was a democratic practice of music.

CT: Can you tell me about some of the democratic aspects of the project?

TA: I would bring scores, but some of them cannot read them. So I would sing, myself, each part. And they modified it in their ways and we practiced it many times, then they influenced each other. Some people had some strong ideas and if one member feels that is better, maybe they would start to imitate that one. I composed an outline, then performers change it in the process of practice . . .

CT: Can you summarise what effect you wanted your Royal Chorus to have on listeners or the other performers?

TA: The basic idea is what we can do with a vocal ensemble without harmonies. Many choral groups spend a lot of time practicing harmonies. I'm not interested in it, but I'm interested in voice. So, I wanted to explore what we can do with it. Also, I must mention the Royal Chorus commissioned works from other composers . . .

CT: Why aren't you interested in harmony?

TA: Why do we need it? I don't understand the meaning of harmony, maybe because of my lack of a sense for harmonies? My thesis in university was about harmony. It was on Jean Jacques Rousseau's "Essay on the Origin of Languages." Jacques Derrida wrote about Rousseau in *Of Grammatology*.

Derrida's discussion was about language, but Rousseau was talking about music actually. Jean Jacques Rousseau's discussion was a romantic idea about community and how it's connected with musical melody and harmony. Rousseau was a composer. Jacques Derrida discussed what was behind that kind of thought, but he treated Rousseau's idea as if it was about language. My intention was that I read Rousseau through Derrida but about music. It's Derrida, so it's not so easy to explain in a few words, but I found a collusion between melody, harmony, and nationalistic thought in Rousseau's thought through Derrida's reading. Rousseau invented the romantic origin of music and language. It is a fabricated origin, more or less. My criticism of harmony is related to this. Even in the Royal Chorus, we had a kind of harmony. But, our harmony meant members can choose it. I like that idea. I didn't write any harmonies by myself, but they happened incidentally. I think it's an interesting point. Also, another thing is that I can't make precise pitches myself. So, how can I approach harmony? It's impossible.

CT: That fact that you don't sing precise pitches, you realise that being able to do so takes time or sometimes training.

TA: I hate training.

CT: You seem concerned with others as well who don't have access to that training or feel an ethico-aesthetic need to resist such training. Maybe the interest in participating in or resisting training or harmony comes from a political imperative.

TA: Yes. That's right . . . It came from political philosophy.

Tomomi Adachi interview excerpts appear with the permission of Tomomi Adachi condensed from a longer interview conducted by the author. More information on Adachi can be found at www.adachitomomi.com.

IN HER OWN WORDS—FAY VICTOR[6]

CT: Can you tell me about how you began to sing?

FV: I've been singing pretty much all my life, but I never wanted to pursue it as a career. My mother died when I was nineteen and that changed everything. This is the reason I became a singer actually. When I was able to breathe again (after the loss of my mother), music was the thing that made me feel whole and happy. Beyond just discovering music, what I discovered—what was really important—was that I began to feel whole again, to feel like sunshine was possible. That discovery gave me the foundation to really look into this, because I had no idea that I'd go after a singing career at all, but it became like nourishment to my life, and I couldn't ignore that. I began to take it very seriously then, by figuring out how to be a good jazz musician and then take it from there.

CT: What were the steps for you to get more deeply involved in music?

FV: Once I figured out that I was interested in singing jazz, then I had to figure out how to develop as a jazz vocalist and in this, I was very fortunate. I started taking vocal lessons and became part of a workshop and community of vocalists and a couple of people who were accompanying us, most importantly was the great pianist/organist Jimmy Sigler. One of his biggest claims to fame was he was the last accompanist for Dinah Washington, for three years. He did a lot of work in Philadelphia, working with people like Phyllis Hyman, Gamble and Huff, Harold Melvin & the Blue Notes. He was brilliant, knew thousands of standards in every key. He didn't need charts; he didn't learn to read music himself until he was 60. So this is where I started, and I received a lot of encouragement. Jimmy and the other musician who ran the workshop, bassist Gerry Eastman, were really serious about us becoming musicians, including introducing jazz theory. So I immersed myself in this space for a few years, which was a great way to start, but the realisation hit that New York is a huge and competitive town, amazing talent pool here. I was starting to get some gigs around but the reality was if I wanted to get better I should try to go somewhere else so I could develop. I didn't think going back to school was the thing to do at that time. I came up in the music with the idea that you learn this music with your ears and on the bandstand so you'll get your own sound. That's how I ended up moving to Europe. That seemed like the place to be able to work and figure out a lot about the music relatively hassle-free. And it turned out to be true. I was able to perform much more than I would have had I stayed in New York and developed my craft. It's also where I became an improviser in the way that I am now. Being there started that process.

CT: What was the name of the workshop?

FV: The Williamsburg Music Center. It was a jazz vocal workshop; they didn't want us to be too adventurous. That was OK at that time; I was a purist then anyway! The great thing about it was that it was every week. Just five dollars to sing a few tunes. A vocalist could develop tons of repertoire because Jimmy Sigler knew so much material. I'm so happy I was able to be part of a community like that at the outset. It was great. It really was.

CT: How did that play out? What directions were you trying and what kind of resistance did you get?

FV: It's good to talk about this. I think the workshop really informed the way I've done everything since then. I'm pretty good at standing up for what I believe is right for myself. Jimmy Sigler also coached a lot of the vocalists with a similar approach. It really worked for some vocalists but not for me. I realised I wanted a discussion about what I wanted to do and not being told what I should do. And I just had a problem with that, so we used to have these arguments! The interesting thing was he thought that because he had more knowledge and more "skin in the game" that I should basically respect what he said and *do* what he said, and I kind of thought that ludicrous because, yes he did *know* much more than I did and I definitely respected that fact, yet I also felt that I'm the one that's onstage, I'm the one that's figuring out my voice and intrinsically I felt it important that I have a say; I have to make sure I feel good about what I do. Standing up to him—at that point he was a big figure—really set the tone for everything else I've gone on to do. I've had to stand up to a lot more people since then and it's been great because it's great to stand up for what you think is right for yourself. It's important to know the things that will cause you to fight and take a stand. It's equally important to be aware of the discovery too. If I didn't have these tussles early on, I may not have had the clarity I had to begin to go my own way. I want to add to that I also learned so much from Jimmy Sigler and he was also encouraging in his own way. May he rest in peace.

CT: Could you be more specific? What were you doing musically that met resistance?

FV: I think when I started to take more musical risks that's when I started to get some resistance. For example, two years into me being part of this workshop I got the opportunity to go to Japan for three months to sing at a hostess bar. It was a fantastic experience and opportunity. I learned a lot because we had to play six nights a week, four sets a night! Plus I was there with the great, great pianist Bertha Hope. Actually, that was the trip I decided to become a jazz singer as a career. So when I came back from that trip I felt stronger after a workout like that. And I remember when I went back to the workshop, the first thing Jimmy Sigler said to me was: "I think you need to do more work. I think you're trying to be too different." . . .

CT: You said you were "taking risks," were you using extended techniques?

FV: No, not at that point. I was still a purist. I was pretty much a purist when I moved to the Netherlands as well and it took a while to open up to other ideas about how to approach singing. I was firmly entrenched in the dogma about what being a jazz vocalist was at that time. But I was still trying to be a musician, trying to sing things in a way that was more about making music than just about being an entertainer. I think they were much more concerned with that. Betty Carter, to me, is a vocalist from the jazz tradition but who sings like an instrumentalist, who approaches the way she phrases, even if she's singing a standard, and the harmonic information in her lines in ways that are more like a trumpet player. I was starting to think in this way, just by ear at that point, and try to take those risks. And they did not like that. I was listening to a lot of horn players. I was listening to much more instrumental jazz than vocal jazz. That still holds true.

CT: So it was issues of phrasing and harmonic content that found resistance?

FV: Yeah, also the idea of singing longer. With a lot of jazz vocals, you sing only one chorus or two. Singing longer and really trying to feel like part of the band and not just as window dressing on top of it . . .

CT: When you bring up the term "window dressing" you highlight the gender politics of the situation, the politics of display. Were there issues around that too? You weren't following the politics of display they were expecting?

FV: I think so. Not being comfortable with a woman who was trying to be an equal. I mean, I was not capable of being an equal in that sense, but I was certainly fighting to be one. I didn't mind the musical resistance, because that's okay, that's how you learn. But not this "you should know your place." Those things are hurtful, but I always fight them. They're not penetrating in a deep way to me because I try to fight them and not internalise it. I just say, "that's bullshit." I guess I've always felt as long as I put in the work, I have as much right to be on the bandstand as anyone else and I've owned that and, again, will stand up for that.

CT: I read you chose Amsterdam because you had a friend there. Were there other factors that drew you to Amsterdam?

FV: Well, when I made the discovery that if I really wanted to get better at this I would need to perform more, work more, and Europe would be a good place to go; I started to figure out how I could make that happen. I met an American musician who lived in Amsterdam as a singer. We became not only great friends, he was a major help. The first two times I went there was through him. And then I just fell in love with the Netherlands. It was a great place to live, amazing quality of life there. So that worked out. And once I started living there I began to get a lot of work, at first really still in the purist jazz, traditional realm I was coming out of. Then a couple of things happened. A German blues musician asked me to join a blues band that he ran in Münster, Germany. This began a deep immersion into the blues and blues-based forms, which was something I became very excited about. My husband, who is an ethnomusicologist by education, also exposed me to a lot of music from around the world. Gradually I started to open my ideas of what a vocalist should be. At the same time, I was listening to more improvisers. I was getting into the Dutch improv scene slowly (Instant Composer's Pool, Willem Breuker Collectif, Misha Mengelberg, Han Bennick) and listening to people like Eric Dolphy, Jackie Maclean, Albert Ayler, late Coltrane, Jimmy Lyons, Cecil Taylor, all those sort of people. I discovered Jeanne Lee and I discovered Cathy Berberian in the '90s as well, both huge for me as well.

CT: How did you discover Jeanne and Cathy and what were your initial reactions to their work?

FV: I had a boyfriend before who was a big fan of Luciano Berio's *Folk Songs* that he played for me. I fell in love with those, just the way she sang was really beautiful and soulful. Then later on I discovered Berio's *Sequenzas*. Those are amazing pieces and the vocal *Sequenza III* was the composition that initially formed my budding improvisational language. But, what really blew me away about the way she sings, besides how great her technique is, is how down to earth she sounded. That was a revelation to me. I thought: "Wow, that's really possible." And then Jeanne Lee was a major discovery. I actually saw Jeanne Lee live once with Mal Waldron. I got some records and I was trying to pursue studying with her because she was teaching in the conservatory in The Hague while I still lived in Holland. But she died before we could connect. That still stings. Then I found and studied with a brilliant opera teacher in the Netherlands for a few years and still see him when I go back to the Netherlands. He's incredible and he's helped me open my voice in a natural way and open my instrument as an improviser as well as develop similar techniques to what a Cathy Berberian can do. It was all happening around the same time, all of these discoveries. And let me just say one thing about living in Europe: I always tell people it was my "woodshedding period," it was the luxury of having time to invest and explore all these myriad paths and ideas without having to worry about things such as healthcare—you're Canadian, you know—or access to good food, really made it easy. I feel lucky to have had that time.

CT: So your entire time in the Netherlands you never got too involved with the improvisation scene there?

FV: Not really. I did connect with Misha Mengelberg. He became a mentor and he was actually really instrumental in helping me really feel confident as a vocalist that takes risks. He's now transitioned and I miss him so. Rest in peace.

CT: Could you tell me more about his role as a mentor for you?

FV: I'm a big fan of Herbie Nichols. Actually I have a Herbie Nichols project, and so we connected because of that. He was also a musician and teacher that understood how to peel back the onion of his students and give them permission to be their own strange self. That was on top of his being a powerful cultural and musical force in the Netherlands with an amazing ability to always be himself. He is deeply influential and important to me. We met in person because I wanted to do a project with him. I remember our first concert together in the BIMhuis in 2005. At the end of it—this will give an idea of what the relationship is—he said: "Yes, your music too is also valid. You must keep doing it." He became important as a person that was helpful to building my confidence as a vocal improviser. Vocal improvisers were not easily accepted as equals with instrumental improvisers. Which I think is ridiculous. I think you can judge it after you've had an experience with the improviser, not, because there's an improviser with the voice, have a preconceived notion of what that's going to be . . .

CT: Why do you think vocal improvisation is sometimes ignored in some improvisation contexts?

FV: I get really angry. Sometimes I feel that if I was a saxophonist I'd be much further. Even releasing records in the scene, it's weird; we have this weird dichotomy where people want vocalists to be more creative, but then if a vocalist
creates something they don't want to hear, people are anti-vocal. I even have
reviews regularly where they say things like, "this is a set great enough to win
over all but the most anti-vocal listener." On the surface, it sounds like it's a
great review but you should just hear something and if you like it you like
it, if you don't like it you don't like it. The idea that you immediately put it
down because it's vocal is, for me, just strange. With the voice, I can't tell you
how many times I met this resistance when I'm trying to get on festivals and
people don't want to have the voice, or they do but they want it a certain way.
I will just keep on fighting for my work.

Fay Victor interview excerpts appear with the permission of Fay Victor condensed from a longer interview conducted by the author. More information on
vocalist, composer, and educator Fay Victor can be found at www.fayvictor.com.

IN HIS OWN WORDS—GABRIEL DHARMOO[7]

CT: When did you start using your voice?

GD: Probably around 2000. I would have been 20ish. Well, I've always sung songs,
but singing in a free extended voice kind of way came later. That would have
started with Framboos, a band we had as composition students at Université
Laval around 2001 to 2003-ish. I remember us collaborating with poets and
exploring voice in that context. It's a small city, Québec City, but there were
different connections with different arts, which is something I was lacking in
my early years in a bigger city. In Montréal there was a sufficient amount of
people in contemporary music, so I sort of stayed within those bounds. But
over there it was good, I got to meet the performance artists that were studying visual arts and my network of artist friends was more mixed. That opened
me to use the voice in an experimental way which wasn't something I knew
existed from what I learned in music.

CT: Tell me more about that. How did that space specifically open you to using
your voice in that way? You just implied interdisciplinarity played a role. Why
would that lead to you using your voice in an extended way?

GD: It seems I wasn't interested in simply sticking to what I learned in the
music faculty; even when it came to contemporary music, we didn't learn
that much through the official courses. Something really struck me when
I took art history classes at university and realised we talked more about
John Cage in that class than we ever had in music. Cage had some sort of

impact on how music is made, and though I'm kind of "take some, leave some" with him personally, it was a revelation to see how sound art and music could appeal to visual artists. Whereas in visual arts and performance art or poetry, sound poetry, you can do all these sounds with your voice and improvise them and it's totally accepted, I think there is a bit of a stigma towards that in music. I felt like music, or the general scene in Québec City was not aware of these things or they didn't value it as much, and it's really through these other arts that I've developed it. And at that time I didn't know anything about people like Phil Minton; I wasn't exposed to it. That knowledge came later. There were four people in Framboos, and two of us—Elizabeth Lima who's also in Joker now, we go way back—we did this vocal exploration together . . .

CT: What then brought you to Montréal?

GD: Composition. I came here to study with Serge Provost at the Conservatoire. So I was seeking more compositional skills at that point, and then maybe two years in there was a new class, a new improv class with René Lussier, so for me that was like "I have to do this." . . . If that class had been in Québec City, I probably would have done it on cello. And then I was like: "maybe I should develop this voice thing that I still do" . . . I think it mostly started there with René and him being very supportive in me going out there and trying it because I gained more confidence as I did it, and more ideas. And he's the one that told me "you're not the only person that does this" [*laughs*]. It's true. When you're young you don't know! He said, "here's a Phil Minton CD, go and listen to it." Yeah, when you know you're not the only person who does this it's as reassuring as it is inspiring. It gives you lots of confidence . . . I actually knew I was more comfortable improvising on voice than on cello. I felt my ideas were more original. I didn't resort to the same kind of patterns. You know, on the cello I feel like there are these six things that I could do that I varied. Like ponticello, tremolo, or tapping . . . I segmented more because there's this technical use of your instrument and the tools, the bow and whatever. And I felt with voice the flow between ideas was more fluid; there's no tool, it's a direct kind of expression. I liked that a lot. I also felt it was rare in a way. Of course, with time, I keep being surprised at how many people do this . . .

CT: Let's talk about *Anthropologies Imaginaires*.[8] Tell me again about what led you towards this current project.

GD: I'm so amazed at how the voice is used throughout the world and I find it really important to have people be aware of how the voice can be used in different ways. Not just that, that any preconceived idea about anything can be re-questioned through how things are done somewhere else in time or in space. So that's the deeper kind of layer, but I feel that—how can I say this—nobody's right. Nobody has the truth on anything, on how we sing, but also what we choose to value in life. For example, right now there's lots of value put into money, yet other people in other places, times or circumstances have a different type of focus. We can learn from that. Similarly, I'm interested in how people sing everywhere. In a given place, if voice has developed to be beautiful in a specific way, or if that's how you use it for different functions and different meanings, then that really represents a deeper kind of, I don't know how to explain it, it's like you can learn a lot from observing a specific thing like voice. For this project, I keep things very ambiguous because it's all fake, but as I was saying it's also somewhat plausible. As an experiment I'd love to compare the perception of field recordings of traditional music and other pieces in the likes of Berio or vocal improvisers and have people take a quiz: avant-garde or tradition from some other place? I think we'd be surprised with the results. I haven't done the study yet but I really think it would throw people for a loop, because there are some really bizarre things out there that you'd expect to be experimental, but are century-old practices, and vice versa. The bottom line is they sound bizarre to whoever is foreign to it, of course. I like reminding people of that. That we don't hold any kind of truth. I find that every culture, even in India, which is not the dominating culture, there's a sense of self-righteousness, like [*he says the following with a dismissive tone*] "Oh they do it like that over there." But I feel that there is so much value to all of these expressions. And whether they range from the perceived "primitive" to the very "sophisticated," it's just a different context. That's why I'm terrified of exploring these questions artistically, because it could be easily become racist, it could easily be insensitive to actual populations that are, for example, oppressed or verging on extinction, but my goal is kind of the opposite. I see value in what they do, and that's why, in the theatrical framing and sober scenography of the piece, I keep the line very blurred on whether they're singing in a cave or in a palace because they both could happen, but audiences might assume the former.

CT: So after you play the clips of the people speaking as if they're ethnomusicologists, what is the vocal content? What are you using? Are you just improvising using any technique or are there specific techniques you're going to use at specific times?

GD: Yeah, I'm still developing the different sections at this point. I want to restrain the materials so that you actually feel like you're hearing eleven different people. I don't want blurred lines; I want them to be very specific and be able to develop within the segment. For some of them, it's easier. The one where I'm using water, I just have to say "I'm using water" that's going to be the special thing, but I still want to keep the nasal voice maybe and some sort of type of melodic treatment. There would be variation and freedom, and that's fine as long as I don't mix too much with what I was going to do in another section . . .

CT: One of the things a piece like this brings up is race. In what ways do you think race has played a role in performances you've given?

GD: My race?

CT: Your race, the races of the audience and those coming together. Oftentimes audiences will register unconventional vocality as the music of the Other. It becomes "ethnological" no matter what it is. Have you had experiences where you're doing this music that is largely contemporary and avant-garde but vis-à-vis your race people interpret it as traditional or "ethnic music" somehow?

GD: I'm not the person to ask, in a way … Being mixed race has always been significant. I play a lot with this ambiguity. People can't always pinpoint where I'm from and it's even funnier with my name being a French name. At a gig in Berlin with Tomomi Adachi, Alessandra Eramo, and Valeri Scherstjanoi, something happened. I wasn't there, but my friend Callum told me about it. There was one piece, the piece by Alessandra, where we were all speaking in our native tongues. My friend was outside, and he overheard a conversation between two friends, one of which had not seen the first part; he had just arrived. They were talking about that piece and they were saying "there was that Chinese guy," I assume that was Tomomi, "and there was this Indian guy talking in French." I think they were French; my friend mentioned they were speaking "France French." They went "he had good French but with some sort of Indian accent." They just couldn't grasp what my background was. Then, when Callum passed them on his way back in, he said" *"Il est Québécois"* (He's Québécois). He himself is Anglo-Canadian but he speaks French well. Anyways, I found that really funny. But, yeah, I think in a way I can pull that off. I'm allowed to play with these questions and these lines. I think everyone should be allowed, but in reality background is important, so not everyone can do it with the same sensibility or respect. Everything I do comes from a place of respect for this music that I find admirable in one way or another. I mean, there are things that are so wacky, but I never think it's ugly or stupid. That's why I love it. I want my work to create some sort of awareness of this diversity. Even in our own cultural setting, if you go fifty years back there was a different singing style. So, you know, it's like we have a tendency of thinking there's always one way to do things, a standardisation.

Gabriel Dharmoo interview excerpts appear with the permission of Gabriel Dharmoo condensed from a longer interview conducted by the author. More information on Dharmoo can be found at www.gabrieldharmoo.org.

IN HER OWN WORDS—DB BOYKO[9]

CT: I'd like to start by discussing the choirs you've been leading.

DB: So there's two choirs. There's the Voice Over Mind Choir, which I started in 2010 for the first Voice Over Mind Festival … and 2009 was the first year that

I was hired to do the Arts and Health project: the Express Your Voice project for seniors and people dealing with chronic health issues . . . Express Your Voice operates eight months out of the year, every week . . . There are some people who have some sort of musical experience, but most people don't . . . I was nervous about even presenting material that had any Western functional harmony to it because there were a lot of people who have been told that they can't sing or are worried about their lack of knowledge around music theory. So, working within the Element Choir conduction signals lexicon there's a lot of room, you don't need to be following specific pitches, which is fantastic. It's incredibly liberating and it's also an amazing form for those with vocal prowess to contribute; it's just such a beautiful, open forum for everyone. I could talk at length about how important that has been for me, working with the seniors, allowing me to go for broke and try new ideas. The word "community" gets so overused at this point, but having worked at the Western Front for many years (the bastion of experimental practice), the institution has become, to my mind, incredibly isolated. So the opportunity to open up the doors for other people to be accepted, to start to engage their creative selves, has been remarkable, and incredibly fulfilling for me.

The first year that [Express Your Voice] started, 2009, we started at the Roundhouse and thirty people showed up, and many were Chinese speaking. So immediately we had to find a translator. We weren't expecting it to be a cross-cultural project. It was an interesting mix of women, some Caucasian who were on the verge of retiring, a lot of health professionals who were quite acculturated, who had an understanding of contemporary practice, and then the Chinese elders, who didn't have that kind of experience, but obviously had musical experience. Over time we worked together, often dovetailing with my curatorial projects at the Western Front. We did a big event at Vancouver Public Library. We commissioned composers Alvin Curran from Italy and Scott Good (outgoing composer-in-residence from the Vancouver Symphony). There were one hundred and fifty kids from high school bands and an elementary school choir and Scott wanted to do a piece using First Nations Coast Salish mythology and I'm going: "Well, we can't just do that, we have to go to the source." So we extended an invitation to William Wasden, a cultural chief and a powerful Namgis singer from Alert Bay, B.C., who is a keeper of tradition and songs. Wasden offered one of his family stories of Dzunukwa, a creature of the woods. So Scott asked me to use my choirs. We brought two choirs together, Voice Over Mind and Express Your Voice choirs became the sounds of the forest. Everyone was very excited to work together.

The week following the performances I met with the seniors and I decided to take them for a soundwalk. When we returned we started to talk about their experience of participating in the production. One of the women started to open up about her experience working with Voice Over Mind choir members, in particular a young man who was cross-dressing. She divulged how she had misjudged him and had met him the day following one of the rehearsals and discovered what a lovely young man he was. And this triggered a pivotal conversation. Suddenly I was reminded of what my mentors Marie Lopes and Diana Vanderveen from the Roundhouse had been describing as the signposts of true engagement, "what you're working towards are those points where they start to have epiphanies (as a group) together." When the woman told this story, the ice broke and they all started to talk about identity politics. It was this big huge release for them: having questions, having doubts around their understanding of gays, lesbians, transgender, and First Nations people. And I'm holding back the tears of "wow, this is really happening." Then we reflected upon the soundwalk we had just taken, talking about what the experience was to just stop and to listen, to do the soundwalk, and then Shirley— this was the first time that she had ever spoken in English—said: "I'm not at home. I'm not washing dishes. I'm here connecting." And then other group members came to her side and helped translate and articulate that she was feeling part of a group, part of this community. And then she said: "when my foot touches the ground, I feel closer to God." Like holy fuck, it happened. We all knew what was happening. We all embraced that moment . . ."

CT: Do you know when it became important to you to have part of your practice be creating a space for people who were told they can't sing to sing? . . .

DB: I think I had always felt that way. I guess the moment that I started to work with sound making, at the end of my university career in the '80s, I recognised that anybody can do this . . . the Bīja, the seed of the practice is accessible to anybody. It's babies in a crib making sound. If you start from that place, everybody has that creative genius inside them to do it. And I was at that place starting to wonder where contemporary music practice was and thinking a lot about outreach and how do we do that . . . If you play Balinese gamelan music, there are hocketing parts. The two parts of the betel nut have to fit together, playing together. That is missing in so much of contemporary music practice. So if there's a way to bring that into the work and everybody can have access to it, the invitation to embrace a musical experience opens up to new listeners and new participants. That happens in free improvisation, but less so in the jazz improvisatory world. Jazz is so much based upon the rigorous understanding of harmonic structure, which makes fantastic, beautiful music and it also makes it very exclusive or exclusionary. So if there's ways to work improvisationally, in structures that allow more people to participate, why not let that happen?

CT: Could you tell me how you came to voice?

DB: I did my degree in theatre in the 1970s and had a fantastic singing teacher by the name of Suzanne Berg, although at that time I never considered singing as a career. I worked in theatre for a while, worked as a stage manager and various production roles, and then decided to go back to school to study kinesiology and ended up in the Simon Fraser University dance program, a four-year degree in choreography, and partway through that Meredith Monk came to Simon Fraser University. I didn't know anything about her work at that time, but I quickly learned. She was really at the forefront of cross-disciplinary practice. So my understanding of her as a dancer changed when I saw her perform a solo concert vocal work. She totally blew me away: "oh my God." So that set things in motion and I started improvising vocally with a bunch of musicians which became a group called Hextremities. I think we were the first ones doing what we called "comprovisation" on the West Coast in the early 1980s.

When I finished university in 1984, I went to Banff and studied with Cecil Taylor. It was the jazz program. I loved jazz as a kid but I wasn't really versed or introduced to the contemporary jazz world, but I went because I was bur-geoning as an improvising vocalist. We had the luxury of working together—about five or six singers, all women as it almost always is—these sessions with Cecil Taylor in these little practice rooms. Then we'd have these big group sessions and there were like a million saxophonists and guitarists. We did this big concert. Cecil Taylor started with a solo performance sitting at the piano. Or, at least we thought that's what he was going to do. And then he got up and he started to dance and he started to vocalise. He was conjuring his shamanic self, dancing his way to the piano and eventually conducting us. It was very pivotal in terms of recognising that all the boundaries were wide open. I had this history of studying in theatre and then a history of studying in dance and then realising that it didn't really matter what you were doing, all of it was applicable and Cecil Taylor was a big informant for me.

CT: When did extended techniques come in for you?

DB: Almost immediately. Right in around that time . . . Joan LaBarbara came to town . . . She taught a workshop about extended vocal techniques. There was a handful of us participating, including singers who came from a classical background who were terrified of things like vocal frys. She gave us a really good primer on vocal exploration and reassured us to not be afraid of work-ing with the voice. It allowed me the freedom to start playing with sound. I can't say what led or what followed, but this was at the same time that I started listening to music from other parts of the world and became inter-ested in Indian music, informing myself of other ways of vocalising. Listening to Pansori. Les Mystère des Voix Bulgares, all the Bulgarian music. This was a time, this was in the '80s when all these recordings were becoming available for the first time. Chinese music. Burmese music. Indonesian music. Around that time when I began curating at the Western Front I was getting intro-duced to electronic music and playing with musicians. I became a member of an electro-acoustic jazz world music ensemble called Hextremities. Two guys in the band were some of the first to have DX7s and the other members, me included, were interested in extending the capabilities of their instruments. So electronic music was also informing me, becoming part of my sound palette. Hearing it and imagining it. It's the same thing if you're going to be a high jumper, you see it and you make the jump. If you surround yourself by all sorts of different sounds, then anything is possible. You hear it, you sing it.

DB Boyko interview excerpts appear with the permission of DB Boyko condensed from a longer interview conducted by the author. One of Canada's most adventuresome vocalists, DB Boyko has explored the boundaries of vocal music as a performer and a creative collaborator. Most enduring is the vocal tour-de-force with singer Christine Duncan. Their projects *Idiollala, Hubbub* and the Canadian tour of "Stall" set in public washrooms invite whimsy and serious listening. DB's community projects include *Express Your Voice* and the *VOICE OVER mind choir* dedicated to generating spontaneous choral works. For twenty-four years DB also championed experimental practice in her role as Director/Curator of Western Front New Music (Vancouver).

Notes

1. This interview took place in Toronto on 11 August 2014. Duncan subsequently reviewed and edited the transcript.
2. This interview took place 26 September 2013 in Chicago. Ndosi subsequently reviewed and edited the transcript.
3. This interview took place over two days, 29 September 2013 in Chicago and 2 October 2013 in Guelph, Ontario. Adachi subsequently reviewed and edited the transcript.
4. In the body of this interview, Japanese names are displayed with the surname first in full caps, followed by given name. This is in accordance to the formatting preferred by ADACHI.
5. In ADACHI's *Song for Everyone* a turntablist improvises into a headphone array worn by a number of singers. The singers attempt to vocalise what they are hearing. The audience hears only the vocalists. See www.youtube.com/watch?v=WKGEE7EvpT0.
6. This interview took place 8 November 2013 in Brooklyn, New York. Victor subsequently reviewed and edited the transcript.
7. This interview took place on 28 October 2013 in Montreal, Quebec. Dharmoo subsequently reviewed and edited the transcript.
8. In this multimedia work, Dharmoo performs live a number of improvisations, with some pre-determined elements, as actors appear onscreen, portraying what we assume are anthropologists and other scholarly voices and frame the improvisations as the traditional music of eleven different fictional cultures. The piece provokes audiences to think about their perceptions of bodies and vocal sounds and the power dynamics in the history of anthropological and ethnomusicological scholarship. For more on this piece, see Dharmoo 2019.
9. This interview took place 18, 21, and 22 March 2015 in Vancouver, British Columbia. Boyko subsequently reviewed and edited the transcript.

CONCLUSION

A Short Prayer for Social Virtuosity

Eric Porter's essay "Jeanne Lee's Voice" argues that Lee "was not fully audible to various interpretive communities" (2013, 88). He argues her glorious signal was dimmed because of her gender, her race, the fact she was a working mother, and the unorthodox interdisciplinary aspects of many of her performances (Ibid., 89). He beautifully discusses the "cultural politics of her work" (Ibid.), characterising them as invested in the pursuit of less exclusive conceptions of human value, and he clearly situates her "eccentric vocal performance" as "an extension of her social vision" (Ibid., 106).

What I find most compelling about the broader "eccentric vocal" practice that Lee helped to give rise to is the extent to which it is not about displays of virtuosity and control, spectacles of the elite and specialised knowledge a singer possesses or their ability to sing in ways others cannot. Free jazz singing *is* sometimes about all of these things—I am not arguing these don't factor into the creation and reception of free jazz voice—but the social visions of the singers I have concentrated on here frequently do not fixate on these common aspects of musical cultures. They embrace accidents as much as control, ordinary sounds as often as virtuosic sounds, autodidactic learning more than elite knowledge, disparaged sounds more often than idealised sounds, and inclusivity more often than exclusivity.

I am also not suggesting that singers and singing practices that lean in this direction are the only ones deserving of attention. Every form of singing does social work; we benefit from a greater understanding of how that plays out in all musical contexts. But in a period where the concentration of wealth and power in the hands of the few is re-approaching new and frightening extremes, it is practices that help us identify with inclusive rather than elite social formations that can contribute the most to resisting these developments.

This urgent need is not disconnected from the series of solo singing albums Phil Minton released in his career: *A Doughnut in Both Hands* (1981), *A Doughnut in One Hand* (1998), *No Doughnuts in Hand* (2008), and *A Doughnut's End* (2015). In the accompanying notes to *A Doughnut's End*, Minton recounts the story that inspired the title:

> I was in New York in 1980, standing on a street corner in the then notorious Bowery area waiting for a lift to a gig. It had been snowing and the street was deep in slush. Simultaneously, a Bowery character and a jogger passed in front of me on the pavement, the jogger splashing slush onto the old chap's clothing. "What the fuck," he shouted as the jogger disappeared up the street, then turning to me he said, "the fuckin' asshole, what the fuck does he think he's doin', you gotta run to the South Bronx and back five fuckin' times before you lose a couple of fuckin' pounds. The trouble is people eat too fuckin' much. The other day the mission took us out on a trip to Coney Island and some of the guys had fuckin' donuts in both hands!"

Understanding the social visions that have led certain free jazz soundsingers to "eccentric vocal" sounds might help us make kin with the sounds and differences we fear; their practices might help us identify in new ways. Knowing Minton feels his vocal explorations are connected to being more empathetic and more equitable, or that Annick Nozati feels her "strange song" brought her "pleasure and peace for the first time in physical, intellectual, and moral form" might take away the urge to correct and contain these sounds or the people that embrace them. It might even stimulate the urge to take up the invitation I opened this book with—improvised soundsinging is here for you if you want it.

If soundsinging tomorrow has no socio-political potential, that'd be great. It would mean it no longer exists in the philosophical sense of the term, and all singing is heard, accepted, and enjoyed as singing, offending no-one and threatening nothing. The irreducible uniqueness of each moment would be more palpable and energising and our interconnectedness to rather than our separateness from all the dynamisms of the world around us would be the focus of our attention. The joggers would foster the global awareness and inner peace they need to avoid spraying slush, and there would be a doughnut in one of each of our hands and never in both.

BIBLIOGRAPHY

Acquaviva, Frédéric. "Wolman in the Open." In *Gil J. Wolman: I Am Immortal and Alive*. Barcelona: Actarbirkhauser, 2010.

Ades, Dawn, ed. *The Dada Reader*. London: Tate, 2006.

Adorno, Theodor W., and Max Horkheimer. *The Dialectic of Enlightenment*. Stanford, CA: Stanford University Press, 2002.

Aguetaï, Christian. "Review of Carte Orange Annick Nozati." *Jazz Magazine*, No. 319, June 1983, p. 14.

Amirkhanian, Charles. "Ode to Gravity: Bob Cobbing." *RadioOM, KPFA*, 20 September 1972. radiom.org/detail.php?omid=OTG.1972.09.20.c1. Accessed 19 May 2014.

Anhalt, Istvan. *Alternative Voices: Essays on Contemporary Vocal and Choral Composition*. Toronto: University of Toronto Press, 1984.

Antufieva, Nadezhda. "Not Like Everybody Else." *The New Research of Tuva*, 9 June 2011. en.tuva.asia/135-namchylak1.html. Accessed 18 September 2018.

Ball, Hugo. "Cabaret Voltaire." 1916. In *The Dada Reader*, edited by Dawn Ades, translated by Christina Mills, p. 20. London: Tate, 2006.

Barrett, Lindon. *Blackness and Value*. New York, NY: Cambridge University Press, 1999.

———. *Racial Blackness and the Discontinuity of Western Modernity*. Chicago, IL: University of Illinois Press, 2014.

Barthes, Roland. *Image, Music, Text*. New York, NY: Hill and Wang, 1977.

Berndt, John. "John Berndt Interviews Jack Wright in 2001." *Spring Garden Music*. www.springgardenmusic.com/berndt%20interview%202001.htm. Accessed 5 October 2018.

Bijma, Greetje. "Singing With the Wind." *Contemporary Music Review*, Vol. 25, Nos. 5–6, 2006, pp. 549–50.

Bithell, Caroline. *A Different Voice, a Different Song: Reclaiming Community Through the Natural Voice and World Song*. Oxford: Oxford University Press, 2014.

Blackford, Chris. "Annick Nozati: An Economy of Means - Interview by Chris Blackford." *Rubberneck*, Vol. 24, June 1997, pp. 4–7.

Blaney, John. *John Lennon: Listen to This Book*. Guildford: Biddles Ltd., Paper Jukebox, 2005.

Bohn, Willard. *Modern Visual Poetry*. Newark, DE: University of Delaware Press, 2001.

Brockway, Merrill, director. *The Living Theatre*. Creative Arts Television, 1969.

Broomer, Stuart. "Ezz-thetics: An Interview with Phil Minton." *Point of Departure: An Online Music Journal*, No. 40, May 2012. www.pointofdeparture.org/archives/PoD-40/PoD40Ezz-thetics.html. Accessed 20 December 2018.

Brothers, Thomas. *Louis Armstrong, Master of Modernism*. New York, NY: W.W. Norton & Company, 2014.

Brown, Linda Ann. *The Beautiful in Strangeness: The Extended Vocal Techniques of Joan LaBarbara*. University of Florida, Ph.D. Dissertation, 2002.

Cartwright, George. "Meltable Snaps It at the Kitchen." *GeorgeCartwright.com*. www.georgecartwright.com/msi-somewhere. Accessed 21 January 2019.

Ceolin, Elena, Gaziano Tisato, and Laura Zattra. "Demetrio Stratos Rethinks Voice Techniques: A Historical Investigation at ISTC in Padova." Sound and Music Computing Conference, University of Padova, 7 July 2011.

Charlton, Hannah. "Maggie Nichols: Liberating Women's Music." *Jazz Forum*, 1982, republished online in The Women's Liberation Music Archive. womensliberationmusicarchive.co.uk/m-2. Accessed 23 November 2015.

Chiriacò, Gianpaolo. "The Creator Has a Master Plan: Black Avant-garde and Cosmopolitanism in the Work of Leon Thomas." Society for American Music Fortieth Annual Conference, 7 March 2014, Lancaster Marriott, Lancaster, PA.

Cobbing, Bob. "Some Statements on Sound Poetry." In *Sound Poetry: A Catalogue*, edited by Steve McCaffery and bpNichol. Toronto: Underwich Editions, 1978.

Cobbing, Bob, and Peter Mayer. *Concerning Concrete Poetry*. 1978. London: Slimvolume, 2014.

Cohen, Scott. "Living Poets Society: Screamin' Jay Hawkins." *Spin*, Vol. 6, No. 1, April 1990, p. 98.

Connor, Steven. *Beyond Words: Sobs, Hums, Stutters and Other Vocalizations*. London: Reaktion Books, 2014.

Corbett, John. *Extended Play: Sounding Off from John Cage to Dr. Funkenstein*. Durham, NC: Duke University Press, 1994.

———. *Microgroove: Forays Into Other Music*. Durham, NC: Duke University Press, 2015.

Cowley, Julian. "Open to the Muse: The Vocal and Social Art of Maggie Nicols." *Musicworks*, Vol. 101, Summer 2008, pp. 13–16.

Crohn, Burrill L., director. *Animalsong: Kirk Newrock and the Natural Sound Ensemble in Performance at the Bronx Zoo*. New York: National Video Industries, 1982.

Crump, Melanie. *When Words Are Not Enough: Tracing the Development of Extended Vocal Techniques in Twentieth-Century America*. University of North Carolina, Greensboro, Ph.D. Dissertation, 2008.

Demain, Bill. "The Disputed History of the Tarzan Yell." *Mentalfloss*, 22 August 2012. mentalfloss.com/article/12328/disputed-history-tarzan-yell. Accessed 19 October 2018.

Denberg, Jody. "Interview With Yoko Ono." *a-i-u.net*, 1997. www.a-i-u.net/ryko97. Accessed 14 April 2010.

Dharmoo, Gabriel. "Anthropologies imaginaires: Une critique de la pensée coloniale par la voix et la satire." *Anthropologie et Sociétés*, Vol. 43, No. 1, 2019.

Doherty, Mike. "An Attempt to Break the Sound Barrier." *National Post*, 15 May 2003, p. AL3.

Dufrêne, François. "Fausse Route: Demi-Tour Gauche Pour Un Cri Automatique." *Soulevement de la Jeunesse*, No. 5, March 1953.

———. "Pragmatique Du Crirythme." *OU Magazine*, Vol. 22, 1966.

Dutton, Paul. *Liner Notes: Blues, Roots, Legends, Shouts & Hollers.* Toronto: Starborne Productions, 1980.

———. "Beyond Doo Wop or How I Came to Realize Hank Williams Is Avant-Garde." *Musicworks,* Vol. 54, Autumn 1992, pp. 8–19.

———. "The Speech-Music Continuum." In *Listening up, Writing Down, and Looking Beyond: Interfaces of the Oral, Written, and Visual,* edited by Susan Gingell and Wendy Roy, pp. 123–34. Waterloo: Wilfrid Laurier University Press, 2012.

Dutton, Paul, and Randy Raine-Reusch. "Tearing Down Borders, Opening the Soul: An Interview With Sainkho Namtchylak." *Musicworks,* Vol. 68, Summer 1997, pp. 5–9.

Eatock, Colin. *New Music Concerts of Toronto: A Critical Study.* McMaster University, Canada, Master's Thesis, 1984.

Feather, Leonard. *The Jazz Years: Earwitness to an Era.* Cambridge, MA: Da Capo Press, 1987.

Feld, Steven. "Pygmy Pop: A Genealogy of Schizophonic Mimesis." *Yearbook for Traditional Music,* Vol. 28, 1996, pp. 1–35.

Fleischer, Dave. "I'll Be Glad When You're Dead You Rascal You." U.M. & M. TV Corp., 1932.

Foote, Lona. "Jeanne Lee-Meet the Composer." *Ear Magazine,* May 1988, pp. 28–29.

Garabedian, John. "Way out in Central Park." *New York Post,* 10 September 1966, p. 63.

Garland, Phyl. "Early Jazz in Film Shorts." *Stereo Review,* Vol. 45, No. 4, October 1980, p. 104.

Graham, Neil, and Derreck Roemer, directors. *Last Call at the Gladstone Hotel.* Last Call Productions, 2007.

Gresty, Hilary. "Introduction." In *1965–1972: When Attitudes Became Form.* Cambridge: Kettle's Yard Gallery, 1984.

Grunebaum, Dan. "Hikashu: Enter the Strange Vocal World of Koichi Makigami at Your Own Risk." *Metropolis,* 28 August 2009. archive.metropolis.co.jp/tokyo/781/music_beat. Accessed 20 December, 2018.

Hadfield, James. "Hikashu: The Interview." *Time out Tokyo,* 4 April 2012. www.timeout.jp/en/tokyo/feature/5583/Hikashu-the-interview. Accessed 8 August 2012.

Haraway, Donna. *Simians, Cyborgs, and Women: The Reinvention of Nature.* New York, NY: Routledge, 1991.

———. *The Companion Species Manifesto: Dogs, People, and Significant Otherness.* Chicago, IL: Prickly Paradigm Press, 2003.

Higgins, Dick. *Modular Poems.* Barton, VT: Unpublished Editions, 1974.

Howard, Anne Marie. "Question and Answer Session With Phil Minton." *Frakture.* www.frakture.org/workshops/feral/feral_reviews.html. Accessed 2 May 2016.

Hyder, Ken. "Maggie: Speed Is the Essence." *Melody Maker,* 8 September 1973, p. 47.

Iles, Chrissie. *Yoko Ono: Have You Seen the Horizon Lately?* Oxford: Museum of Modern Art, 1997.

Ilic, David. "Maggie Nicols: The Singer of Scit-Scat Chit-Chat Spells out a Little of Her History to David Ilic." *The Wire,* 24 February 1986, pp. 22–23, 27.

Iran Chamber Society. "Sussan Deyhim: A Creative and Sensible Artist." *IranChamber.com.* www.iranchamber.com/music/sdeyhim/sussan_deyhim.php. Accessed 21 January 2019.

Irwin, Jim, editor. *The Mojo Collection: The Ultimate Music Companion.* Edinburgh: Canongate, 2009.

Jaji, Tsitsi Ella. *Africa in Stereo: Modernism, Music, and Pan-African Solidarity.* New York, NY: Oxford University Press, 2014.

Jarman-Ivens, Freya. *Queer Voices: Technologies, Vocalities, and the Musical Flaw.* New York, NY: Palgrave Macmillan, 2011.

Johnston, Jill. "'Life and Art,' Review of Yoko Ono's November 24, 1961 Carnegie Recital Hall Concert." *The Village Voice*, 7 December 1961, p. 18.

Kalo, Laura C., George Whiteside, and Ivan Midderigh. "The Roy Hart Theatre: Teaching the Totality of Self." In *The Vocal Vision: Views on Voice*, edited by Marion Hampton and Barbara Acker, pp. 185–99. New York, NY: Applause Theatre Book Publishers, 1997.

Kostelanetz, Richard. "Text-Sound Art: A Survey (Concluded)." *Performing Arts Journal*, Vol. 2, No. 3, Winter 1978, pp. 71–84.

Kristeva, Julia. "Robert Wilson." *ArtPress*, No. 191, 1994, pp. 64–65.

Kronengold, Charles. "Exchange Theories in Disco, New Wave, and Album-Oriented Rock." *Criticism*, Vol. 50, No. 1, Winter 2008, pp. 43–82.

La Bash, Heather. *Yoko Ono: Transnational Artist in a World of Stickiness.* University of Kansas, Master's Thesis, 2008.

Lake, Steve. "Cow Orchestra." *Melody Maker*, 19 March 1977, p. 6.

Lazarius, Damian. "Leon Thomas: It's My Life I'm Fighting for." *Straight No Chaser*, No. 33, Autumn 1995, p. 30.

Lefebvre, Henri. *Introduction to Modernity.* New York, NY: Verso, 1995.

Lewis, George E. "Improvised Music After 1950: Afrological and Eurological Perspectives." 1996. In *The Other Side of Nowhere: Jazz, Improvisation, and Communities in Dialogue*, edited by Daniel Fischlin and Ajay Heble. Middletown: Wesleyan University Press, 2004.

Lock, Graham. "Sweet Thunder." *The Wire*, No. 14, April 1985, pp. 10–15.

Lushetich, Natasha. *Fluxus: The Practice of Non-Duality.* New York, NY: Rodopi, 2014.

Mac Low, Jackson. *Thing of Beauty.* Berkeley, CA: University of California Press, 2008.

McCaffery, Steve. "Sound Poetry-A Survey." In *Sound Poetry: A Catalogue*, edited by Steve McCaffery and bpNichol. Toronto: Underwich Editions, 1978.

McGregor, Alayne. "Christine Duncan's Element Choir Is Looking for Singers." *Ottawa-JazzScene.ca*, 10 July 2013. ottawajazzscene.ca/news/7592-christine-duncans-element-choir-is-looking-for-singers. Accessed 22 January 2019.

McKay, George. *Circular Breathing: The Cultural Politics of Jazz in Britain.* Durham, NC: Duke University Press, 2005.

———. "Interview With Maggie Nicols." *GeorgeMcKay.org*, 23 November 2002. georgemckay.org/interviews/maggie-nicols. Accessed 13 September 2012.

Menhinick, Scott. "Biography: Ran Blake." *RanBlake.com*, 2002. ranblake.com/biography. Accessed 27 April 2014.

Milani, Matteo, and Federico Placidi. "An Interview With Trevor Wishart." *Unidentified Sound Object*, 26 January 2009. usoproject.blogspot.com/2009/01/interview-with-trevor-wishart-pt1.html. Accessed 7 May 2014.

Mitchell, Joseph. "Professor Sea Gull." *The New Yorker*, 12 December 1942, p. 28.

Morgenstern, Dan. "Joe Carroll: Man With a Happy Sound, Dan Morgenstern Talks to a Jazz Singer Without Ulcers." *Metronome*, Vol. 78, August 1961, pp. 20–21.

Morton, Jelly Roll, and Alan Lomax. "Library of Congress Narrative." 1938. Transcribed and annotated by Michael Hill, Roger Richard, and Mike Medding. www.doctorjazz.co.uk/locspeech1.html. Accessed 18 January 2018.

Moten, Fred. *In the Break: The Aesthetics of the Black Radical Tradition.* Minneapolis: University of Minnesota Press, 2003.

Nicholson, Stuart. *Ella Fitzgerald: A Biography of the First Lady of Jazz, Updated Edition.* London: Routledge, 2004.

Nozati, Annick. "La Voix Humaine." *Les Allumès du Jazz*, Vol. 4, No. 4, 2000. Article reprinted on gsavio.free.fr/nozati. Accessed 8 November 2015.

Olsson, Jesper. "The Audiographic Impulse: Doing Literature With the Tape Recorder." In *Audiobooks, Literature, and Sound Studies*, edited by Matthew Rubery, pp. 61–75. London: Routledge, 2011.

Perrone, Pierre. "Obituary: Leon Thomas." *The Independent*, 2 June 1999. www.independent.co.uk/arts-entertainment/obituary-leon-thomas-1097568.html. Accessed 31 January 2019.

Piekut, Benjamin. *Experimentalism Otherwise: The New York Avant-Garde and Its Limits.* Berkeley, CA: University of California Press, 2011.

Pikes, Noah. *Dark Voices: The Genesis of the Roy Hart Theatre.* 1999. New Orleans, LA: Spring Journal, 2004.

Porter, Eric. "Jeanne Lee's Voice." 2006. In *People Get Ready: The Future of Jazz Is Now!* edited by Ajay Heble and Rob Wallace. Durham, NC: Duke University Press, 2013.

Rancière, Jacques. *Disagreement: Politics and Philosophy.* Minneapolis, MN: University of Minnesota Press, 1999.

———. *Dissensus: On Politics and Aesthetics.* New York, NY: Continuum International Publishing, 2010.

Robinson, Jacqueline. *Modern Dance in France: An Adventure 1920–1970.* Translated by Catherine Dale. Amsterdam: Overseas Publishers Association, 1997.

Rosenkrantz, Timme. *Harlem Jazz Adventures: A European Baron's Memoir, 1934–1969.* Lanham, MD: The Scarecrow Press, 2012.

Rusch, Bob. "Louis Armstrong Interview." *Cadence*, Vol. 12, No. 1, January 1986, pp. 5–12.

Schechner, Richard. *Performance Studies: An Introduction.* New York, NY: Routledge, 2002.

Schuiling, Floris. *The Instant Composers Pool and Improvisation Beyond Jazz.* New York, NY: Routledge, 2019.

Scott, Richard. "Maggie Nicols." *Richard Scott.net*, 23 January 1990. richard-scott.net/interviews/maggie-nicols. Accessed 23 November 2015.

Scotto, Aubrey. *A Rhapsody in Black and Blue.* U.M. & M. TV Corp., 1932.

Shaw, Arnold. *52nd Street, the Street of Jazz.* New York, NY: Da Capo, 1971.

Smith, Hazel. "Performance, Improvisation and Technology: American Contemporary Avant-Garde Poetry." *Australasian Journal of American Studies*, Vol. 12, No. 2, December 1993, pp. 15–31.

Smith, Julie Dawn. "Perverse Hysterics: The Noisy Cri of Les Diaboliques." *Big Ears: Listening for Gender in Jazz Studies.* Durham, NC: Duke University Press, 2008.

———. "Playing Like a Girl: The Queer Laughter of the Feminist Improvising Group." In *The Other Side of Nowhere: Jazz, Improvisation, and Communities in Dialogue*, edited by Daniel Fischlin and Ajay Heble. Middletown: Wesleyan University Press, 2004.

Stern, Howard. "The Howard Stern Show." *SiriusXM Radio*, 29 October 2014.

Stewart-Baxter, Derrick. "Blues & Views." *Jazz Journal*, Vol. 23, No. 12, December 1970, p. 25.

Sutherland, W. Mark. "The Point About Criticism Is That It Is Frequently Wrong: Bob Cobbing Interviewed By W. Mark Sutherland." *Ubu*, 19 April 2001. www.ubu.com/papers/cobbing_sutherland.html. Accessed 19 January 2019.

Thomas, Greg. "Eyearun: Bob Cobbing and Concrete Poetry." *Journal of British and Irish Innovative Poetry*, Vol. 4, No. 2, 2012, pp. 203–27.

Thurber, Jim. "The Rube: Memoirs of the 60s." In *Berkeley Daze: Profiles of Poets in Berkeley in the '60s*, edited by Richard Denner. Sebastopol: dPress, 2008.

Tkweme, W.S. *Vindicating Karma: Jazz and the Black Arts Movement*. University of Massachusetts, Amherst, Ph.D. Dissertation, 2007.

Tomlinson, Gary. "Musicology, Anthropology, History." In *The Cultural Study of Music: A Critical Introduction, Second Edition*, edited by Martin Clayton, Trevor Herbert, and Richard Middleton. New York, NY: Routledge, 2012.

Tonelli, Chris. "Ableism and the Reception of Improvised Soundsinging." *Music & Politics*, Vol. X, No. 2, Summer 2016. doi:10.3998/mp.9460447.0010.204

———. "Social Virtuosity and the Improvising Voice: Phil Minton & Maggie Nicols Interviewed by Chris Tonelli." *Critical Studies in Improvisation*, Vol. 10, No. 2, 2015. doi:10.21083/csieci.v10i2.3212

———. "Unimagining Song: Making Kin in the Vocal Scene." *Yearbook for Traditional Music*, Vol. 49, 2017, pp. 149–61.

Tresham, Scott. "Phil Minton and the Feral Choir in Ottawa and Victoriaville." *Music.Cbc Blogs*, 9 May 2012. music.cbc.ca/#/blogs/2012/5/Phil-Minton-and-the-Feral-Choir-in-Ottawa-and-Victoriaville. Accessed 14 January 2014.

Tuynman, Carol E. "Tamia of a Thousand and One Voices: From an Interview With Tamia by Carol E. Tuynman." *Ear Magazine*, Vol. 10, No. 3, January-February-March 1986.

Tzara, Tristan. "Note for the Bourgeoisie." 1916. In *The Dada Reader*, edited and translated by Dawn Ades, p. 21. London: Tate, 2006.

Ueland, Hanne Beate. "The Future of Music Belongs to Imaginary Sounds: About Yoko Ono's Music in the Meaning of Traditions." In *Yoko Ono: Horizontal Memories*, pp. 125–33. Oslo: Astrup Fearnley Museum of Modern Art, 2005.

Vassilandonakis, Yiorgos. "An Interview With Trevor Wishart." *Computer Music Journal*, Vol. 33, No. 2, Summer 2009, pp. 8–23.

Wagner, Bryan. *Disturbing the Peace: Black Culture and the Police Power After Slavery*. Cambridge, MA: Harvard University Press, 2009.

Waterman, Ellen. *Sounds Provocative: The Ecology of Experimental Music Performance*. Bloomington, IN: Indiana University Press, Forthcoming.

Weheliye, Alexander G. *Habeas Viscus: Racializing Assemblages: Biopolitics, and Black Feminist Theories of the Human*. Durham, NC: Duke University Press, 2014.

Weiss, Allen, editor. *Experimental Sound and Radio*. Cambridge, MA: Massachusetts Institute of Technology Press, 2001.

Wickes, John. *Innovations in British Jazz, Volume One, 1960–1980*. Chelmsford: Soundworld Publishers, 1999.

Williams, Richard. "Maggie Helps Herself." *Melody Maker*, 22 April 1972, p. 34.

Wilmer, Valerie. *As Serious As Your Life: Black Music and the Free Jazz Revolution, 1957–1977*. London: Allison & Busby, 1977.

Wishart, Trevor. *On Sonic Art*. Amsterdam: Harwood Academic Publishers, 1996.

Young, Paul. *The Cinema Dreams Its Rivals: Media Fantasy Films from Radio to the Internet*. Minneapolis, MN: University of Minnesota Press, 2006.

INDEX